Armed Groups and Contemporary Conflicts

Armed groups operating beyond the state have become the most important actors in most contemporary wars and violent conflicts, from Iraq and Afghanistan to Colombia and Somalia. They come in a dizzying array of forms: some informally linked to the state and state power, others in opposition to the state; some pursuing classic political goals, others primarily predatory and large-scale criminal enterprises. All groups, however, challenge the state's Weberian monopoly of the legitimate use of force, yet their origins, evolution, violent dynamics, and relations with state power are poorly understood.

This interdisciplinary collection includes both conceptual and empirical studies of contemporary armed groups, examining cases in Latin America, Asia and Africa. It brings sociological, political economy, and ethnographic approaches to bear on larger questions including armed groups and the changing nature of warfare, the economic dimensions of their activities, and means of engagement with armed actors. It both broadens and sharpens our understanding of how force and violence are used in today's contemporary armed conflicts.

This book was published as a special issue of Contemporary Security Policy.

Keith Krause is Professor, and Director of the Centre on Conflict, Development and Peacebuilding at the Graduate Institute of International and Development Studies, Geneva, Switzerland.

Armed Groups and Contemporary Conflicts

Challenging the Weberian State

Edited by Keith Krause

Routledge
Taylor & Francis Group

LONDON AND NEW YORK

First published 2010 by Routledge
2 Park Square, Milton Park, Abingdon, Oxfordshire OX14 4RN

Simultaneously published in the USA and Canada
by Routledge
711 Third Avenue, New York, NY 10017

Routledge is an imprint of the Taylor & Francis Group, an informa business

© 2010 Taylor & Francis

First issued in paperback 2012

This book is a reproduction of *Contemporary Security Policy*, vol. 30, issue 2. The Publisher
requests to those authors who may be citing this book to state, also, the bibliographical details
of the special issue on which the book was based

Typeset in TimesNewRomanPS by Value Chain, India

British Library Cataloguing in Publication Data
A catalogue record for this book is available from the British Library

ISBN 13: 978-0-415-57457-0 (hbk)
ISBN 13: 978-0-415-81592-5 (pbk)

CONTENTS

Abstracts of Articles

Introduction: The Challenge of Non-State Armed Groups
by Keith Krause and Jennifer Milliken

The study of non-state armed groups (NSAGs) has traditionally been limited to those actors with a political agenda that pose a specific threat to the state and undermine its ability to claim a monopoly over the legitimate use of force within its territory. In contrast, this introduction – and the articles that follow – expands upon this narrow conceptualization and redefines NSAGs to encompass such actors as militias, warlords, private security providers, urban gangs, and transnational and criminal networks. This understanding facilitates a wider exploration of how such groups form in relation to the state, and how the state in turn is shaped through its interactions and conflict with the armed group(s). This article provides an overview of a set of research issues, frameworks, and methods that represent a starting place for a broadened agenda on armed groups which moves beyond those actors who mount direct challenges to the Weberian state. A more nuanced understanding of the different forms and historical trajectories of the interactions between armed group and states also highlights the dynamics through which various types of violent actors influence the use of force and violence in contemporary world politics.

Non-State Armed Actors, New Imagined Communities, and Shifting Patterns of Sovereignty and Insecurity in the Modern World
by Diane E. Davis

In a world of growing security challenges, non-state armed actors have captured significant attention from scholars concerned with regime stability and the consolidation of national states. But the preoccupation with national political dynamics has eclipsed the study of non-state armed actors who struggle to secure economic dominion, and whose activities reveal alternative networks of power, authority, independence, and self-governance unfolding on a variety of territorial scales both smaller and larger than the nation-state. With a focus on actors as wide-ranging as private police, gangs, and mafias, this article charts the proliferation and significance of non-state armed action structured around economic activities, and assesses the nature of violence and insecurity generated by these activities in comparison to more conventional politically oriented non-state action. Drawing evidence primarily from middle-income countries of the global south, where political regimes are relatively more stable but a wide variety of non-state armed actors still proliferate, it examines the new 'spatiality' of non-armed state action directed toward economic sovereignty, argues that it forms the basis for alternative imagined communities of allegiance, and assesses the implications for the future of the traditional nation-state. After highlighting the overlap and co-existence of multiple categories of non-state armed actors and how they impact the security, legitimacy, and stability of nation-states, the essay concludes with questions about conventional categorizations of states, armed and non-armed actors, and the nature of sovereignty in the contemporary era.

With the State against the State? The Formation of Armed Groups
by Klaus Schlichte

Non-state war actors have trajectories. While recent research contributions stress the role of material interest as the driving force for the formation of non-state war actors, this article attempts to sketch an alternative explanation for their formation. Based on a data-set of 80 cases and comparative case discussion it focuses on the relationships that leaders and staff members of armed groups entertain before the actual formation of such groups. Three mechanisms of formation are consecutively distinguished, depending on the degree and kind of social relationships that precede their formation. The article discusses the causal settings of each mechanism and reveals in how far state policies in medium term and long run horizons produce what they want to curb: the formation of violent challenges.

Grasping the Financing and Mobilization Cost of Armed Groups: A New Perspective on Conflict Dynamics
by Achim Wennmann

This paper approaches conflict financing as a combination of available revenue sources and the cost to start and maintain armed conflict. The paper therefore goes beyond conceptualizations of conflict financing that only look at the total available revenue of armed groups. Based on recent small arms research, the paper sketches a tool to estimate the mobilization cost of armed groups with the objective to establish data points for barriers to entry into armed conflict and the cost of competition during armed conflict. The paper argues that what matters in conflict financing is to identify the financing and mobilization costs together, and if an armed group can pay for the type of conflict required to reaching its objective. The paper contributes to an evolving literature on the feasibility of conflict and provides a new perspective on conflict dynamics with implications for peace processes, peacebuilding, and policy against conflict financing.

From Social Movement to Armed Group: A Case Study from Nigeria
by Jennifer M. Hazen

Violence is one of a range of tactics available to social movements. The important question is not whether violence is a tactic, but why certain groups within particular social movements choose a violent path. Using the cycle of protest model this study maps the progression from localized protest to armed group in a case study of the Niger Delta People's Volunteer Force. The case study demonstrates how an armed group emerges from a broader social movement, what influences this evolution, and what enables the armed group to sustain itself when facing significantly higher costs for survival. For the Niger Delta People's Volunteer Force, competition for scarce resources, its ideology justifying an aggressive posture toward government, and its capacity to mobilize necessary resources to engage in a violent struggle with the government all played significant roles in the emergence and survival of the group.

Gangs as Non-State Armed Groups: The Central American Case
by Dennis Rodgers and Robert Muggah

Gangs are popularly considered to be the major security threat facing the Central American region. In focusing on the origins and dynamics of gangs in the region, this article seeks to broaden conceptualizations of non-state armed groups by expanding the theoretical optic from a narrow focus on war and post-war contexts to a wider spectrum of settings, actors, and motivations. It highlights a category of actors that does not explicitly seek to overthrow the state, but rather progressively undermines or assumes certain state functions. The article also reveals how efforts to contain and regulate gangs flow from their imputed motives, with interventions influenced by whether they are conceived as a criminal or political threat. At the same time, coercive regulation tend to be favoured even when such repressive interventions exacerbate gang violence, for reasons that reveal the deeper under-lying political, social, and economic challenges facing the Central American region.

The Role of Non-State Actors in 'Community-Based Policing' – An Exploration of the *Arbakai* (Tribal Police) in South-Eastern Afghanistan
by Susanne Schmeidl and Masood Karokhail

Despite the ousting of the Taliban and a subsequent peace agreement reached at the end of 2001, Afghanistan continues to struggle with insecurity. The existing security deficit of the Afghan state is currently filled by a wide array of (armed) non-state actors (ANSA). Even though much of the Afghan experience with ANSA has been negative, the inability of the state to provide comprehensive security necessitates a consideration of alternatives. One of such possible alternative, the community-based policing structure in south-eastern Afghanistan (*arbakai*) is explored in this article. We conclude that it is important to understand the context-specificity of ANSA before promoting overarching policies such as advocating a transferability of the *arbakai* outside their unique cultural and regional context. We also caution against the use ANSA beyond their capacities, such as for counter-insurgency pur-poses and formalize engagement with clear parameters to ensure accountability.

Staging Society: Sources of Loyalty in the Angolan UNITA
by Teresa Koloma Beck

This article explores the importance of the social environment for the stability of armed groups as organizations. A case study of the Angolan UNITA explores how this armed group engaged and transformed existing social structures to recruit members and create a stable and loyal following. Contrary to the image of UNITA as a tribal organization, it is shown that UNITA's most loyal followership was created in a far-reaching project of social engineering, designed to control the combatants' entire lifeworld. UNITA created a state within a state, a society within society. To policymakers in the post-war context, this situation poses a major challenge. To facilitate a rapprochement of UNITA people to the majority society and the institutions of the state will take time and effort. The latter will have to be as intensive as UNITA's original social project had been.

Explaining Patterns of Violence in Collapsed States
by William Reno

Analyses of predatory violence that stress individual fighters' pursuits of short-term opportunities for enrichment explain why insurgents seem to be so uninterested in taking time to propagandize, recruit, and organize local populations to fight. International efforts to resolve this kind of conflict often aim to sever this link between resources, conflict, and these short-term goals. Quick opportunities do attract certain kinds of people and shape how they organize and how they fight. But critical cases often are overlooked in analyses linking local resources to propensities for predation. This behaviour may indicate the construction of new institutions that contribute to post-conflict stability such that people with guns obey people without guns. Individual interests are not irrelevant, but present an incomplete picture of the behaviour and organization of insurgents. A more complete explanation entails looking more closely at the relation of insurgents to non-combatants and to the politics of patronage, or the 'state' as it has become in the most extreme examples of state collapse. Historically this obedience to community leadership or to political cadres has been integral to the mobilization of insurgents with political programs and liberated zones, and ultimately, the creation of new versions of state authority. The examples in this article generate two propositions. First, local relationships put more constraints on how strongmen mobilize fighters and use violence once conflicts break out. Second, regions more closely connected to prewar capital-based patronage networks were more likely to host predatory armed groups.

The Changing Ownership of War: States, Insurgencies and Technology
by Aaron Karp

As the state loses not only its Weberian monopoly over legitimate violence, but also its control over military initiative and dominance of military technology, what forces lead the redefinition of the ends and means of armed violence? If non-state armed groups are understood as the new owners of war, how must our understanding of the *artefacts of violence* adapt as well? This article examines the effects of changes in the legitimacy of violence on its physical manifestations. Weapons technologies have ceased to be an independent variable of violence and become consequences of strategic and doctrinal choice. As states lose the ability to use technology to regulate warfare, technological virtuosity no longer is defined by the state, but by the initiators of violence. It follows that the most important violent technologies no longer are state-generated. They are adaptations and creations by terrorists and insurgents. This transformation affects priorities and possibilities for control over violent technology. Innovative statist methods – as developed through the Proliferation Security Initiative (PSI) and UNSC 1540 – remain highly relevant, as do Westphalian concepts such as export control and disarmament. Recognizing limits to their effectiveness in an environment where rules are set by non-state actors as much as by states themselves, however, is crucial.

Notes on Contributors

Teresa Koloma Beck studied economics at the University of Witten/Herdecke, Germany, and political science at the Institut d'Etudes Politiques in Paris. From 2004 to 2008, she was part of the research group, Micropolitics of Armed Groups, at Humboldt University, Berlin, focussing on a PhD project about the transformation of societies in civil wars. Currently, she is working on post-conflict society in Mozambique as part of the research project, The Politics of Building Peace, at Philipps University (Marburg, Germany).

Diane E. Davis is Professor of Political Sociology and Head of the International Development in the Department of Urban Studies Group, and formerly Associate Dean of the School of Architecture and Planning. She is the author of *Urban Leviathan: Mexico City in the Twentieth Century* (Temple University Press 1994; Spanish translation 1999) and *Discipline and Development: Middle Classes and Prosperity in East Asia and Latin America* (Cambridge University Press, 2004) as well as co-editor of *Irregular Armed Forces and their Role in Politics and State Formation* (Cambridge University Press, 2003).

Jennifer M. Hazen, PhD Georgetown University, is senior researcher with the Small Arms Survey. Prior to this she has worked with International Crisis Group, the United Nations peacekeeping mission in Sierra Leone, the US State Department, the Center for International Cooperation, Management Systems International, among others.

Aaron Karp is Lecturer in Political Science at Old Dominion University in Norfolk, Virginia, and senior consultant to the Small Arms Survey in Geneva. He is co-editor of the journal *Contemporary Security Policy*. His most recent books are *Global Insurgency and the Future of Armed Conflict* (with Regina Karp and Terry Terriff, Routledge, 2007) and *Inconspicuous Disarmament* (Routledge, 2009).

Masood Karokhail, MBA, Preston University (Pakistan), is deputy director and co-founder of The Liaison Office in Kabul, Afghanistan. During the Taliban times he was the Afghanistan country manager for Unilever. Prior to this he worked in the administration section of the Afghan NGO Development & Humanitarian Services for Afghanistan in Pakistan. From 2002 to 2003, he worked with Swisspeace in setting up and running the Afghan Civil Society Forum, organizing dialogue conferences and civic education outreach campaigns. In 2005 he was a visiting researcher at the Centre for Development Research (ZEF) in Bonn.

Keith Krause, PhD Balliol College, Oxford, is Professor of International Politics at the Graduate Institute of International and Development Studies in Geneva, and Director of its Centre for Conflict, Development and Peacebuilding (CCDP). He is also the founder and Programme Director of the Small Arms Survey project, and has jointly edited its yearbook, *Small Arms Survey* (annual, Cambridge University Press) since 2001. His current research is concentrated in the changing character of political violence, concepts of security, and state formation and insecurity in the post-colonial world. He has published *Arms and the State* (Cambridge) and edited or co-edited *Critical Security Studies* (Minnesota), and *Culture and Security* (Routledge), and authored many journal articles and book chapters.

Jennifer Milliken, PhD University of Minnesota, is founder of Milliken Strategy & Communications. She produces international conferences such as BioMarine 2008, DIFC Week 2008, and The Women's Forum Global Meeting 2009. Along with her business and finance background, Jennifer has expertise in the political economy of globalization and conflict and post-conflict reconstruction. She has published *The Social Construction of the Korean War*, and co-edited *State Failure, Collapse and Reconstruction*. Previous posts include Assistant Professor of International Relations at the Graduate Institute of International Studies in Geneva, Switzerland, and Lecturer in Political Science at York University, Toronto, Canada.

Robert Muggah, PhD Oxford, is Research Director of the Geneva-based Small Arms Survey. He is also a research fellow at the Centre for Conflict, Development and Peacebuilding (Switzerland), and an Associate of the Households in Conflict Network (UK), the Conflict Analysis Resource Centre (Colombia) and The SecDev Group (Canada). He is a senior adviser to the Organization for Economic Cooperation and Development (OECD) in Paris, and has worked for multilateral and bilateral agencies in more than 20 countries. He is the editor of *Security and Post-Conflict Reconstruction: Dealing with Fighters in the Aftermath of War* (Routledge, 2009), *Relocation Failures in Sri Lanka: A Short History of Internal Displacement* (Zed, 2008), and *No Refuge: The Crisis of Refugee Militarization in Africa* (Zed, 2006).

William Reno is a specialist in African politics and the politics of collapsing states. His current work examines violent commercial organizations in Africa, the former Soviet Union, and the Balkans and their relationships to state power and global economic actors. Reno's research takes him to places such as Sierra Leone, Congo, and Central Asia where he talk to insurgents (including so-called 'warlords'), government officials, and foreigners involved in these conflicts. His books include *Corruption and State Politics in Sierra Leone* (Cambridge, 1995) and *Warlord Politics and African States* (Lynne Rienner, 1998). He is completing the forthcoming volume, *The Evolution of Warfare in Independent Africa*.

Dennis Rodgers is Senior Research Fellow in the Brooks World Poverty Institute (BWPI), at the University of Manchester, Visiting Senior Fellow in the Crisis States Research Centre at the London School of Economics, and Research Fellow at the Graduate Institute of International and Development Studies in Geneva, Switzerland. Publications include the edited collection *Youth Violence in Latin America: Gangs and Juvenile Justice in Perspective* (Palgrave Macmillan, 2009), as well as articles in the *Journal of Latin American Studies*, the *New Left Review*, *Critique of Anthropology*, the *Journal of Development Studies*, and the *Bulletin of Latin American Research*. He is currently completing a monograph on Nicaraguan youth gangs based on over a decade of longitudinal ethnographic research.

Klaus Schlichte is Professor at the Institute for Political Science at Otto-von-Guericke-Universität in Magdeburg, Germany. His most recent books include *In the Shadow of Violence. The Politics of Armed Groups* (University of Chicago Press, 2009); *Der Staat in der Weltgesellschaft. Politische Herrschaft in Afrika, Asien und Lateinamerika* (Frankfurt am Main/New York: Campus, 2005), named the best post-doctoral monograph for 2006 by the Deutschen Vereinigung für Politische Wissenschaft; and *Kriege in der Weltgesellschaft. Empirische Analysen und strukturgeschichtliche Erklärung*, (with D. Jung and J. Siegelberg, Westdeutscher Verlag, 2003).

Susanne Schmeidl, PhD in sociology from Ohio State University, is senior advisor and founding members of The Liaison Office (TLO) in Afghanistan as well as visiting fellow with the Asia-Pacific College of Diplomacy at the Australian National University. Between 2002 and 2005 she managed the Swisspeace office in Afghanistan where she also coordinated the Afghan Civil Society Forum. She has published extensively on Afghanistan, gender, civil society, refugee migration, conflict early warning, peacebuilding, and human security.

Achim Wennmann, PhD, is Researcher at the Centre on Conflict, Development and Peacebuilding of the Graduate Institute of International and Development Studies in Geneva. He was co-editor (with Keith Krause and Robert Muggah, 2008) of the *Global Burden of Armed Violence*. Other publications include 'Getting Armed Groups to the Table: Peace Processes, the Political Economy of Conflict and the Mediated State' in *Third World Quarterly*, Vol. 30, No. 6 (2009); 'The Political Economy of Conflict Financing: A Comprehensive Approach Beyond Natural Resources' in *Global Governance*, July 2007, and 'Resourcing the Recurrence of Intra-state Conflict: Parallel Economies and Their Implications for Peacebuilding' in *Security Dialogue*, December 2005.

Preface

The articles compiled for this book originated from a conference held at the Graduate Institute of International and Development Studies in Geneva, Switzerland in April 2008 on 'Transnational and Non-State Armed Groups: Legal and Policy Responses'. The conference was the second workshop in an interdisciplinary project jointly run by the Centre on Conflict, Development and Peacebuilding (CCDP) at the Graduate Institute, and the Program on Humanitarian Policy and Conflict Research (HPCR) at Harvard University.

While the first meeting in March 2007 dealt mainly with the metamorphosis of conflict and the limitations of current laws of war, the 2008 gathering concentrated on the role of non-state armed actors in the contemporary world. Issues discussed at this conference included: non-state armed groups and the changing nature of warfare; case studies of non-state armed groups; perspectives on non-state armed group in human rights and humanitarian law; economic dimensions of contemporary armed conflicts; and mechanisms for engaging with non-state armed groups.

Participants in the conference not only represented a variety of academic disciplines, they also spoke from different standpoints – as scholars and legal experts, field researchers and humanitarian workers. This diversity of approaches allowed for the development of a more robust understanding of the role and influence of armed groups in contemporary world politics, which can be seen throughout the articles selected for this book.

Thanks are due to the participants in the conference, including those who did not prepare articles for publication, and to Liliane Zossou and Juan Carlos Ochoa for overseeing the research project, and organizing the conference itself. Its database on armed groups can be found at: http://www.armed-groups.org/ and other reports and publications from the project can be found at: http://www.hpcrresearch.org/projects/tags.php.

Financial support for the project was provided by the Swiss Agency for Development and Cooperation (SDC). Able editorial support for all of the contributions to the volume was provided by Meghan Pritchard, helpful editorial coordination and inputs by Aaron Karp, and administrative support by Oliver Jütersonke and Sandra Reimann.

Keith Krause

Introduction: The Challenge of Non-State Armed Groups

KEITH KRAUSE AND JENNIFER MILLIKEN

Non-state armed groups pose a direct challenge to the Westphalian project of constructing sovereign states that possess both the Weberian legal and practical monopoly over the legitimate use of force within a given territory. They have tradition-ally been considered relevant to scholars and to the international community only when a group becomes capable of directly challenging this monopoly. This restricted vision of the scope and significance of armed groups is essentially limited to 'state-like' actors engaged as insurgents in a civil war-like context, and is increasingly distant from the reality of contemporary armed groups and the conflicts in which they engage.[1] The world is populated by armed groups that do not mount direct challenges to the Weberian state, but that are still relevant for their violent and destructive capabilities, the predatory and rent-seeking behaviour in which they engage locally, regionally, and trans-nationally, and the damage that they inflict on human rights, public security, the rule of law, and prospects for inclusive social and economic development. Many so-called 'non-state' armed groups are also deeply entangled with state power and state agents in complex ways. Thus, the label 'non-state' represents a barrier to under-standing their multiple roles and functions.

From a social science perspective, the research agenda for armed groups should thus be broadened not only in regards to which groups to study, but also how – with what frameworks, methods and approaches – we should study them. Current work, by scholars such as Stathis Kalyvas and Jeremy Weinstein, focuses mainly on micro-level and modelling approaches to the dynamics of armed groups.[2] There are, however, other approaches in our social science toolbox. Ethnographic fieldwork can give us insights into how armed groups build support, operate, and use violence, adding depth to more conventional approaches. Process reconstruction within a socio-logical framework can enrich our knowledge of the political context of armed group formation, and how different contexts support the emergence of different types of armed groups. A political economy approach can help us understand better how the 'sinews of war' are brought together by non-state armed groups. And grasping the broader implications of armed groups for contemporary warfare requires an historical perspective on the state's relationship to armed groups.[3] Only if we can grasp how armed groups are related to the states in which they take form, and how states are shaped through conflict with non-state armed actors, can we have gain perspective on the evolution of conflict and future trends in armed violence, and, perhaps most importantly, how these trends could be accentuated, checked, or reversed.

The different contributions to this volume represent these various approaches, and touch on a variety of specific themes, including non-state armed groups and the changing nature of warfare, case studies of non-state armed groups, the economic dimensions of contemporary armed conflicts, and forms of engagement with armed groups. They are diverse in subject matter, method and approach, which is not surprising given the different disciplines and approaches brought to bear by the authors. But they share a common view that the study of non-state armed groups should be expanded and expansive, in order to foster a better understanding of some of the dynamics that underpin the use of force and violence in contemporary world politics. This introduction will survey some of the central themes, highlight their significance for our understanding of the dynamics of armed groups, and provide an overview of contributions to the volume.

Non-State Armed Groups: Broadening the Scope of Inquiry[4]

The basic definitions of non-state armed groups – both as objects of study and subjects for engagement – differ between international lawyers, social scientists from different disciplines, and practitioners from international governmental and non-governmental organizations. Among scholars, traditional definitions revolve around the idea that an armed group is 'an armed, non-state actor in contemporary wars . . . [with] a minimal degree of cohesiveness as an organization (to be distinguished as an entity and to have a name, to have some kind of leadership) and a certain duration of its violent campaign'.[5] This understanding finds an echo in (and is conceptually linked to) the equally narrow legalistic focus on groups that can be considered subject to international humanitarian law (IHL). IHL, which 'imposes obligations on certain parties to an internal armed conflict irrespective of any recognition granted by the state they are fighting against or by any third state', is crucial for determining which armed groups can be treated as subject to IHL.[6] The threshold conditions that are generally accepted include: the armed forces or organized armed groups are under responsible command; they are able to exercise control over territory to carry out sustained and concerted military operations; and they are able to implement Additional Protocol II to the Geneva Conventions. The effect of these threshold conditions is to restrict formal engagement to armed groups fighting in internal wars. The jurisprudence on the issue explicitly excludes 'internal armed conflict' banditry and other criminal acts such as riots, internal disturbances, and unorganized and short-lived insurrections.[7]

Nonetheless, other definitions can be found, both among practitioners and scholars. For example, the working definition used by the UN Assistance Mission in Afghanistan (UNAMA), which is responsible for organizing the disarmament and disbanding of armed groups, estimates that there are 1,800 armed groups operating in Afghanistan alone, most of which would not meet the narrow definitions above.[8] In Indonesia, a large proportion of armed groups are effectively paramilitary organizations affiliated (loosely or tightly) with different political factions; sometimes working with state actors, sometimes in opposition to the state.[9] It is hardly surprising therefore that there is no consensus on a definition of non-state armed groups, or on which groups are of interest (and to whom).[10]

At the risk of over-simplification, discussions on which armed groups should be of interest can be summarized in terms of five categories of armed groups: (1) insurgent groups; (2) militant groups; (3) urban gangs and warlords; (4) private militias, police forces and security companies; and (5) transnational groups.[11] Although a taxonomy is not a definition, it is a step towards a broader conceptualization of armed actors.

Insurgent Groups

While the category of insurgent does not carry binding force in international law, both practitioners and researchers working on armed groups still mainly focus on groups having effective control over some part of a state's territory, and possessing the organizational means to carry out sustained attacks against state forces. This traditional concept of armed groups is also associated with notions of armed groups as 'proto-states' or 'states-in-formation': these groups seek to defeat the regime against which they are fighting, or through secession in a national liberation movement. It also covers armed groups which may not be seeking state takeover or secession, but which are engaged in an 'internal war', or a violent mass confrontation with a certain continuity and participation of the forces of a state on one side.

Militant Groups

These are groups that are seeking to redress perceived political and economic injustices through violent means. They endure organizationally and in terms of quasi-regular attacks against the state (and often, other groups). But they may not have effective ongoing control over a base region. The level of killing in which they are involved does not exceed (or has not yet exceeded) the violence threshold by which insurgencies are usually demarcated.

Warlords, Urban Gangs and Criminal Networks

Groups whose main purpose appears to be the pursuit of illicit profits through control over natural resources, drugs, trafficking in people, kidnapping, etc., have traditionally been left to the field of criminologists. They have, however, become increasingly significant in internal war situations, as well as in so-called non-war contexts where the levels of violence involved can approach or surpass the threshold of deaths in war and armed conflicts.[12]

Private Militias, Police Forces and Security Companies

Both powerful and weak states alike are increasingly turning to private security companies to supplement, or sometimes practically to replace, state militaries and police forces. This accompanies the growing recourse by the private sector to 'security for hire' actors who provide security to company or private property and operations. What is often neglected in this analysis, however, are the local and community based militias and police that are also being formed in crime- and conflict-ridden areas. As is noted by the contribution of Susanne Schmeidl and Masood Karokhail to this volume, there has even been experimentation in Afghanistan to promote a traditional form of community police, the Arbakai, in order to provide the public order that the Afghan state cannot achieve.

Transnational Groups

This category includes al Qaeda and similar armed groups such as Jemaah Islamiyah that profess millennial, religious and other ideological goals, and which are networked across different states and territories in their operations. The violence perpetrated by these groups is intentionally spectacular and terror-provoking, even if in actual numbers of deaths the groups are far less destructive than traditional insurgents.

Traditional interest in insurgent groups has many roots, including the 20th century transition to internal war as the dominant mode of warfare, the brutality of some internal wars, and the post-Cold War turn towards human security and 'the responsibility to protect' by Western governments, UN agencies, and non-governmental organizations.[13] Why, however, should we broaden the agenda beyond insurgent groups in the way this taxonomy implies?

A first reason is that the human security consequences of the 'other' forms of organized violence are actually now more significant than those created by internal wars. The largest global estimate of recorded instances of violent death in war (international and intrastate combined) is 52,000 persons per year. Meanwhile, on average approximately 500,000 persons die each year in non-war violence, and a large proportion of these deaths involved non-insurgent armed groups of one sort or another.[14] In Central America, for example, urban gang violence (including gang killings, state repression, and gang responses to such action) is responsible for most of the region's violent deaths. The levels of violence in the region are also as high as during the internal wars of the 1980s.[15]

Second, case studies of different types of armed groups indicate that fundamentally, the dynamics that fuel the resort to violence do not necessarily differ across different types of armed groups. Almost always, at the root is a crisis in the state, out of which particular alienated groups exit (or are kicked out) and turn to violence. Alternatively, those groups in political opposition, or those groups excluded from the political system, mobilize with arms. As Anthony Vinci points out, 'As the state weakens, armed groups – non-state organizations that have the capacity for systematic military action – can become relatively more powerful.'[16] The similarities and interconnections between different types of armed groups and their use of violence can only be understood, however, if the scope of inquiry into armed groups is broadened beyond traditional (and relatively large-scale) insurgent groups. Such understanding is not only academic; it can have considerable relevance for policies and programs of early warning, disarmament, post-conflict reconstruction, and development assistance.

Third, there are good reasons to explore the adequacy of contemporary international legal frameworks in addressing the humanitarian and human rights obligations (or not) of different kinds of non-state armed groups. The recent American use of the category 'unlawful enemy combatant' to cover many individuals detained by US forces highlighted the difficulties encountered in using the traditional framework and distinctions in the circumstances of contemporary conflict.[17] Finally, there are also practical reasons for attempting to understand whether and how the nature, scope and aims of a non-state armed group shape the conditions under which one should or could engage with it to promote crisis prevention, conflict management, and demobilization, or broader efforts to address the causes and consequences of armed violence and promote development.[18]

Studying Armed Groups

Contributors to this volume include urban sociologists, development scholars, anthropologists and political scientists (with parenthetically American, British, and Continental European training). As a genuinely inter-disciplinary and plural group, they are committed to a broadened agenda to the study of armed groups, and their contributions reflect this plurality. Although there was no agreed-upon research agenda, the different articles in this volume identify a set of research issues, frameworks and methods that represent the starting point for a broadened agenda. These include:

- Ethnographic field work on culture and social rules;
- Process reconstruction and the formation of armed groups;
- Political economy of armed groups;
- Historical sociology of the changing relations between armed groups and the state.

The remainder of this introduction briefly presents the contributions, organized around these four themes.

Ethnographic Fieldwork: Culture and Social Rules

Most of the work on armed groups in political science is based on or develops rationalist models of individuals' motivations, or of the strategic choices of groups (in target selection and tactics, for example).[19] These represent 'outside' approaches in the sense that they do not study the social understandings of the members of armed groups. Instead, if a study addresses the issue at all, the reasons for certain behaviours by armed groups are posited by the researcher, often in the name of parsimonious or generalizable explanation. For many contributors to this volume ethnographic fieldwork is a useful corrective and/or a preferred orientation to externalized approaches. Ethnographic study can involve informal interviews with armed groups or government officials in order to uncover their understanding of a situation, and/or to validate external interpretations of the meaning of certain acts. It can also be used to reconstruct the socio-cultural meanings and rules of action for armed groups, as these are defined by the groups and the broader society.[20] In any of its variants the approach is demanding and potentially dangerous when applied to armed groups. But it can also yield significant insights that are not evident from an outside perspective.

A good example comes from the contribution by Susanne Schmeidl and Masood Karokhail on the Arbakai, the tribal police operating with some success to keep order in Loya Paktia province in Afghanistan.[21] Outsiders to the Afghan context usually view the Arbakai as a form of Afghan militia. But Schmeidl and Karokhail explain how, from an insider's perspective, the Arbakai are significantly different from other Afghan militias. While both are irregular non-state armed actors, the

Arbakai are a very old Pashtun tradition with their roots in the pashtunwali justice system. The social constitution of the group ties the Arbakai to a clear chain of command, makes them relatively stable, reliable and predictable, and embeds them in society. Militias in Afghanistan, by contrast, are a more recent form of armed group that has 'no traceable link to any kind of justice system'. They tend to rule through coercion and by instilling fear in the population. With an organization based on a 'person-cult' of the militia leader, and the extending of protection and benefits, militias can be 'rather erratic and unpredictable, especially when leaders are removed'.[22]

Based on this ethnographic examination, Schmeidl and Karokhail provide a clear explanation for why, in a state with such rampant insecurity, the Arbakee have been effective at fulfilling security mandates. Their account focuses on the social rules for mobilizing the Arbakee, selecting men for duty, and determining their mandate and duration of engagement. It emphasizes how, for example, Arbakee 'are raised for *specific* purposes, and the size of the Arbakai and duration of engagement [are] usually matched to the task at hand'.[23] Also of note is that the 'men selected to perform Arbakee duty remain in their own jurisdiction, that is, each group of men is responsible for his own village and the areas associated with the village', creating 'a chain of responsibility' for a village and its jurisdiction.[24] Schmeidl and Karo-khail's insider conclusions about what makes the Arbakai effective also informs their cautions about expanding the Arbakai's role in policing Afghanistan. Several proposals for this have been advanced in policy circles, including by Britain in its concept of 'neighbourhood defence teams'. In Schmeidl and Karokhail's judgment, however, if the Arbakee were used outside of the Loya Paktia region they would lose their accountability structure, risking empowering warlords and their militias. Even within Loya Paktia, there are important potential limitations. One of these is that the Arbakee serve the community interest, not that of a provincial or federal government. In terms of self-defined purpose and geographical understanding, much would have to change to obtain an effective policing network beyond the village jurisdiction.

Teresa Koloma Beck also challenges conventional wisdom in her study of UNITA (National Union for the Total Independence of Angola) in Angola. Most research on UNITA argues that the armed group sustained its membership mainly through tribal ties. Yet Koloma Beck's field interviews indicate that the most loyal followers were the young boys and girls who were forcibly recruited into the movement. When UNITA was driven in 1976 to retreat to the *mata*, the uninhabited regions of the deep south of the country, the movement's leaders realized they had to create 'a social life in this unsociable environment'.[25] They not only built up a veritable city in the territory that they came to control, complete with schools and hospitals, but also promulgated a social structural framework to guide the teenaged recruits' actions. The guiding idea seems to have been 'to guard ... against the derailing of violence ... Yet ... this project of behavioural regulation was not limited to the immediate situations of battle and confrontation, but aimed instead at all domains of the combatant's life'. In addition to participating in military campaigns, UNITA soldiers 'had to attend school and to work on the fields for defined periods of time'. UNITA troops did not live together as male bands, but 'each one was urged, or indeed coerced, to marry and have children ... These social structures were framed by a draconian jurisdiction, within the framework of which, for example, adultery or the abuse of women could be severely punished'.[26] After UNITA was defeated at the polls in 1992, the leadership shrank to a small circle of people from Jonas Savimbi's Bailundo clan. Yet among UNITA troops, loyalty to the movement remained strongest among those recruited and socialized into the organization.

UNITA and the Arbakai could be discounted as exceptional instances of social orderliness among armed groups. Yet urban gangs also follow social rules, as is demonstrated by the research of Dennis Rodgers, and the contribution to this volume by Dennis Rodgers and Robert Muggah. Far from being a manifestation of anarchic violence, as many portray gangs in Central America, Rodgers' study of the *pandillas* in Managua indicates that they have followed highly regular, even ritualized, practices of violence. Gang wars 'revolved around either attacking or protecting a neighbourhood, with fighting generally specifically focused either on harming or limiting damage to both neighbourhood infrastructure and inhabitants, as well as injuring or killing symbolically important *pandilleros*'.[27] Fighting escalated in regular and easily recognizable ways, and gang members also fought in a particular fashion. This idea of 'living in the shadow of death' meant:

> flying in the face of danger and exposing oneself purposefully in order to taunt the enemy, taking risks and displaying bravado, whatever the odds and conse-quences, daring death to do its best. It meant not asking questions or calculating chances, but just going ahead and acting in a cheerfully exuberant manner, with style and panache.[28]

Rodgers concluded that *pandilla* wars were 'scripted performances' which in fact circumscribed the unpredictability of violence and created a 'safe haven' for locals by driving out rival gangs from other neighbourhoods.[29]

Muggah and Rodgers document the way in which these scripted performances are changing, as the *pandillas* are transforming into drug gangs that no longer feel responsible to 'love' their neighbourhood.[30] As their contribution shows, the trans-formation of behaviour of these gangs throughout Central America (mainly in El Salvador, Guatemala, Honduras, and Nicaragua) makes them resemble in some way other armed groups. Although Central American gangs do not fit the traditional understanding of armed groups (as organizations with the explicit purpose of obtaining direct control over state institutions), they do challenge the state's practical monopoly of the use of force (if not with a political agenda). They also have the capacity to progressively undermine or assume certain state functions, and shape the state's relationship with its citizens around the provision of security as a public good. Given this, gangs should be conceived as important armed groups, which – instead of forming out of an ambition to overthrow the state – 'often emerge as a result of state weakness, as gangs seek to potentially fill in for the absence of certain state functions'.[31]

Rodgers and Muggah also point out that most gang members join gangs out of a feeling of exclusion (both socially and economically), and out of a perceived need for security. This poses particular challenges for the way in which states (and inter-national actors) approach the phenomenon of gangs. They argue that the approach of a state to a given group is often based on imputed motives, and in particular defining the group as posing either a political or criminal threat. The recent labelling of Central American gangs by states 'as an enemy "other" in a manner very similar to its treatment of more conventional non-state armed groups such as rebel or insurgent organizations'[32] arguably has had the dangerous by-product of actually encouraging, and not limiting, violent behaviour. Pre-existing feelings of exclusion among gang members are potentially further exacerbated by the repressive policies of the state. This provides insight into the changing nature of gang activity, especially in terms of the increase in violent behaviour noted in Rodgers' research into the *pandillas* in Managua,[33] which can be at least partially be explained as a reaction to changes in state policy. This increase in violence[34] can be traced back to the so-called 'War on Gangs', as manifested in the *'Mano Dura'* ('Iron Fist') of El Salvador, the *'Cero Tolerancia'* ('Zero Tolerance') of Honduras, and the *'Plan Escoba'* ('Operation Broomsweep') of Guatemala. These heavy-handed policy responses – which include extended jail sentences for gang members, provisions allowing minors to be treated as adults, and the deployment of military troops to combat the problem – has been unable to address the root causes of gang perpetuation.

State policies towards gangs, which address only surface issues of gang perpetu-ation, are partly responsible for the increased violence. In the specific cases of Guatemala, Honduras, and El Salvador, Rodgers and Muggah point out that the policies of state-led enforcement operations and coercive regulation serve to conceal the deeper underlying political, social, and economic challenges manifested in gang formation and perpetuation.[35] Although the phenomenon of gangs in Central America is most definitely linked to deep-rooted issues such as the legacy of war in the region, the availability of small arms, and the pervasiveness of *machismo* in Central American societies, it is also a consequence of increasing inequality and exclusion rather than specific political objectives. It is thus important that state and international policy responses address all of these aspects. The actions taken towards gangs have the capacity to have a significant impact (either positive or negative) on the future behaviour, formation and perpetuation of these groups. This point is echoed in the discussion below on the changing relationship between armed groups and the state, and the contributions by Diane Davis and William Reno. Importantly, however, the new 'exclusive' and more violent order in Central America is still simply that – an order of 'practical and symbolic rules and norms', which provides individuals and groups within neighbourhoods with a frame-work for interaction.[36]

Process Reconstruction and the Formation of Armed Groups

Inherent in the work of Susanne Schmeidl and Teresa Koloma Beck is the identifi-cation of action patterns for armed groups that abstract general conclusions based on research observations. This activity, which can also be termed 'process reconstruc-tion', is in sharp contrast to the rationalist modelling of groups, in which patterns of behaviour are taken to reflect the choices made by individuals as they try to maximize their benefits and minimize their costs. There is therefore no need to reconstruct action patterns or to examine processes empirically; all of 'the action', so to speak, is in the choice calculus.

Rationalist models currently dominate in the literature on armed group formation and motivation – a subject of some importance for policymakers as well as scholars. Much work on armed groups has, for example, been focused around the 'greed versus grievance debate'. The 'greed' side, exemplified in the work of Paul Collier and his colleagues, argues that competition over rents and rent-seeking behaviour leads elite leaders to consider armed rebellion as a viable course of action. The movement gains followers when the rebellion is financially viable (especially supported by natural resource-based rents and/or sympathetic diasporas) and also when a 'poverty trap' exists which makes soldiering more attractive.[37] The 'grievance' side, in contrast, emphasizes that relative deprivation linked to ethnic and nationalist identities underlies the motives and actions of most contemporary armed groups. Identity matters as a force for amalgamating groups by differentiating them along lines of race, language, religion, or tribal or regional affiliation.[38]

Contributors to this volume recognized that rent competition and predatory opportunism are part of the story of how and why violent organizations emerge. But there are also good reasons to seek a more differentiated explanation of armed group formation.[39] In some cases, armed groups like the Arbakai provide protection for local communities, even when from an outside perspective they could benefit more from concentrating on profiteering opportunities in their resource-rich areas. In other cases, one finds more predation in resource-poor areas, and less in resource-rich regions (for example, Northern versus Southern Somalia, or Northern Uganda).[40] Similarly, if greed was the main reason for the formation of armed groups, we would expect opportunistic organizations to dominate in all times and places where resources (or the population) were easily exploitable. Yet Sub-Saharan Africa only became the unfortunate poster child for this thesis in the 1990s, whereas elsewhere at the same time, the thesis fits poorly (Lebanon, Palestine, and Southeast Asia). Grievance arguments suffer from their own limitations. Group amalgamation does not necessarily neatly follow lines of tribe, ethnicity, etc., as is demonstrated by the study of Koloma Beck. Armed violence would also be significantly more prevalent if anger and frustration were its main cause. After all, there are large reservoirs of people in the global South who face stagnant or falling incomes and state violence and corruption.

To improve our understanding of armed group formation, the contributions of both Jennifer Hazen and Klaus Schlichte to this volume also chose a political sociology approach. Hazen uses social movement theory to develop an explanation of the rise of the Niger Delta People's Volunteer Force (NDPVF) in Nigeria, exploring why the NDPVF turned to violence, and how it was able to develop into a sustainable militant group. Schlichte's study is part of a large comparative project on armed group formation based on a data set of 80 insurgent groups. He uses Weberian social theory, especially the work of Norbert Elias on figuration, to develop his research strategy.[41]

Hazen's social movement approach situates the NDPVF's development in a political opportunity structure and competition between political groups. The NDPVF movement did not come from nowhere, but rather emerged in a democratic Nigeria where patronage politics remains at the core of the political system. Elections are a key moment for patrons to access money and resources, or to lose access, making them the fulcrum for violence and intimidation. In the run-up to the 2003 elections, political candidates provided arms and cash to various groups to create their own personal militias. After the elections many candidates failed to retrieve the weapons, and elected officials failed to fulfil the promises that had been made during the campaign. This left a number of organized groups armed and disgruntled. Mujahid Asari Dobuko, the leader of the Ijaw Youth Council (IYC), sought in this context to have his organization pursue a more radical agenda. Losing within the IYC on radicalization, he left to form the NDPVF. Asari was able to draw on his reputation and skilfully manage the media to tap widespread local grievances in the Delta and build substantial popular support for his new group.

But why did the NDFVF opt for armed violence when it could have continued to pressure for change as a militant social movement? Hazen focused on the need for the NDPVF to distinguish itself from other social movements, starting with the IYC. The NDPVF also faced 'a serious threat to its survival and to the lives of its leaders' from the Niger Delta Vigilante (NDV) group, also operating in the Ijaw area, as well as the Nigerian government. The latter not only stood behind the NDV as it attacked the NDPVF, it 'initiated its own efforts to eliminate Asari and disband the NDPVF'.[42] Hazen's explanations are processual – they tell us how greed and grievance are brought together in contentious politics. They also point to the inadequacy of the 'non-state' label for armed groups, since in this case, the groups are inextricably intertwined with the formal quest for power in Nigeria.

Schlichte also uses process reconstruction to ground the case studies in his data set. But unlike Hazen, Schlichte abstracts from his cases to specify a set of three ideal types for different patterns of processes of armed group formation. These are worth noting, as they illustrate the ability of an approach like this to generate empirically rich yet parsimonious theoretical categories.[43] They are:

Ad hoc Mechanism

Political crisis in neo-patrimonial systems $=>$ selective exclusion from political class $=>$ leader initiative $=>$ search for military expertise $=>$ armed rebellion.[44] Examples would be the National Patriotic Front of Liberia or the Revolutionary United Front in Sierra Leone.

Repression Mechanism

Rapid social change $=>$ overstrained regime $=>$ political exclusion $=>$ organized opposition $=>$ repression $=>$ radicalization $=>$ armed rebellion.[45] Examples would be the Moro National Liberation Front in the Philippines or the Tamil Tigers in Sri Lanka.

Spin-off Mechanism

War $=>$ informalized state $=>$ delegation of violence $=>$ own reproductive base $=>$ own momentum $=>$ separation.[46] Examples would be the Serbian Volunteer Guard or RENAMO in Mozambique.

Schlichte's categories explain not only a group's formative process, but also the likely outcomes: whether different groups will successfully institutionalize and 'turn their violent power into domination'.[47] His summary conclusion of the odds of success for ad hoc groups, for example, is that they:

> usually have weaker [social] ties from the beginning. They usually consist of connections that are products of circumstances rather than relations cultivated over time. Consequently, their internal functioning is precarious. Shared interest alone does not suffice to create stable organization, and ad hoc groups are therefore more prone to fragmentation and decay. In propitious settings, such as strong support by other states, they can institutionalize and defeat government armies.[48]

Theoretical claims like this can be used in other comparative studies, tested, probed, and refined – an accomplishment for research of this kind on armed groups. And while Schlichte's project only addresses insurgent groups, the approach might also be applicable to other types of groups as well. Certainly Hazen's presentation of the NDFVF includes all the elements of the ad hoc mechanism, while her observations on the possible fate of the group clearly echo Schlichte's fragmentation pathway thesis.

The Political Economy of Armed Groups

In addition to insider accounts of armed groups action repertoires and motivations, it is also important to consider the material foundations for, and constraints on, armed groups. Achim Wennmann examines how armed groups pay for and profit from conflict, a topic that has become a major policy issue in recent years. Significant attention has been given to how diamonds, oil, timber, and other resources have fuelled violence in states such as Angola, Sierra Leone, and the Democratic Republic of Congo. Natural resources such as 'conflict diamonds', however, are only one of the means by which armed groups can finance their operations, and Wennmann's project attempts to create a more comprehensive mapping of revenue sources, including developing tools for survey research in this area.[49]

His 'accounting approach' is particularly innovative for its inclusion of other means of conflict finance such as taxation, diaspora funding, and kidnapping. Going further, it also distinguishes between the effectiveness of different sources in funding a major or minor conflict. He concludes that some methods of financing, such as easily exploitable resources (diamonds, drugs, and external support) provide easily centralized control and prospects for rapid (and significant) revenue streams, and tend to be highly effective. By contrast, methods such as local taxation or diaspora financing are more difficult to exercise central control over; although they offer a consistent revenue stream, it is usually less lucrative, and therefore of only moderate effectiveness. At the lower end, we find 'taxation' of humanitarian relief, kidnapping, looting, and individual contributions, which offer the lowest possible revenue streams, and although of limited effectiveness, it still provides the possibility of sustaining a low-intensity conflict.[50]

Wennmann's analysis illustrates that the conditions for starting and sustaining an armed conflict vary considerably, and that there is no necessary linear relationship between the prospects of resource capture and the formation of armed groups (or their violent behaviour). Along with mapping different revenue sources, he develops a tool for estimating the cost of conflict, distinguishing between the costs of starting and of perpetuating the use of force. On this account, it costs substantially more to continue than to start a major war, while low-intensity conflicts have both lower barrier-to-entry and 'operating' costs. Overall, the incentives (and disincentives) for launching an armed conflict thus must be conceived of dynamically, 'depending on the conflict intensity, the rate of replacement for soldiers and materiel and the development of prices of weapons, ammunition and other items'.[51] Armed groups may not be able to finance escalation to a war, but many will be able to fund a conflict 'start up' and to keep operating as gangs, militant groups, etc. 'Cutting off marginal sums of money seems wishful thinking when considering the illicit opportunities for money making in conflict or post-conflict societies, or in the global illicit market place.'[52]

A study of conflict financing like this can provide an important complement to insider approaches, especially when it comes to explaining why certain armed groups succeed or fail. For example, from a conflict financing perspective on UNITA, it was not only the organization's methods of sustaining membership which determined its ability to keep fighting: an equally important factor was its diamond-based conflict funding. UNITA 'was unable to maintain the armed conflict because diamonds did not generate enough revenue to escalate the conflict between 1993 and 1999. It was also unable to control alluvial diamond mines once attacked by the government, and with its financial backbone undermined, UNITA's functioning as an armed group was affected.'[53]

The Sociology of Changing Relations between Armed Groups and the State

The internal conflicts that erupted after the end of the Cold War generated a series of studies reflecting on structural, political, and socio-economic change and its effects on states and armed groups. The 'New Wars' literature brought to the forefront the roles of transnational networks, economic globalization, and the fragmentation of the legitimacy and political authority of states as important contextual factors for the emergence of new armed groups and their resilience vis-à-vis weak Southern states.[54] This literature might now seem outdated, since the incidence of internal wars has been reversed or stabilized. But the impetus to think about historical changes in the relations between armed groups and the state has remained as a scholarly preoccupation. These concerns are reflected in the contributions of Diane Davis, Aaron Karp, and William Reno to this volume.

One line of reflection concerns the value of an historical conception of the state as a form of political order formed and reformed in response to war-making, technological change, and resource extraction struggles and bargaining between groups. This approach is most often associated with the work of Charles Tilly, but with the proviso that most states in the global South do not fit the ideal type of the modern Western nation state.[55] The European process of state formation yielded states that broadly provide public goods: domestic order, security from foreign attack, education, health, welfare, and economic development. Many Southern states can only provide such public goods in a limited way, and important basic services are often in practice privatized through political arrangements developed by ruling elites in order to stay in power and capture monopoly rents. By encouraging comparative historical analysis, a state formation perspective can illuminate the development trajectories and roles of new armed groups in this context of states-in-formation.

Diane Davis, for example, links the growing role of private police in many Southern states to the 'war' that authoritarian states had made on their rebellious citizens during the Cold War era.[56] Seeking to advance as late industrializers, state elites enforced compliance from labour through repression and violence carried out by police, militaries, and paramilitaries. Democratization ended some of this, but left a legacy of corruption and impunity. Meanwhile, the neo-liberal turn increased social and income polarity dramatically, creating a context in which private police have become increasingly important as guards for corporate assets and to 'act on behalf of citizen clients, protecting their homes, workplaces, and transport routes'.[57] What public policing remains provides order for the wealthy, leaving the poorest to fend for themselves.

The issue for Davis is that while in some states such as South Africa, the public and private police may be working together and in the process strengthening the commitment to rule of law and democracy, in other states such as Mexico, the already-eroded legitimacy of the state continues to degrade. In border areas and the cities, private police mix with gangs and so-called mafias to 'sell' security selectively and unevenly. This does not occur in isolation from, or competition with, the state, since the networks of non-state armed actors are often well connected with state actors, with police officers moonlighting as private security agents, or ex-police or military directly employed as private police. As a result, however, 'when the same individuals or networks of armed professionals move back and forth between the state and civil society, sharing knowledge and personal relations, it is harder for citizens to leverage institutional accountability, and abuse of coercive power is more likely to continue'.[58] Echoing the New Wars arguments, Davis predicts that the state's complicity in violence networks will delegitimize it further, even while encouraging the proliferation of more non-state armed actors. The ultimate result of the 'oligopolization of the means of violence' will be 'new compromises or complicities between state and non-state coercive actors' that 'driv[e] a vicious cycle of state de-legitimization and the appearance of alternative imagined communities of reciprocity, many of which are protected by their own non-state armed actors'.[59]

Building upon this, Will Reno's contribution delves into the subject of violence within collapsed states. Instead of following an explanatory mechanism that focuses on individual interests – actors engaging in violent hostilities in search of short-term (often economic) gain – Reno argues that such approaches only provide a partial understanding of the behaviour and understandings of insurgents. He argues that state collapse is in fact a consequence, and not a cause, of certain coercive and predatory behaviours. Essentially, Reno posits that to understand violent behaviour by armed groups, it is important to account not only for the potential motives of the armed actors, but for the particular social structures in which actors are located. Specifically, he argues that the extremes of predation are better understood as a consequence of certain political strategies and local political economies that they created in patronage-based political systems. In this interpretation of insurgent behaviour, 'context matters a lot, particularly the manner and degree to which local networks of authority control the uses of resources and those who benefit from them'.[60]

In this way, Reno's argument for the importance of context in understanding transnational and non-state armed group formation and behaviour ties in nicely with the findings presented by Schmeidl and Karokhail's contributions, as well as that of Koloma Beck. It also echoes the assertion of Rodgers and Muggah that Central American gang violence is better understood not as simply existing within the non-state armed group distinction, but as related to a specific social context, usually defined by elements of social and economic exclusion. All of these scholars argued for the importance of context specific analysis in studying this topic.

A different historical perspective on the state in relation to armed groups comes from Aaron Karp's examination, through the lens of military history, of the epochal transformations in war-making and military technology.[61] Karp's starting point is that increasingly the United States and its allies decide to go to war and prosecute conflicts based on 'post-modern, humanitarian sensibilities'. War has to be made acceptable to domestic and international audiences, and therefore the successful use of force is defined as 'minimal death and destruction', rather than the total crushing of the power of the enemy.[62] State-of-the-art technologies thus paradoxically serve not to assure victory, but rather to make it impossible for insurgents to win militarily – while reducing the risks to Western forces.

The political limitations that Western powers place on warfare contrast for Karp with the freedom of action of many contemporary armed groups. While they cannot defeat their opponents outright, the adversaries of Western states in the Middle East and Afghanistan face few legitimacy obstacles in choosing strategy or innovating in weapons and tactics. This 'migration of military-technical initiative' to armed groups enables them to use guerrilla warfare to try and 'inflict enough pain and humiliation to convince the adversary to give up'.[63] When sniping and suicide bombing lose their impact, the insurgents change their approach, controlling the pace of innovation on the battlefield. In Iraq, for example, sniper and rifle attacks were first replaced in tactical leadership terms by suicide bombings and then by the increased use of improvised explosive devices (IEDs) to attack coalition forces. A similar process in Lebanon and Gaza resulted in rocket attacks being used as the tactical innovation. The al-Qassam rockets used by Hamas in Gaza 'are hardly impressive ... Except for an explosive warhead of 2–5 kg, they are little different from large hobby rockets popular among North American enthusiasts ... [But] as primarily political weapons, they only have to work well enough to encourage Palestinian unity and keep pressure on Israel for political concessions.'[64]

Are insurgents and terrorists likely to continue to hold the advantage in tactical innovation, especially of a low-tech variety, over the United States and its allies? Karp placed developments in the Middle East and Afghanistan in the context of the transition from 'third generation' to 'fourth generation warfare'.[65] Third generation warfare is industrial and network-centric warfare (as in recent US military doctrine for fighting in Iraq). Fourth generation warfare is guerrilla warfare, whether the classic variant (such as in Maoist doctrine) or contemporary approaches in which guerrillas need never try to defeat the opponent militarily. For Karp, the rise of fourth generation warfare may be part of the process of overturning the utility of war planning and war as an instrument of statecraft. More immediately, it gives a new advantage to insurgents, 'the ability to pick dominant weapons', making it more likely for armed conflicts to become 'stalemated, continuing without much hope of resolution'.[66]

Conclusion

If we align Aaron Karp's and Diane Davis's historical arguments with the political economy conclusions of Achim Wennmann, we arrive at a fairly bleak picture for the future of global armed violence. Major civil wars may be increasingly less frequent, but it is also increasingly easy for armed groups of all stripes to keep conflicts going as low-intensity contests, whether primarily political or primarily economic in nature. Southern states are ill-equipped to prosecute these wars. And militarily more powerful Western states will probably not be able to achieve military victory, given their self-imposed political limitations and the difficulties in countering asymmetric tactical innovations. Social violence meanwhile appears to be on the rise outside of what are defined conventionally as conflict zones, and the line between different sorts of armed groups, and different forms of armed violence, is increasingly blurred.[67]

Although some states could develop the means to check the expansion of armed groups in their cities and regional hinterlands, in too many cases social violence seems likely to continue or expand, as a result of the declining ability of the state to manifest in practice its theoretical Weberian monopoly on the legitimate use of force. At the root of this may be the relative lack or long-term decay of the public good of security, which opens spaces into which new predatory or protective actors emerge. A complete picture of these historical trends, and the role of armed groups in them, is still beyond our grasp. As Will Reno also points out, more knowledge needs to be gained by examining violence (in its predatory form) by looking at those states that are exceptions to the rule rather than those that affirm it. These states can serve as important counterfactual examples to the overarching assumption that such things as natural resource wealth, or weak or absent state structures (especially in the case of Africa), create the necessary and perhaps even sufficient conditions for armed violence. As Reno points out, we need not to take for granted the state or to naturalize such categories as 'weak state' or 'failed state'.

Rather, researchers must map out how state institutions actually work to provide public order and security (or not), and how states interact with potential and actual challengers to the state's monopoly on the legitimate use of violence. This is not just a good rule for studying Southern states. It is also a useful perspective to adopt in the broader project of expanding the research agenda on armed groups, and for theorizing the relationship between armed groups, states, and state formation processes. We may not arrive at a less bleak picture of the future for armed violence worldwide. But we may develop a somewhat more nuanced account of its potential manifestations, be able to identify new and emerging violent social formations, and be better able to recognize their prospects as well as their limitations.

NOTES

1. For a good overview of the controversies surrounding the definition of non-state armed groups from a legal perspective, see Andrea J. Dew and Mohammad-Mahmoud Ould Mohamedou, 'Empowered Groups, Tested Laws, and Policy Options: The Challenges of Transnational and Non-State Armed Groups' (Boston, MA and Geneva: Program on Humanitarian Policy and Conflict Research, Harvard University, and Graduate Institute of International Studies, Geneva, 2007); Pablo Policzer, 'Neither Terrorists Nor Freedom Fighters', Working Paper 5, Armed Groups Project, University of Calgary, March 2005.

2. See, for example, Jeremy Weinstein, 'Resources and the Information Problem in Rebel Recruitment', *Journal of Conflict Resolution*, Vol. 49, No. 4 (August 2005), pp. 598–624; Stathis Kalyvas and Matthew Adam Kocher, 'How "Free" is Free Riding in Civil Wars: Violence: Insurgency and the Collective Action Problem', *World Politics*, Vol. 59, No. 4 (January 2007), pp. 177–216; Stathis Kalyvas, 'Wanton and Senseless? The Logic of Massacres in Algeria', *Rationality and Society*, Vol. 11, No. 3 (1999), pp. 243–85.

3. See Diane E. Davis and Anthony Pereira, *Irregular Armed Forces and their Role in Politics and State Formation* (Cambridge: Cambridge University Press, 2003); Janice Thomson, *Mercenaries, Pirates and Sovereignty* (Princeton, NJ: Princeton University Press, 1994).

4. Articles in this volume were (with two exceptions) originally presented at an April 2008 conference, 'Transnational and Non-State Armed Groups: Legal and Policy Responses', sponsored by the Graduate Institute of International and Development Studies in Geneva and the Program on Humanitarian Policy and Conflict Research, Harvard University.

5. Stefan Malthanner, 'The "Armed Groups Database": Aims, Sources, and Methodology', Junior Research Group, 'Micropolitics of Armed Groups', Working Papers Micropolitics No. 2/2007, 11-12, available online at: http://www.ipw.ovgu.de/forschung/inhalt/projekte_konferenzen/mikropolitik/publikationen.html. This is the same database that underlies the study by Klaus Schlichte in this volume.

6. Andrew Clapham, 'Human Rights Obligations of Non-State Actors in Conflict Situations', *International Review of the Red Cross*, Vol. 88, No. 863 (September 2006), pp. 491–523, p. 493.

7. For more on this issue, see International Committee of the Red Cross (ICRC), *Rules of International Humanitarian Law and Other Rules Relating to the Conduct of Hostilities* (Geneva: ICRC, 2005).

8. See the Disbandment of Illegal Armed Groups (DIAG) website (http://www.diag.gov.af/diagproject) and strategy. DIAG defines an illegal armed group 'as a group of five or more armed individuals forming an association outside of the lawful state security organs, drawing its cohesion from (a) loyalty to the commander, (b) receipt of material benefits, (c) impunity enjoyed by members, (d) shared ethnic or social background'.

9. Ian Douglas Wilson, 'Continuity and Change: The Changing Contours of Organized Violence in Post-New Order Indonesia', *Critical Asian Studies*, Vol. 38, No. 2 (2006), pp. 265–97.

10. Most of the debate on legitimacy, however, turns on legal versus sociological concepts of legitimacy (roughly, the legitimacy of actors and courses of action for the international society of states versus the legitimacy of states vis-à-vis their citizens).

11. For a different taxonomy (insurgents, terrorists, militias, organized criminal groups) see Shultz, Richard H., Douglas Farah & Itamara Lochard, 'Armed Groups: A Tier-One Security Priority' Colorado, USAF Institute for National Security Studies, Occasional Paper 57, 2004.

12. For recent contributions on warlordism see William Reno, *Warlord Politics and African States* (Boulder, CO: Lynne Rienner, 1999), pp. 1–44; Kimberly Marten, 'Warlordism in Comparative

Perspective', *International Security*, Vol. 31, No. 3 (Winter 2006-2007), pp. 41–73; Daniel Brió, 'The (Un)bearable Lightness of Violence: Warlordism as an Alternative Form of Governance in the "Westphalian Periphery"', in *State Failure Revisited II: Actors of Violence and Alternative Forms of Governance*, INEF Report 89/2007, pp. 7–49.

13. See 'The Responsibility to Protect: Report of the International Commission on Intervention and State Sovereignty' (Ottawa: International Development Research Centre, 2001), available online at http://www.iciss.ca/report-en.asp.

14. Geneva Secretariat, *The Global Burden of Armed Violence* (Geneva: Geneva Declaration Secretariat, 2008), p. 2. An additional 200,000 persons on average die in conflict zones from non-violent causes (such as malnutrition, dysentery, or other easily preventable diseases). The report is available online at http://www.genevadeclaration.org/pdfs/Global-Burden-of-Armed-Violence.pdf.

15. Dennis Rodgers, 'Living in the Shadow of Death: Gangs, Violence, and Social Order in Urban Nicaragua, 1996–2002', *Journal of Latin American Studies*, Vol. 38, No. 2 (2006), pp. 267–92.

16. Anthony Vinci, 'Anarchy, Failed States, and Armed Groups: Reconsidering Conventional Analysis', *International Studies Quarterly*, Vol. 52, No. 2 (2008), p. 299.

17. For an example of the American government's perspective before recent Supreme Court rulings forced changes in American practice, see Scott Reid, 'Terrorists as Enemy Combatants: An Analysis of How the United States Applies the Law of Armed Conflict in the Global War on Terrorism', Naval War College, 2004, available online at http://www.fas.org/man/eprint/reid.pdf.

18. See Jörn Grävingholt, 'Engaging Armed Groups in Development Cooperation', Paper presented at the conference, 'Exploring Criteria and Conditions for Engaging Non-State Actors (NSAs) to Respect Humanitarian Law and Human Rights Law', Graduate Institute of International Studies, Geneva, Switzerland, June 2007.

19. Kalyvas and Kocher, 'How "Free" is Free Riding in Civil Wars' (note 2); Weinstein, 'Resources and the Information Problem in Rebel Recruitment' (note 2); See also Robert Pape, 'The Strategic Logic of Suicide Terrorism,' *American Political Science Review*, Vol. 97, No. 3 (August 2003), pp. 1–19.

20. See, for examples, Maria Eriksson Baaz and Maria Stern, 'Making Sense of Violence: Voices of Soldiers in the Congo (DRC)', *Journal of Modern African Studies*, Vol. 46, No. 1 (2008), pp. 57–86; Benedict R. O'G Anderson (ed.), *Violence and the State in Suharto's Indonesia* (Ithaca, NY: Cornell University Press, 2001); and for the larger debate, Patrick Chabal and Jean-Pascal Daloz, *Culture Troubles: Politics and the Interpretation of Meaning* (Chicago, IL: University of Chicago Press, 2006).

21. Susanne Schmeidl and Masood Karokhail, 'Armed Non-State Actors and "Community-based Policing" – An Exploration of the Arbakai (Tribal Police) in South-eastern Afghanistan', *Contemporary Security Policy*, Vol. 30, No. 2 (August 2009), pp. 318–42

22. Ibid., p. 331.

23. Ibid., p. 322.

24. Ibid., p. 325.

25. Teresa Koloma Beck, 'Staging Society: Sources of Loyalty in the Angolan UNITA', *Contemporary Security Policy*, Vol. 30, No. 2 (August 2009), pp. 343–55.

26. Ibid., 351.

27. Rodgers, 'Living in the Shadow of Death' (note 15), pp. 276.

28. Ibid.

29. Ibid., pp. 278, 277.

30. Ibid., p. 281.

31. Dennis Rodgers and Robert Muggah, 'Gangs as Non-State Armed Groups: The Central American Case', *Contemporary Security Policy*, Vol. 30, No. 2 (August 2009), p. 11.

32. Ibid., p. 312.

33. Rodgers, 'Living in the Shadow of Death' (note 15).

34. For a further discussion on the increase in violent behavior that accompanied the movement towards more hardline policies by these governments towards gangs, see R. Gutierrez, 'Central America: Harsher Measures Don't Cut Crime', Inter Press Service News Agency (IPS News), 1 November 2006, available online at: http://ipsnews.net/news.asp?idnews=35337.

35. Rodgers and Muggah, 'Gangs as Non-State Armed Groups' (note 31).

36. Ibid.

37. See, for example, Paul Collier, *Economic Causes of Civil Conflict and Their Implications for Policy* (Washington, DC: World Bank, 2000); Paul Collier and Anke Hoeffler, 'Greed and Grievance in Civil War', *Oxford Economic Papers*, Vol. 46, No. 4 (2004), pp. 563–95 and Paul Collier, *The Bottom Billion: Why The Poorest Countries Are Failing and What Can Be Done About It* (Oxford: Oxford University Press, 2007).

38. See, for example, Ted R. Gurr, *Why Men Rebel* (Princeton, NJ: Princeton University Press, 1970); Ted R. Gurr, *Peoples versus States: Minorities at Risk in the New Century* (Washington, DC: United States Institute for Peace Press, 2000); Roger Peterson, *Understanding Ethnic Violence: Fear, Hatred, and Resentment in Twentieth-Century Eastern Europe* (Cambridge: Cambridge University Press, 2004); Lars-Erik Cederman and Luc Girardin, 'Measuring Grievance: Ethno-Political Exclusion and Civil War Onset', Paper presented at the International Conference organized by the Swiss Federal Institute of Technology, Zurich, Switzerland, 15–17 September 2005, 'Mapping the Complexity of Civil Wars', available online at http://www.icr.ethz.ch/mccw/papers/cederman.pdf.

39. For scholarly treatment of some of the weaknesses of the debate, see Christopher Cramer, 'Homo Economicus Goes to War: Methodological Individualism, Rational Choice and the Political Economy of War', *World Development*, Vol. 30, No. 11 (2002), pp. 1845–64, and Karen Ballentine and Jake Sherman (eds), *The Political Economy of Armed Conflict: Beyond Greed and Grievance* (Boulder, CO: Lynne Rienner Publishers, 2003). Will Reno also provides a critique of the debate in a paper aiming to advance the rationalist framework: 'Explaining Patterns of Violence in Collapsed States', Paper presented at a seminar of the Program on Order, Conflict and Violence, Yale University, 30 January 2008, available online at http://www.yale.edu/macmillan/ocvprogram/papers/Reno_OCV.pdf.

40. On predation in resource poor environments, see Anthony Vinci, 'Existential Motivations in the Lord's Resistance Army's Continuing Conflict', *Studies in Conflict and Terrorism*, Vol. 30, No. 4 (April 2007), pp. 337–52.

41. Jennifer Hazen, 'From Social Movement to Armed Group: A Case Study from Nigeria', *Contemporary Security Policy*, Vol. 30, No. 2 (August 2009), pp. 281–300; Klaus Schlichte, 'With the State against the State? The Formation of Armed Groups', *Contemporary Security Policy*, Vol. 30, No. 2 (August 2009), pp. 246–64.

42. Hazen, 'From Social Movement to Armed Group', (note 41), p. 292.

43. Another notable feature of Schlichte's research is his sociological examination of what Eric Wolf called 'fields of leverage': places where frustrated people can be organized and ideologues can instill a commitment to fight. Two of the most important fields for leaders to develop are universities and militaries. Many armed group leaders have a university education (55.4 per cent in Schlichte's study), and/or a military training (66 per cent in the same study). Followers, in contrast, come first from the countryside (being categorized as peasants) but they may also have a student background (52.1 per cent) or come from the urban subclasses (41.1 per cent) and already be a member of another violent group when recruited (32.9 per cent).

44. Schlichte, 'With the State against the State?' (note 41), pp. 253–55.

45. Ibid., pp. 250–53.

46. Ibid., pp. 256–59.

47. Ibid., p. 260.

48. Ibid.

49. Achim Wennmann, 'Grasping the Financing of Non-state Armed Groups: A New Perspective on Conflict Dynamics', *Contemporary Security Policy*, Vol. 30, No. 2 (August 2009), pp. 265–80.

50. Ibid., p. 274.

51. Ibid., p. 268.

52. Ibid., p. 276.

53. Ibid., p. 273.

54. See, for example, Mary Kaldor, *New and Old Wars: Organized Violence in a Global Era* (Cambridge: Polity Press, 1999), Herfried Münkler, *The New* Wars (Cambridge: Polity, 2005); Mark Duffield, *Global Governance and the New Wars: The Merging of Development and Security* (London: Zed Books, 2001).

55. Charles Tilly, *Coercion, Capital and European States, AD 990-1992* (Oxford: Blackwell, 1992). On the applicability of his approach, see Brian Taylor and Roxana Botea, 'Tilly Tally: War-Making and State-Making in the Contemporary Third World', *International Studies Review*, Vol. 10, No. 1 (March 2008), pp. 27–56; Georg Sorensen, 'War and State-Making: Why Doesn't it Work in the Third World?' *Security Dialogue*, Vol. 32, No. 3 (2001), pp. 341–54; Michael Niemann, 'War Making and State Making in Central Africa', *Africa Today*, Vol. 53, No. 3 (Spring 2007), pp. 21–39.

56. Diane Davis, 'Beyond the Democracy-Development Mantra: The Challenges of Violence and Insecurity in the Contemporary Global South', Unpublished paper, 2008; Diane Davis, 'Non-State Armed Actors, New Imagined Communities, and Shifting Patterns of Sovereignty and Insecurity in the Modern World, *Contemporary Security Policy*, Vol. 30, No. 2 (August 2009), pp. 221–45. The basis for Davis's arguments is developed further in Diane Davis and Anthony W. Peirera (eds),

Irregular Armed Forces and their Role in Politics and State Formation (Cambridge: Cambridge University Press, 2003).

57. Davis, 'Non-State Armed Actors' (note 56), p. 237.
58. Ibid., p. 240.
59. Ibid., p. 226.
60. William Reno, 'Explaining Patterns of Violence in Collapsed States', *Contemporary Security Policy*, Vol. 30, No. 2 (August 2009), pp. 356–74.
61. Aaron Karp, 'The Changing Ownership of War: States, Insurgencies and Technology', *Contemporary Security Policy*, Vol. 30, No. 2 (August 2009), pp. 375–94.
62. Ibid., p. 377.
63. Ibid., p. 382.
64. Ibid., p. 387.
65. For more on this concept, see William S. Lind, John F. Schmitt, Joseph W. Sutton and Gary I. Wilson, 'The Changing Face of War: Into the Fourth Generation', *Marine Corps Gazette* (October 1989), pp. 22–6 and Robert B. Polk, *Fourth Generation Warfare and its Impact on the Army* (Fort Leavenworth, KS: General Staff College, Fort Leavenworth KS School of Advanced Military Studies, 2000).
66. Karp, 'The Changing Ownership of War' (note 61), p. 389.
67. See Michael Brzoska, 'Collective Violence Beyond the Standard Definition of Armed Conflict', in Stockholm International Peace Research Institute, *SIPRI Yearbook 2007* (Stockholm: SIPRI, 2007), pp. 94–106.

Non-State Armed Actors, New Imagined Communities, and Shifting Patterns of Sovereignty and Insecurity in the Modern World

DIANE E. DAVIS

Introduction: Rethinking Assumptions about Non-State Armed Actors

In a world of growing security challenges where random and targeted violence generate public anxiety and government concern, non-state armed actors have captured significant scholarly attention, particularly in failed or fragile states where institutions of governance and overall state legitimacy are weakened or under siege.[1] The challenges posed by non-state armed actors are seen as particularly de-stabilizing in low-income late developers where extreme poverty has intersected with political dissatisfaction, authoritarian practices, and ethno-national exclusion to drive violent attacks on states and governing regimes both within home territories and abroad.[2] In both contexts, whether it is the economy or the state that is considered weak, non-state armed actors are identified as central protagonists of regime instability, political disorder, violent conflict, and overall conditions of insecurity and violence.

The assumed relationship between poverty, weak or unstable states and the proliferation of non-state armed actors has translated into a set of geopolitical, developmental, and even disciplinary biases in the literature. Those most likely to undertake research on non-state armed actors are either political scientists with an interest in terrorism, national security, domestic rebellion, and state power,[3] or human rights lawyers and theoreticians who face the thorny challenge of articulating and insuring rights-based codes of conduct and behavioural expectations among armed political groups who challenge the legitimacy and legislative reach of nation-states.[4] In their studies, both groups focus most attention on the poorest and most politically unstable regions of Africa, South or Central Asia, and the Middle East, where poverty, state weakness, military or autocratic rule, and rebel opposition to authoritarian states are widespread. Finally, solutions centre around remedying the political and economic conditions most correlated with state fragility, violent opposition, civil war, and/or the human rights abuses and high levels of impunity associated with these activities. The most popular range from the establishment of good governance and poverty alleviation programs to the deployment of human rights advocates or international peacekeeping forces (or some other form of effective mechanism to produce a cessation of violence) to the diplomatic or military strengthening of regimes in power so that sovereignty or government authority is no longer in question.

But non-state armed actors who fuel insecurity and engage in violence are by no means a problem only in the poorest or most politically unstable (and least democratic) countries of the world; nor are terrorists, revolutionaries, guerrilla rebels or other politically self-defined actors seeking to undermine or overthrow states and regimes the only non-state armed actors of relevance. Armed actors not formally employed by the state contribute to insecurity and endemic violence in a variety of regime-types around the world, some more stable and democratic than others, and some with considerable evidence of economic development and wealth. Moreover, many non-state actors are motivated neither by anti-government ideals nor by regime change, nor are their targets or 'arenas' of action always directed at the level of the national state.

Among non-state armed actors who proliferate in the contemporary period, a large and growing number focus their attention on urban economies[5] and transnational networks of trade and accumulation,[6] with some of them even structured around clandestine networks of remittances,[7] thereby flying under the radar screen (if not catapulting over) the broadly cast domains of governance and sovereignty associated with the nation-state. Likewise, a considerable number of these non-state armed actors use violence to secure markets, networks, and the supply of goods or activities for economic survival, suggesting that their targets are as likely to be other market or supply chain competitors (and sometimes even other actors in civil society, including other non-state armed actors) as the sovereign state itself.[8]

Examples of these non-state armed actors include armed drug lords in urban Brazil and Mexico, international smuggling rings in Central and Southeast Asia, new mafia organizations in Russia, community-based vigilantes in South Africa, Guatemala, and Indonesia, and most striking perhaps, an astounding number of armed private security forces or citizen militias taking on policing functions in politically stable and unstable countries alike, ranging from Mexico to Pakistan to Iraq. All these activities rely on armed actors who fuel violence and generate conditions akin to warfare, but without identifying the state or political upheaval as their main objective.

The range of activities in which today's armed actors engage raises important questions about the rather simplistic 'greed versus grievance' dichotomy that has dominated the literature on non-state armed actors, suggesting not only that grievance is hardly a universal motivation behind the mobilization of non-state armed actors, but also that the concept of greed may be just as misguided. 'Greed' may capture the motivations behind the drug trade, because of the enormous sums of money involved. But as a notion it makes much less sense when the non-state armed actor is involved in smuggling low-rent contraband (e.g. CDs, designer knock-offs, etc.) or when community justice – as in vigilantism or even citizen militias – is the underlying aim.

Further complicating conventional wisdom on the subject, preliminary evidence suggests that some of the above-mentioned categories of non-state armed actors have been known to act clandestinely *on behalf of* states – or in conjunction with the state's own armed actors, sometimes as formal or informal contract employees – as much as against the regime in power. Examples not only include the government's deployment of paid mercenaries to fill gaps where official military operations have failed, but also the use of citizen militias, privately contracted paramilitaries, neighbourhood 'posses', and other civil society-based associations or independent providers of security to achieve the policing or military aims necessary for establishing the state's hegemony.[9] Perhaps the most complicated of such arrangements is that currently seen in Iraq, where the so-called 'Awakening' militias can be considered both a social movement and an enforcer group working both for citizens and the state, albeit indirectly and with the formal identity as a non-state armed actor.[10]

Lest one think that such instances are epiphenomenal, or tied specifically to the current conflict in Iraq and Afghanistan, evidence suggests that these types of coercive actors, straddling both the state and civil society, are far more common than has been generally recognized in the contemporary literature on non-state actors, let alone in the literature on violence and insecurity. Recent research by Desmond Arias show that armed groups in Brazil interact directly with the state in 'social networks', providing financial or narcotic kick-backs to security forces, who in turn provide armed groups with weaponry and a modicum of unconstrained manoeuvrability in their respective communities;[11] while Ralph Rozema has identified a version of such collaborations in his study of the relations between criminal networks and paramilitaries in Colombia.[12] Historical evidence further shows that the state-sanctioned deployment of citizen militias or privately operated paramilitary forces has been a common response to political instability and/or industrial, agrarian, and communal violence in cases as diverse as 19th-century Greece, 20th-century Mexico and Peru, and contemporary Colombia.[13] The current United States government's reliance on paid mercenaries and other contract employees to achieve its military aims in Iraq and Afghanistan, and the general use of paid mercenaries by militaries around the world, suggests that the practice continues in new forms and should not be relegated to the past.[14]

Finally, the accelerating growth of private security forces on a world-wide scale may be the most important challenge to conventional thinking on non-state armed actors, in theoretical if not empirical terms, because it signals the widespread transfer of security functions from the state to civil society.[15] The fact that private police are evident in rich and poor countries alike, democratic and otherwise, further suggests that this shift may be as much about contemporary times and reflective of larger patterns of security re-organization seen in the widespread transfer of policing functions from the public to the private sphere, as it is about poverty, state fragility, and democratic institutions and practices (or their lack thereof). To the extent that private police exist alongside public police, rather than in replacement of them, also means that this phenomenon blurs the line between a state and non-state monopoly of the means of violence, thereby challenging the categorical imperative underlying long-standing use.

With all these shifts, many of the concepts and assumptions used to study both social and political change, not to mention coercion, non-state armed action, or the state itself, are turned on their heads – especially in the context of political conflict, the arena that has hosted most of the literature on non-state armed actors. To the extent that security and policing functions are undertaken by individual citizens, clans, and other community or identity-based groups, they move to the larger analytical domain of civil society but undertake actions with a private rather than public purpose, sometimes even engaging in 'uncivil' activities while at other times providing key public goods. Complicating the analytical terrain, because in conflict situations civil society is frequently the source of rebellion and opposition to predatory or authoritarian rule, it is often viewed as enabling those in the public sphere to struggle against the 'lifeworld colonizing' forces of an unjust state (to use Habermas' notion). But armed actors who answer to private contractors can never serve the entire public. Likewise, to the extent that the state loses its monopoly on coercion, whether to privately contracted police or armed mafia, it can no longer guarantee a critical public good, security; still, precisely because in conflict situations it is common for the state to use its armed forces to protect private interests (i.e. those loyalists embedded in the regime or on the receiving end of political or economic largesse) rather than all citizens, whether this truly means the loss of public goods is not entirely clear.

Given the complexity of this picture, it may be time to re-think prevailing assumptions about non-state armed actors and consider a new analytical agenda for studying who they are and what their impact is on security and violence in the contemporary era. We must be prepared to question our definition of what, exactly, constitutes a non-state armed actor and whether such actors, despite the nomenclature, might also systematically maintain some clandestine or informal relationship to the state, even in the absence of formal linkages. How hard and fast is the analytical distinction between state and non-state armed actors; and what is the theoretical rationale for preserving it in future scholarship? Why do we distinguish between political versus economic motivations in our categorization of non-state armed actors? Are clans, tribes, warlords, and rebels all that different from mafias, gangs, and drug lords; in what ways and why? Further, we must be prepared to examine and perhaps move beyond conventional understandings of the conditions under which non-state armed actors will emerge, thrive, employ violence, and thus contribute to conditions of insecurity. In today's world, the functions and territorial reach of nation-states are in flux; progress on democratic transition has itself generated a proliferation of non-state armed state actors; new global economic practices and international networks link non-state actors with varying economic or political agendas to each other in commodity or supply chains that know no territorial bounds; and insecurity abounds, even for the wealthiest, but more tragically so for the poor.[16] Given these changes, are the assumptions about states and their arms-wielding opponents – drawn from cold war and post-cold war frameworks about the legitimacy and hegemony of the nation-state – still robust enough to lead us to a good understanding of contemporary security challenges?

In this essay, I try to answer these questions by arguing that the emergence and proliferation of non-state armed action focuses as much on economic as political claims, and that the forms and spatial patterns of violence and insecurity these actors generate can be considered both product and producer of the changing nature of states and sovereignty in the contemporary era. This larger claim is structured around several specific propositions linked by a single narrative linking discrete sections of this essay. After accounting for the recent appearance of a much wider range of non-state armed actors whose objectives depart significantly from the armed rebels and anti-state movements that preoccupied contemporary security studies writings on non-state armed actors in prior decades, I turn to the contemporary global dynamics that drive this phenomenon. After tracing the source and nature of these activities to emergent transnational dynamics and new territorial locations on both local and global scales, I then argue that the new 'spatiality' of non-armed state action forms the basis for new imagined communities of allegiance and new forms and scales of sovereignty, each of which challenge the power and legitimacy of the traditional nation-state. To explain why this has occurred, I examine historical trajectories of political and economic development over the past two decades and how they undermined old notions of sovereignty and political allegiance while creating new ones. Finally, I assess the implications of these developments for contemporary security challenges.

The bulk of evidence in this essay is drawn from middle-income late developers, mainly in Latin America, but with some additional reference to South Africa and other countries of the global south where the developmental state has made some progress. These countries serve as the main focus not just because this is where we see a rise in non-state armed action structured around economic activities, but also because the democratic character, relative political stability, and modest but clear economic progress in these countries makes the emergence of non-state armed actors both a political concern and an important qualifying challenge to conventional wisdom. In highlighting the main forms of non-state armed action in these contexts, and their uniqueness in light of the prevailing assumptions, I focus heavily on private police as an increasingly visible non-state armed actor. As an object of study, private police have fallen below the scholarly radar in most literature on state stability and security conditions. Yet their emergence is on the rise in the contemporary world because of changing state and sovereignty conditions, and their existence and activities underscore a fundamental lacuna in the literature on the origins of violence and political stability offered by security scholars and practitioners alike.

States, Sovereignties, and Non-Armed State Actors: Theoretical and Conceptual Foundations

To analytically ground the empirical evidence and narrative presented in this paper, we begin by turning attention to theories of the state, and to the relationship between the nature, functions, and priorities of non-state armed actors and sovereignty. The rationale for making this connection lies in the important works of Max Weber and his more contemporary interpreter Charles Tilly, who showed that state-making has been connected to war-making to a great degree; that successful state formation depends on monopolization of the means of coercion; and that the conditions of sovereignty enabled by successful state formation depend on the forging of reciprocal connections between rulers and ruled.[17]

The basic argument is that in order to defend or establish its sovereignty, a state engages in warfare (usually against other existent or putative states), with inter-state violence fuelling both the fires of warfare and modern state-formation. To the extent that engaging armed actors to fight war requires resources, the state in turn creates new institutions (government bureaucracies), new revenue sources (taxes), and new avenues for securing legitimacy (citizenship rights) that allow it to extract funds and moral support from the citizenry, in the process building stronger state-society connections. These institutions, revenues, and legitimacy claims form the basic building blocks of the modern state, whose capacity to endure and strengthen its sovereignty rests on the capacity of its own coercive forces (military, police, and other state armed actors) to monopolize the means of violence. In short, the struggle to establish state sovereignty rests on armed force, even as the institutional and fiscal capacity to use armed force rests on state power. A closer examination of non-state armed actors suggests that a parallel dynamic may be at play, albeit in non-state domains, where armed actors without allegiance to the nation-state are also engaged in struggles over sovereignty and allegiance.

To be more specific: in a globalizing world where neoliberal political and economic policies are ascendant, citizens become less connected to national states as a source of political support or social and economic claim-making,[18] and more tied to alternative 'imagined communities' of loyalties built either on essentialist identities like ethnicity, race or religion or on spatially-circumscribed allegiances and networks of social and economic production and reproduction.[19] These processes are speeded by 'the societal changes associated with the accessibility of information technology that stimulate networked organizational forms', in turn affecting the nature of conflict and crime by empowering 'non-state entities' and altering the global political landscape.[20] To the extent that alternative imagined communities of allegiance and reciprocity provide new forms of welfare, employment, and meaning, they often operate as the functional equivalents of states, thus encouraging new forms of 'non-state sovereignty'[21] that contrast to the imagined national communities that sustained modern nation-state formation and traditional patterns of sovereignty, along the lines articulated by Benedict Anderson.[22] When these new imagined communities exist apart from (if not in opposition to) traditional nation-states, they often choose (or are forced) to rely on their own armed actors to sustain, nurture, or protect their activities and dominion, especially when they conflict with national state priorities.

This dynamic could readily describe the sets of allegiances, loyalties, and impacts of guerrilla forces and other more conventionally defined non-state armed actors who might conceptualize themselves as an alternative 'imagined community' of rebels fighting against an oppressive nation-state, as seen in Sudan, Somalia, Congo, and other countries caught in the vicious cycle of civil war or politicized armed conflicts.[23] But it is becoming increasingly clear that these same general dynamics are evident in the activities and priorities of those who have not conventionally been studied in the literature on non-state armed actors, including drug smugglers, mafias, youth gangs, and citizen militias in more stable democratic countries who use armed force but also share social loyalties and common economic objectives in ways that sustain alternative reciprocities and solidarity to each other rather than the state.

Granted the concept of imagined communities was developed in order to account for the emergence of a territorially bounded nationalism predominant in the 19th and

20th centuries, built around a limited and sovereign political community based on 'deep, horizontal comradeship'.[24] That is, this notion was built on an understanding of strong and visceral connections within and between citizens and the state, and thus it is hard to think of drug lords and street gangs fitting neatly into such a conceptual apparatus, not just in terms of their disengagement with formal nationalism but also in terms of strong connections with a wide range of citizens. All too often, in fact, these types of activities alienate neighbours and residents who are caught up in the violence generated by these non-state armed actors. But if we look carefully at Anderson's original work and its meaning, there are significant elements that suggest the continued relevance of the concept of imagined community, albeit rethought to account for the shifting territorial bases of sovereignty and allegiance that also make more contemporary imagined communities 'new' or different from the past.

Foremost, Anderson's deployment of this concept drew its rationale and definitional contours not from universal claims about the conditions under which citizens and the state would always unite, but as a descriptor of a particular historical moment during which territorially based nationalism became ascendant in the 19th and early 20th century. As such, Anderson conceived of the networks of political reciprocity that created the imagined national community as both limited and sovereign precisely because those were the territorialities of the times: in his words, limited because 'no nation imagine[d] itself co-terminous with mankind' and sovereign because the Enlightenment had shifted legitimate authority out of religious institutions and into the state. The territorialities of today suggest that political communities of reciprocity are no longer limited in the same way as before, owing to globalization and transnational flows of peoples and ideas, and to the fact that states are neither uniformly legitimate nor the only authority in an increasingly inter-connected and globalized world. But this does not mean political communities of reciprocity (or imagined communities) have disappeared, only that they are transforming in scale and scope – hence our desire to accommodate an understanding of these changes and recast them in the context of a 'new imagined community' nomenclature. Stated somewhat differently, rather than conceptually throwing the proverbial baby out with the bath water, we seek to explain how and why the connections that tie citizens together and to other forms of sovereignty or authority may bring them into a political imaginary that stands as separate to the nation state in a new or alternative imagined community, if you will.

The issue of deep, horizontal comradeship identified by Anderson as key to his notion of the imagined communities may be more of a conceptual challenge, because as noted above the types of violence-laden activities examined here are not generally thought of as providing the basis for extensive social connection. Moreover, that many of the new activities and forms of networking are transnational in character suggests that there inevitably will be trade-offs between closeness in social relations (or comradeship) and territorial extension of networks or reciprocities that fuel gang, mafia, and other forms of non-state armed action. As Mark Granovetter's notion of the 'strength of weak ties' suggests,[25] this does not necessarily mean that there are not forms of comradeship or connection among the purveyors of these activities and/or the communities from which they emanate. In addition to the inadvertent solidarities created through weak ties, much depends on the scale and nature of the activities under question. Private police working for community clients can create a general sense of civic solidarity, especially if they self-define their aims as protecting larger values in society, as occurred in South Africa after the end of apartheid rule,[26] or as is now current among private police in Mexico City who see themselves on the fault lines of 'war' against criminal forces who threaten to disrupt daily life.[27] And even among those whose activities span larger territorial distances, 'community without propinquity' can emerge, something Melvin Webber proclaimed long ago.[28]

Remember also that Anderson was offering a much more materialist argument for the rise of nationalism/imagined communities, built on an understanding of the emergence of print capitalism and the utility of shared language, not on intrinsic social or cultural identities, blood ties, or other essentialist forms of fraternity. Not only should this caution us against romanticizing or essentializing the notion of community, it also should remind us to seek the material underpinnings of these connections. In the contemporary era, new technologies and new trade connections link networks of citizens and their activities to home-based communities where deep personal ties may still persist, despite the distances covered. Some have even argued that technological changes have reconfigured local community relations and networks in ways that mark a significant spatial departure from the past, while still preserving the notion of community more generally.[29] Overall, scholarship on territorial and technological trends suggest that social ties and the scales upon which they operate have not disappeared so much as been transformed, thereby creating alternative foundations for imagined communities that differ in significant ways from those of prior periods. We have this in mind when we speak of 'new' imagined communities.

An example of just this type of new imagined community, built on both local and transnationally linked armed actions and loyalties, appeared last spring in the Mexican industrial city of Laredo, in the Northern state of Nuevo Laredo not far from the US-Mexican border. A renowned drug mafia cartel called the *Zetas* hung a banner on a downtown pedestrian bridge calling for 'military recruits and ex-military men...seeking a good salary, food, and help for their families' to join them and support their activities. The banner promised no more 'suffering maltreatment or hunger', while a local phone number was posted for contact.[30] The hubris of a drug mafia publicly announcing efforts to recruit new loyalists to a countervailing social and political project defined in direct opposition to a sovereign state and its rule of law, but using the same principles of welfare reciprocity and solidarity, would have been almost unimaginable a decade ago. But in the contemporary era, transnational crime networks are as visible – and almost as legitimate – as national states in many parts of the world, finding loyalty and a sense of community among citizen supporters whose lives become spatially or socially embedded in their powerful criminal orbits.[31] Indeed, after the Laredo announcement citizens in 11 other cities across Mexico responded by hanging public banners asking the country's president to take a 'neutral' stance in the fight against drug-traffickers, so as not to tip the balance towards either the military or the *narcos*, a plea they justified by under-scoring the fact that many of Mexico own military personnel were as corrupted and involved in the drug trade as the *Zetas*.[32]

To a certain extent, elements of this situation hark back to medieval, absolutist, and pre-modern periods before successful state formation, described by Perry Ander-son and others, when princely elites, regional warlords, or other territorially circum-scribed power-brokers wielded control of territories, markets, and subjects. They were the quintessential 'non-state armed actors' because they existed in a world before the advent of the modern state. But there is a parallel in today's world. Non-state armed actors in new imagined communities are operating in ways that pose a challenge to longstanding institutions of sovereignty structured around citizen and armed force loyalty to the modern-nation state and the state-society social contract. If we loosen the strict definition of sovereignty to accommodate the more general concepts of 'power and authority', 'self-government', and the exist-ence of 'independent' territories,[33] this means we are living in world of new sover-eignties, a point already advanced by Arjun Appadurai[34] and taken an empirical step further in Dennis Rogers' work on 'social sovereignty'.[35]

What *most* distinguishes the contemporary situation from the pre-modern, however, as well as the immediate past is the fact that these new imagined commu-nities are struggling for 'alternative forms of sovereignty' – power, authority, inde-pendence, and self-governance on a variety of territorial scales, whether formal or informal – in an environment *where traditional institutions of national sovereignty and the power of the nation-state still exist and must be reckoned with*.[36] Stated simply, the new imagined communities of the contemporary world do not exist in an historical vacuum. They co-exist and overlap with the modern state, and by so doing have a feedback effect on 'old' imagined communities (e.g. the national state) and their relationship to society, by virtue of their capacity to de-legitimize, weaken, or challenge political allegiance to the nation-state. The challenge for con-temporary security studies scholarship is to examine both overlapping and competing states, sovereignties, and non-state armed actors, and to examine their impact on violence and insecurity both with respect to nation-states and society as a whole. Just as important, scholars must examine the practical and theoretical implications of these developments.

In the service of both aims, in the remaining pages I will establish where the activities of contemporary non-state armed actors focused on securing economic dominion are emerging with most frequency, explain why, and show how they challenge the stability and efficacy of consolidated and/or democratic states, with different dynamics perhaps, but similarly de-stabilizing effects as in poor, politically contested, and/or authoritarian states. I also will argue that de-legitimization or weakening of the national state in the face of alternative imagined communities of non-state actors suggests a shift in the action domain of armed force from state to civil society, as well as a potential blurring of the line between different categories of armed actors and between public and private. I end with a discussion of the ways that these shifts make it more difficult to establish conditions of security and stability, even as they raise new analytical questions about conventional categorizations of states, armed and non-armed actors, and the nature of sovereignty in the modern world.

New Territorial Dynamics of Non-State Armed Action: The Urban Frontlines of Conflict

In prior epochs of more conventional war-making, when state armed actors monopolized the means of violence, sovereignty used to be about asserting and legitimizing political power over a fixed territorial domain that established the same national boundaries of allegiance for citizens and state alike. Capital, whether globally or locally extracted, served as a source of funds for arming state actors who engaged in war to protect national boundaries and the citizens within them. States frequently made alliances with local capitalists to supplant the state's territorial sovereignty and war-making aims; in return they protected markets, so that flows of resources could be guaranteed for state activities, war-related or not. All this constituted what Charles Tilly so aptly identified as a protection racket.[37] In today's world, many non-state armed actors also rely on sources of global and local capital, and by so doing they diminish both the legitimacy and resource-extraction capacities of national states, even as they relocate the territorial domain and reach of protection rackets to other scales, both sub-national and international. This has brought new networks of individuals and economic activities connected in and across transnational or sub-national territories, in which armed actors acting on behalf of these new networks – or protection rackets – sometimes wield as much coercive power than do their 'host' nation-states, at least in particular locations and territories.

Such trends are evident by focusing on the main purveyors of violence in the contemporary era, and by highlighting their territorial location. Two or more decades ago, the military, paramilitary, and police tended to monopolize the means of violence, using repressive actions against rebellious citizens identified with warlike terminology as 'enemies of the state'. Much of this conflict centred in rural areas or in regions excluded from the urban-based or elite-dominated developmental gains that accompanied late development. Today, although civil wars, agrarian or rural-based rebel movements still persist in a select subset of countries around the world, violence and 'warfare' are more likely to unfold in cities, especially capital cities.[38] They also are just as likely to be associated with the activities of drug cartels, mafias, non-state militias, citizens acting as vigilantes, and private police (providing protection for both individuals and firms) as with political insurgency. Moreover, whereas in the past much of the armed violence was associated with roaming rebel or guerrilla opposition, in today's world non-state armed actors locate their command and control functions in fixed settings, in neighbourhoods and communities strategically located in large cities and/or in strategic border or exchange areas, many of which sustain their transnational reach.

Several of these dynamics are embodied in the activities and identities of the Mara Salvatrucha, known widely as 'los Maras', a gang whose social and economic activities link a network of Spanish-speaking youth from their origins in Los Angeles through Mexico down into the major cities of Guatemala and El Salvador in a self-identified community of loyalties, whose strength has only accelerated in the wake of state efforts to incarcerate urban gang members (where they only strengthen their networks, plan new operations, and become more strategic opponents to the state). But what is most significant about the Maras is not so much their self-identified gang status but their origins as a group of city-based youth who turned to criminal activity because of the lack of employment alternatives in the large metropolitan areas of California, Mexico, and Central America. Both the urban and employment aspects of their formation as a transnational 'alternative imagined community' speak loudly to the prevalence of city-based, non-state armed actors all over the burgeoning metropolises of the global south, even as they underscore the temporality of this phenomenon.[39] Indeed the rapid growth of cities in the developing world has become one of the major social, economic, and demographic challenges of the contemporary era. We are entering an age where almost half the world is urban and where the majority of population growth will be concentrated in large cities in formerly poor countries of the world, most predominantly in East Asia, South Asia, Latin America, and the Middle East. Rapid urbanization has brought with it a huge set of problems, primarily employment and housing scarcities, which if not resolved will destroy old bonds of community and solidarity among citizens, and which also fuel insecurity and the resort to armed force.[40]

In the rapidly transforming urban environments of the global south, residents find few job opportunities in the industrial sector, a situation which forces larger numbers of residents into informal employment (in commerce and trade primarily) or other means of securing their livelihood.[41] In Mexico City, for example, official estimates identify close to 70 per cent of the urban labour force as employed in the informal sector, and within this category, petty commerce and street vending often predominate. Such employment, which barely meets subsistence needs for many stuck within it, has become ever more 'illicit' as protectionist barriers drop and fewer domestic goods for re-sale are produced, and as the globalization of trade in contraband and illegal goods picks up the slack. As a result, much informal employment is physically and socially situated within an illicit world of violence and impunity, not just because of the sheer illegality of many of the goods traded, but also because to be involved in guns, drugs, and other contraband products (pirated CDs, knock-off designer goods, valuable gems in the case of natural resource-rich African cities) frequently necessitates the deployment of one's own 'armed forces' for protection against the long arm of the state, whether the police or customs inspectors.[42] These forces also fight amongst themselves for control of illicit supply chains, further creating an environment of violence.

Well-organized cadres involved in these illicit activities often take on the functionally equivalent role of mini-states by monopolizing the means of violence and providing protection in exchange for loyalty and territorial dominion.[43] But as mini-states they also participate in their own form of 'foreign policy', that is negotiating, baiting, or cooperating with the sovereign states in whose territory they operate. The result is often the development of clandestine connections between local police, mafias, and the informal sector, as well as the isolation of certain territorial areas as locations for these activities.[44]

The physical concentration of dangerous illegal activities in territorial locations that function as 'no man's lands' outside state control further drives the problems of impunity, insecurity, and violence on the part of non-state armed actors. Histori- cally, border areas between nation-states have played this role, with constantly shift- ing populations preventing networks of reciprocity and social control to strengthen sufficiently to insure that violence and danger would still flourish, despite the efforts of authorities to control movement in and out of border areas. But as urban- ization changes cities into dense conglomerations of peoples and activities, and as illicit trade becomes a principal source of livelihood, we see the same patterns in cities. Certain areas begin to serve the refuge for illegal activities and shifting flows of people and goods. In many cities of the global south, these dangerous areas sit nestled against old central business districts (CBD), where local chambers of commerce face a declining manufacturing base and are especially desperate to attract high-end corporate investors and financial services. Some of this owes to the importance of maintaining a physical proximity to large markets of consumers who will buy informal or illegal goods. But whatever the origin, these spacial dynamics further drive the conflict as the upper and lower ends of the commercial spectrum compete to control the same space. When the successful introduction of urban mega-projects or other downtown development schemes physically displaces those who earn their living in informal sector, their sources of economic livelihood are disrupted, driving more and more to illegal activities and the use of violence to maintain their supply chains. Yet the presence of so much informality and violence in centrally located areas of large cities is often what motivates high-end developers to push for urban renewal and other major renovations of central business districts in the first place.[45]

Globalization has added even more urgency to these contradictory processes as real estate development and the physical creation of upscale 'global cities' has emerged as a key source of grease for the wheels of capital accumulation in the global economy.[46] The upshot is a clash of forces, if not development models, between competing sets of actors both seeking to maintain their dominion in strate- gically located urban spaces, with non-state armed actors involved in protecting illegal and informal activities a key set of actors embroiled in this larger conflict.[47]

These struggles parallel yet depart from the traditional forms of political struggle waged by non-state armed actors against states discussed in much of the conventional literature. On one hand, the state is involved in this conflict by virtue of its deploy- ment of urban planners and police to displace the local populations who fight to main- tain their locations and activities downtown. But the non-state armed actors who are involved in protecting their turf and physical territory, and who assert their political and economic power through illicit rather than licit networks of trade and distribution, are not struggling for political dominion, control of the state, or a reversal in patterns of political exclusion. Rather, they seek economic dominion, and their desire is to not to politically control national territory (as states do), so much as to control key local nodes and transnational networks that make their economic activities possible.[48] Accordingly, they are as likely to use armed force in a defensive way, that is, to keep the state out of their affairs, rather than to insert themselves in the state's affairs.

To be sure, not all informal sector workers in cities of the global south should be classified as non-state armed actors involved in illegal or illicit activities. Nor do they all operate in a transnational orbit of illegality that drives them to use armed force to protect themselves and their means of livelihood from state intervention. But what many of these poor urban residents do hold in common in the contemporary era is a network of obligations and reciprocities in a given spatial context that is not necessarily coincident with the nation-state.[49] The more transnational the supply chain of goods in which these citizens are involved, the more likely that money and/or commodity exchange fuels the connections; while the larger the sums of money are involved, the more likely will these networks of reciprocity will fuel an environment illegality and thus violence. And to the extent that these communities of non-state armed actors involved in transnational networks of violence have the capacity to challenge the national-state's control of the means of coercion, the state and its hold on sovereignty and security is under direct challenge.

In these and other regards, the problems produced by many of these 'non-conventional' non-state armed actors may be as debilitating and threatening to the institutional capacities and democratic character of the state as were the more 'conventional' non-state armed actors (guerrillas, rebels, etc.) that dominated the literature in prior decades. This has been clearly shown in Mexico, in the actions of drug mafias and other armed actors, who have waged war against local police and military in an ongoing battle that has pushed the state to introduce authoritarian measures and legislation that limit general civil liberties and concentrate power in a small circle of high-level officials.[50] Such patterns are also clear in other countries or regions of the world, with Brazil, Argentina, Russia, and South Africa only a few of the many nations where smuggling rings that rely on armed protection have come into violent conflict with the state or citizens.[51] Additionally, in some of these settings the power and influence of mafias has at times been so great, owing to the huge sums of money involved, that mafia elements directly infiltrate those state's agencies charged with coercion.[52] Infiltration or rampant rent-seeking further limits the state's capacity to reduce overall violence and insecurity. With inside knowledge of the state's strategies and intelligence gathering breached, the state cannot function as an all-powerful sovereign entity, nor is it capable of upholding a rule of law, despite its democratic status and electorally legitimate hold on power.

Such conditions not only undermine the state's effective sovereignty; they also require new political or legislative strategies for dealing with these highly elusive yet economically consequential non-state armed actors, ranging from restructuring or eliminating entire state agencies to instituting new legal measures or constitutional changes for defining criminality and empowering the courts, police, and military to fight against non-state armed actors without violating the established norms of governance. These requisites have a direct feedback affect on the nature of the state and its institutional structures, the most visible of which are reflected in efforts to centralize power and authority in new coercive apparatuses capable of controlling or eliminating non-state armed actors. Yet these reforms hold the capacity to undermine the state's democratic underpinnings by promoting the unfettered use of state violence to stem a losing battle against corruption, mafias, and drug trade.

Urban Nation, State Formation, and the Peculiarities of Late Development

The proliferation of non-state armed actors rooted in cities throughout the global south, but who operate transnationally and thus escape effective regulation, is not merely a problem for individual cities or states and their capacities to govern and/ or monopolize the means of coercion. The presence of so many armed actors involved in illegal and illicit supply chains has dramatically transformed the quality of life more generally, with the declining security situation generating citizen unhappiness with the state and, at times, even with democratic institutions. Not that long ago optimism reigned in many developing countries about benefits to be gained by the democratic transition; but dreams of progress have steadily dimmed as problems of violence, crime, and insecurity have proliferated with a vengeance, especially in cities.[53]

Citizens are frustrated with the state, mainly because little headway has been made in eliminating urban crime and violence. This is a result not just of the infiltration of criminal elements into the governing state apparatus, as noted earlier, but also because those charged with keeping order and guaranteeing the rule of law on behalf of the state, that is the police and/or the military, are themselves frequently implicated in abusive practices or criminality.[54] And although patterns of urban violence are linked to illicit activities undertaken by mafias and criminal gangs who run the supply and distribution of contraband, these activities persist with the tacit support of the police and even the military, whose priorities are often protection of their own institutional sovereignty and/or involvement in these black market activities rather than protection of citizens who suffer in the precarious urban environment where informality flourishes and the rule of law remains elusive.

The result is growing cynicism and a renewed sense of hopelessness about both the future and the potential of a democratic political system to deal with extra-legal violence and impunity. State legitimacy is on the decline; instead of letting elected officials and their regulatory agents fight the problems of crime, growing numbers of citizens reject formal political channels and look for their own answers to the problems of insecurity in everyday life. The upside of this trend may be that citizens mobilize among themselves or become directly involved in civil society efforts to monitor crime and reduce insecurity.[55] But there also is a downside. Anxiety about the urban security situation and the state's inability to guarantee order has become so extreme in certain contexts that citizens turn to violence themselves – whether in the form of vigilantism, seen as a last-gasp measure for achieving some sense of citizen justice, whether by self-arming or other forms of protection, or whether through the embrace of a life of crime, so as to be on the giving rather than the receiving end of a growing environment of insecurity – in order to establish some control over their daily existence.[56] In this way, violence originally generated by non-state armed actors involved in illegal, illicit activities lays the contours for a declining urban security situation, which in turn widens the circle of armed action by pushing urban citizens into the world of violence as well, sometimes even motivating them to deploy violence against others out of sheer frustration with the state's incapacity to deliver security.

One result is yet another type of vicious cycle, one that parallels the 'conflict trap' identified by Paul Collier in his seminal work on violence in the poor and unstable countries of the African continent, but whose dynamics unfold in middle-income cities within and between urban residents who are trying to control the security situation in the face of everyday violence linked to trade and a relatively well-capitalized urban economy. This type of urban insecurity is more a problem for civil society than the state, because it permeates and transforms everyday life by fuelling homicides, accelerating crime rates (despite a decline in reportage by victims), justifying lynching and other vigilante acts, and impacting inter-personal violence, all in ways that restrict citizens' abilities to move freely without fear of armed robbery, violent attack, or extortion.[57] In this environment, it is no surprise that citizens arm themselves, hire private security guards, act offensively as much as defensively in battling insecurity, and barricade themselves in gated private communities, all actions which contribute – in perception if not reality – to the environment of fear and insecurity.

That these problems are as likely to emerge in the newly democratized and aspiring middle-income nations of Central and South America, South Africa, and Southeast Asia, as in the poorer and not yet democratic nations of the world, returns us to our originating concerns with questions about the origins of these new patterns of non-state armed action, violence, and insecurity. If these problems neither emerge nor concentrate in the types of regimes proposed in the conventional literature, why not? And why would other regime-types, even democratic ones, become host to such problems?

The answer to these questions lies partly in the ways that past development trajectories rotted the coercive apparatuses of the developmental state from within, bringing corrupt regimes that may now be formally democratic, but that have been incapable of squelching the capacities of non-state armed actors and citizens to take the situation into their own hands. These states could be considered to have lost much of their sovereignty, in *de facto* if not *de jure* terms, at least to the extent that everyday citizens and non-state armed actors bypass the state in their search for security, relying instead on their own networks and communities of identity and/or coercive action. And to find the origins of these shifting patterns, and the reasons why they are most likely to plague developmental states that have made considerable political and economic progress, we must turn to history, and to the ways that prior battles over state formation and sovereignty laid the foundations for the shifts we see today.

For large portions of the 19th and early 20th century, most countries of the developing world suffered through continuous conflicts over sovereignty, seen initially in struggles for independence from colonial powers, in the form of civil wars and other similarly weighty regional conflicts, and, in a few cases, in revolution or other protracted battles leading to a major political rupture with a colonial or liberal past. Most of these countries shared a history of centre-region tensions over the mercantilist nature of the national economy and the efforts to centralize power; longstanding battles between agrarian and industrial elites about the nature of the state and the direction of the economy; pervasive social uprisings and rebellion on the part of the nation's most impoverished citizens, whose exclusion from the governing pact fuelled their collective ire; and the emergence of professional military linked to the power elite (regionally, nationally, or both). All of these conflicts gave life to a single important fact: the persistence of ongoing struggles over the nature, character, and direction of state power.

While the roots of contestation over state-building and state power may have initially traced to the colonial period, struggles persisted beyond formal independence and marked the political and economic landscape of most of the developing world throughout the 20th century, producing a highly conflictive political environment in which an abusive state apparatus, untrammelled coercive power, and violence all flowered. In an effort to advance and protect their state-building efforts, most governments in the developing world exercised considerable coercive power against real and potential enemies, and these practices ultimately helped institutionalize police corruption and the coercive power of an authoritarian state whose pervasive use of violence and disregard for the rule of law ultimately permeated civil society as well. Complicating matters, most states – whether consolidated with a recognized sovereignty or struggling to hold onto power – were also faced with the challenges of rapid economic development. This meant that in addition to consolidating state power vis-à-vis political or ideological enemies, most late developmental states found it essential to manage if not control the rural labour force, a nascent working class, and/or an organized agrarian elite, all while trying to mobilize capitalists. Having a strong military and police were essential to these goals as well as undermining any citizen opposition to this larger developmental project. Accordingly, economic development aims reinforced regime consolidation aims and vice-versa, with both justifying a greater coercive power of the state.[58]

Finally, and just as important for our understanding of the coercive aspects of the state, in many countries of the world the dual challenges of consolidating state power and growing the economy frequently unfolded within the context of rapid urbanization, precisely because economies of scale and consumer markets concentrated industrial development in a few cities. This was particularly the case in the countries of Latin America, South Asia, and Southeast Asia, and much less so in Africa, where rapid and intense urbanization came late and where the locus of political and economic power remained rural. In the developing countries where urbanization served as a third leg of modernization, along with political and economic development, police were as significant as the military in fulfilling the state's political, economic, and even social aims, and thereby extending the coercive arm of the state into the everyday life of large portions of the nation's citizens. This was so not only because large cities served as home to much of the industrial working class and the owners of industrial establishments that the police sought to protect. Police also became central actors because the rapidly urbanizing locales required additional forms of control and regulation – relating to the production and consumption of new goods and services, the provision and management of transportation and traffic, the inspection of markets, and the monitoring of the urban unemployed and indigent, to name but a few – that were necessary in order to grow the commercial economy and guarantee social order in an environment where rural migrants, informal sector workers, and other new social actors appeared on the scene in droves.

In this complicated environment of rapid urbanization, industrialization, and state formation, in which the government's longevity and successes depended on its coercive capacities to hold onto state power, grow the economy, and manage the rapid population shift from countryside to city, the power of the police expanded by leaps and bounds, often to the point where tensions developed vis-à-vis the military – although sometimes, as in Brazil, the corpus of 'beat police' are actually a bureaucratic arm of the military. With police becoming more and more involved in everyday urban life, and the military struggling to keep its privileged position as the arm of the state used to root out enemies and defend the national interest, tensions often emerged within these coercive arms of the state as well as between them and the citizenry. One result is that the military and the police – as individuals and institutionally – were given extraordinary leeway and operated with very little state-imposed discipline.

These legacies empowered the late developmental state's coercive apparatuses in ways that undermined the judicial system and facilitated corruption and impunity both within the state and society. Indeed, with cities expanding ever more rapidly and hosting more informality, police soon learned that rent-seeking with respect to this growing and vulnerable sector of society was an activity that served both their interests. Informal sellers would bribe officials if it meant avoiding court-based pro-secution for urban violations; yet the police also gained more from diverting 'justice' away from the higher courts, where they similarly had little influence, to the streets where face-to-face negotiation with citizens usually produced some sort of financial transaction.[59]

From the State to Civil Society? Shifting Domains of Armed Force and the Decline of State Sovereignty

Such abuses of power may have served the state and citizens during the difficult times when both poverty and employment patterns made face-to-face accommodation a rational response to scarcity and uncertainty, but over time they delegitimized the court system, reinforced corruption and impunity in the police, undermined the rule of law, and ultimately led citizens to reduce trust in the state's coercive forces while also seeking to find their own agents of security and protection. Under these conditions, coercive practices and *de facto* sovereignty allegiances began shifting away from the state and a stable state-society contract, and more toward citizens who network among themselves to provide services and welfare. Such dynamics are well evidenced by the exponential growth of private police, who increasingly taking on activities previously provided by the state, including protecting private homes, workplaces, and transport routes. To be sure, the rise of private police is a world-wide phenomenon. But it is especially evident in those urban environments of the global south where citizens feel they cannot count on public police for protec-tion, owing to the high degrees of corruption and impunity. As such, this phenomenon is of particular visibility and significance in developing countries with a history of authoritarianism, even those where political and economic transition has been successful, because the authoritarian state frequently encouraged a culture of impunity within its coercive apparatuses.

When citizens bypass state channels and turn to non-state actors like private police for protection, the state itself loses a key function and some of its legitimacy, even if the logic seems quite appropriate. To some extent, this is a vicious cycle: if citizens do not struggle for government accountability and transparency in rooting out corruption and cleaning up the police, the state will not go the extra mile in attacking the police, since this is a costly and uphill battle. Yet in the absence of concrete gains in rooting out police corruption, citizens become further alienated from the government, driving them to alternative imagined communities of reciprocity to solve the insecurity problem. This new imagined community might be one of outraged citizens mobilizing against the state for greater security, as seen recently in Mexico City in the mass mobilizations of hundreds of thousands. It might be seen in the form of creating new business-citizen partnerships around security provision, a model used in Johannesburg in the form of a Business Improvement District (BID). Yet it might also be seen in the form of local citizens taking on policing activities themselves, whether in the form of lynching or vigilantism.

But such anarchic citizen responses have a direct impact on the state and its legitimate sovereignty, even as they raise troubling questions about democracy and the rule of law more generally. When ever more individuals start bearing arms as a condition of their employment in private security services, and citizens themselves start to carry guns for self-protection from criminals and police alike, violent 'resolutions' to questions of public insecurity become the norm, thereby fuelling the vicious circle of violence and insecurity. The overall security situation can deteriorate further when 'private' police compete with 'public' police for a monopoly over the means of violence and the legitimacy to use force. In both Mexico City and Johannesburg, two highly violent cities, there have been instances of 'public' and 'private' police forces, not to mention communities themselves, engaging in conflict over who has the right to protect and arrest citizens. Such tensions between different 'imagined communities' of reciprocity bring a collision of loyalties and allegiances, with private police serving and protecting their clients and public police acting on behalf of a sovereign state and its rule of law. The upshot is an environment of fear and insecurity where competing or overlapping imagined communities struggle to hold dominion. Such a situation is well seen in the *favelas* of Rio de Janeiro and Sao Paolo, where citizens are as likely to support local drug lords because they guarantee protection and 'local sovereignty' better than do police or the state.[60]

Complicating matters, as private police grow in numbers and citizens rely on them for protection, there is less discussion about the larger social contract in which security is to be guaranteed as well as increasing ambiguity about the conditions under which private police can take on public police functions, or vice-versa. In the most democratic nations, where there is strong and relatively widespread commitment to a shared social and political contract between ruler and ruled, as in

South Africa, citizens are trying to monitor the situation so as to limit private police powers. Citizens and politicians have worked to impose legislative controls on private police, and they have deliberated over how to insure that public police still protect citizens, in ways that reinforce the state's role as guarantor of the constitution and rule of law. But in those nations where democracy is less well entrenched, where the state remains weak, or where the citizenry is divided about how much trust it will put in the police or the state, very little headway has been made in limiting the power of private police vis-à-vis public police.

In Mexico, for example, where democratic transition has exacerbated vicious conflict between political parties and interest groups so as to make police reform almost impossible, corruption remains rampant and people turn to private police for security. As a result, it is hard to find public support to limit private police actions, and they have become almost as unaccountable as public police. This fact is evidenced by rising complaints about human-rights abuses lodged against private police by citizens, a state of affairs echoed in Brazil as well, where some citizens claim that off-duty cops who take on the role of private police are responsible for more extra-judicial killings than the public police. In an environment where there is insufficient state or citizen capacity to limit private security forces, we also see private police withholding evidence from public police in order to protect their own 'monopolization' of the means of coercion, meaning prior legal procedures and democratic fundamentals associated with a single rule of law start to break down. This only encourages the fragmentation of the citizenry into distinct imagined communities, if you will – further legitimizing the proliferation of more non-state armed actors, each protecting their sub-national or transnational network of clients, imagined communities, and alternative sovereignties.

The problem is not just competition between state and non-state armed actors, however. In some countries the problem is the overlap, or a blurring of lines, between armed forces working in and outside the state. This is not only clear in those countries like Mexico, where poorly paid public police frequently moonlight as private police at night; it also occurs in situations when those who are expelled from public police service for corruption (as in Mexico) or after regime change (as in South Africa after apartheid) become private police. Whatever the source, when the same individuals or networks of armed professionals move back and forth between the state and civil society, sharing knowledge and personal relations, it is harder for citizens to leverage institutional accountability, and abuse of coercive power is more likely to continue.

The *de facto* blurring of lines between public and private police, much like the overlaps between civilian and state-based armed actors evidenced by the clandestine reciprocities between criminals and police, poses several challenges to conventional research on state and non-state armed actors. First, both examples support our originating concerns about the ambiguities in definition, even as they raise questions about which category of armed state actors would be most likely to undermine (or uphold) a stable and sovereign state and its rule of law. Increasingly, it is hard for citizens to know whether public police, private police, the military, local vigilante groups, or even criminal mafias will be most likely to protect them from harm, or to know whether any or all of these armed actors will use violence against them. In the absence of any certainty about which armed actors or state/non-state institutions are most likely to guarantee protection and security, citizens turn to their own informal institutions and mechanisms for protection. By and large, these informal practices bypass the nation-state, further undermining its legitimate sovereignty.

More important perhaps, the conceptual blurring of lines between different types of armed actors poses new security concerns that have implications for both theory and practical action. One of the most troubling is evident in yet a third form of categorical 'boundary crossing', one that has become increasingly common in the contemporary era as new armed state action continues to grow in importance and visibility: the growing interconnections between conventionally defined armed actors politically focused on battles for state power, and 'alternative' non-state armed actors focused on securing or strengthening economic dominion. With global smuggling on the rise in a world of ever more fluid national boundaries, and with the imagined community of the nation-state decreasing in relation to alternative local and transnational networks of allegiance, there are increasing opportunities for old-style political insurgents with nationalist political projects to take advantage of the power and activities of non-state armed actors.[61] This is evidenced by the fact that rebels, terrorists and guerrillas – or those more conventionally defined as non-state armed actors concerned with political regime change – increasingly fuel their political activities through connections with 'newer' forms of non-state armed actors who seek economic advantage, that is, those involved in contraband and illicit trade activities, and vice-versa. Some examples include Hezbollah's reliance on Colombia drug traffickers for funds, the Taliban's use of the opium trade for financial resources, and Somali rebels' engagement with pirates and other criminal groups who control trade running through waters off the African coast.

These activities not only call into question prior scholarly efforts to categorize armed action as having either political *or* economic motivations; they also make much more difficult the efforts of states – or even global actors and institutions – to eliminate the sources of insecurity. When a battle is purely political or purely economic, it is easier to identify 'counter-insurgent' strategies to isolate or undermine these forces, either through direct military action or by mobilizing citizens to contribute to the isolation or de-legitimization of rebel forces. The same is true when an enemy operates only on one scale, whether local, national, *or* transnational. But when these networks of actors collude, or when imagined communities who define themselves around economic sovereignty start sharing networks with those seeking political sovereignty, and when this strongly networked set of armed actors operate on multiple scales simultaneously (using transnational economic activities to fight local politics, for example, or local politics to sustain transnational economic activities), the challenges are immense. Both strategically and analytically, it is difficult to decipher which territorial or ideological point of entry might give the best leverage, indicating in turn that scholars and practitioners need to identify new strategies for establishing security and fighting non-state armed action.

Concluding Thoughts on the 'Coercive Transition', Non-State Armed Actors, and Insecurity in the Modern World

These examples suggest that one key challenge of the contemporary epoch is to come to terms with the fact that we are living in a 'coercive transition'. That is, we seem to be exiting a Westphalian world where most coercive force has been monopolized in the hands of nation-states, and entering a new epoch where local and transnational non-state actors take on those roles, either because the nation-state is weak or non-state actors are overly strong, or because the strength of the latter fuels the weakness of the former, and vice-versa.[62] This pattern, which dominated in the pre-modern era before the rise of nation-states, used to be confined primarily to the poor and non-democratic countries and regions of the world that never fully consolidated state power. But now it is expanding in geographic scope, and appears in middle-income countries of the global south. To the extent that the wealthier and more democratic nations of the world, whether England or the United States, are being pulled into this global orbit through transnational activities that cross developmental boundaries, then we really must see this as a global and temporal transition that affects us all. In the face of these changes, new questions arise. How will security be guaranteed on a local, national, or global scale if these scales are connected not only through transnational networks but also through fused imagined communities that reject standard allegiances to a single nation-state? And what will this mean for the future for democracy, security, and the global order?

It is still too early to find definitive answers. This is precisely the task for further research. But as scholars and practitioners think about the ways that different nations are 'managing' this transition, and as they develop new strategies to confront insecurity in the modern world, there is value in remembering the basic root of the problem.

First, a wide variety of non-state armed actors are increasingly engaging in violence and thus challenging the state's role in monopolizing the means of coercion. These changes both result from and drive the limited capacities of states to respond to citizen concerns, driving a vicious cycle of state de-legitimization and the appearance of alternative imagined communities of reciprocity, many of which are protected by their own non-state armed actors. Second, the non-state armed actors increasingly involved in violence in today's world are not those necessarily struggling over state power or for political inclusion. A large number are motivated either by economic requisites or a desire for self-protection in a deteriorating security environment in which the state seems increasingly unwilling or incapable of doing so. Third, it is precisely these changes in the nature and origins of non-state armed action that create new forms of conflict over the monopolization of coercive capacity, in turn pitting state and non-state 'imagined communities' and their armed forces against each other.

The latter dynamic drives the use of violence by non-state armed actors who seek to defend their dominion, thus laying the groundwork for more conflict between and among non-state armed actors (both locally and transnationally). The result is often the forging of new compromises or complicities between state and non-state coercive actors, with such relationships reinforcing a tendency toward oligopoly in the means of violence. These relationships also change the nature of the state by blurring the line between state and non-state actors, and by compromising the state's monopoly role as the guarantor of the rule of law, thereby limiting the state's capacity to enforce a pluralistic social contract where all are protected and included, not merely those who have access to protection or security.

Finally, to study these developments scholars must accommodate a more nuanced understanding of space and territorial dynamics, precisely because the new imagined communities that non-state armed actors defend, and the battles the state in turn is forced to engage in, are likely to exist in spatial orbits that are both smaller and larger than the nation-state, at times cross-cutting countries and regions to create new networks of obligation and reciprocity that can only be understood when the spatial correlates of their action and allegiance are spelled out. This, finally, may be the greatest security challenge for the nation-state: learning how to operate in new sub- and trans-national territorial domains, and determining whether existent institutions, political authority, and social legitimacy available to them now are ready for the 21st-century task that lies ahead. Such a task calls for creative new ways of strengthening states, of forging new citizen-state relations, and creating new institutions or flexible procedures that allow national states to legitimately struggle against non-state armed actors at a variety of scales simultaneously, both local and transnational. In the process, new state forms and new sovereignty arrangements will undoubtedly emerge, but hopefully in the context of peace and security rather than unrestrained armed force.

ACKNOWLEDGEMENTS

Portions of the research for this paper, particularly those sections focused on private police and police corruption, were undertaken with support from the Carnegie Corporation of New York and the John D. and Catherine T. MacArthur Foundation. Direct all inquiries to: Email: dedavis@mit.edu.

NOTES

1. Peter Huber and Cordula Reimann, *Non-State Armed Actors: An Annotated Bibliography* (Geneva: Swiss Piece Center for Peacebuilding, 2006); William Reno, 'The Changing Nature of Warfare and the Absence of State-building in West Africa,' in Diane E. Davis and Anthony W. Pereira (eds), *Irregular Armed Forces and their Role in Politics and State Formation* (Cambridge: Cambridge University Press, 2004), pp. 322–45.
2. Paul Collier, V.L. Elliott, Håvard Hegre, Anke Hoeffler, Marta Reynal-Querol, and Nicholas Sambanis, *Breaking the Conflict Trap: Civil War and Development Policy* (Washington, DC and Oxford: World Bank and Oxford University Press, 2003); James Fearon and David Laitin, 'Ethnicity, Insurgency, and Civil War', *American Political Science Review*, Vol. 97, No. 1 (2003), pp. 75–90.
3. Reno, The Changing Nature of Warfare (note 1); Pablo Policzer, 'Democracy and Non-State Armed Groups', in Michaelene Cox (ed.), *State of Corruption, State of Chaos: The Terror of Political Malfeasance* (Lanham, MD: Rowman and Littlefield, 2008), pp. 35–51; Jeremy Weinstein, *Inside Rebellion: The Politics of Insurgent Violence* (Cambridge: Cambridge University Press, 2007); Macartan Humphries and Jeremy Weinstein, 'Who Fights: The Determinants of Participation in Civil War', *American Journal of Political Science*, Vol. 52 No. 2 (April 2008), pp. 436–55; Elizabeth Jean Wood, *Insurgent Collective Action and Civil War in El Salvador* (Cambridge: Cambridge University

Press, 2003); Jorn Gravingholt, Claudia Hofman, and Stephen Klingebiel, *Development Cooperation and Non-State Armed Groups*, Working Paper, German Development Institute, Bonn, 2006.

4. George Anderopoulos, Zehra Kabasakal Arat, and Peter Juviler (eds), *Non-State Actors in the Human Rights Universe* (Sterling, VA: Kumarian Press, 2006); Andrew Clapham, 'Human Rights Obligations of Non-State Actors in Conflict Situations', *International Review of the Red Cross*, Vol. 88, No. 863 (September 2006), pp. 491–523; Max P. Glaeser, *Negotiated Access-Humanitarian Engagement with Non-State Armed Actors* (Cambridge, MA: Carr Center for Human Rights, KSG, Harvard University, May 2004); Chandra Lekha Sriran, *Confronting Past Human Rights Violations: Justice vs. Peace in Times of Transition* (London: Frank Cass, 2004).

5. Vadim Volkov, *Violent Entrepreneurs: The Use of Force in Making Russian Capitalism* (Ithaca, NY: Cornell University Press, 2002).

6. Peter Lupsha, 'Transnational Crime versus the Nation-State', *Transnational Organized Crime*, Vol. 2, No. 1 (Spring 1996), pp. 21–48; Marcel Fafchamps, 'Networks, Communities and Markets in Sub-Saharan Africa: Implications for Firm Growth and Investment', *Journal of African Economies*, Vol. 10, AERC Supplement 2 (2001), pp. 109–42.

7. Abdou Maliq Simone, 'Pirate Towns: Reworking Social and Symbolic Infrastructures in Johannesburg and Douala', *Urban Studies*, Vol. 43, No. 2 (February 2006), pp. 357–70; S. Maimbo (ed.) 'Remittances and Economic Development in Somalia: An Overview', *Social Development Papers* No. 38 (Washington DC: World Bank, 2006).

8. Enrique Desmond Arias, 'The Dynamics of Criminal Governance: Networks and Social Order in Rio de Janeiro', *Journal of Latin American Studies*, Vol. 38, No. 2 (2006) pp. 1–32; Nat J. Coletta and Michelle L. Cullen. 'The Nexus Between Violent Conflict, Social Capital and Social Cohesion: Case Studies from Cambodia and Rwanda', Social Capital Working Paper No. 23. (Washington DC: World Bank, 2000), p. A1.

9. Jane Perlez and Pir Subair Shah, 'As Taliban Overwhelm the Police, Pakistanis Fight Back', *New York Times*, 2 November 2008.

10. Erica Goode, 'Handshake Defuses a Standoff in Baghdad', *New York Times*, 4 September 2008, p. 1.

11. Enrique Desmond Arias, *Drugs and Democracy in Rio de Janeiro: Trafficking, Social Networks, and Public Security* (Durham, NC: University of North Carolina Press, 2006).

12. Ralph Rozema, 'Urban DDR-Processes: Paramilitaries and Criminal Networks in Medellin, Colombia', *Journal of Latin American Studies*, Vol. 40, No. 3 (2008), pp. 423–52.

13. Diane E. Davis and Anthony W. Pereira (eds), *Irregular Armed Forces and their Role in Politics and State Formation* (Cambridge: Cambridge University Press, 2004).

14. Marc von Voencken, 'The Business of War,' *Peace and Conflict Monitor*, 15 December 2003; Report of the United Nations Working Group on the Use of Mercenaries, 24 August 2007; 'Iraqi Premier Says Blackwater Shootings Challenge His Nation's Sovereignty', *New York Times*, 24 September 2007.

15. Simon Chesterman and Chia Lehnardt, *From Mercenaries to Market: The Rise and Regulation of Private Security Companies* (New York: Oxford University Press, 2007).

16. Diane E. Davis, 'Speaking to the Silences: Do We Need a Sociology for the Post-9/11 World?' *International Journal of Politics, Culture, and Society*, Vol. 18, Nos. 3–4 (2005), pp. 293–311.

17. Charles Tilly, *Capital, Coercion, and European States, AD 990-1992* (Cambridge: Basil Blackwell, 1990).

18. Saskia Sassen, *Territory, Authority, Rights: From Medieval to Global Assemblages* (Princeton, NJ: Princeton University Press, 2007); Matthew Sparke, *In the Space of theory: Post-foundational Geographies of the Nation-state* (Minneapolis: University of Minnesota Press, 2005).

19. Margaret Keck and Kathryn Sikkink, *Transnational Issue Networks in International Politics* (Princeton, NJ: Princeton University Press, 1997); Andrew Linklater, *The Transformation of Political Community: Ethical Foundations of the Post-Westphalian Era* (Cambridge: Cambridge University Press, 1993); Matthew Sparke, 'A Neoliberal Nexus: Citizenship, Security and the Future of the Border', *Political Geography*, Vol. 25, No. 2 (2006), pp. 151–80.

20. John P. Sullivan and Robert J. Bunker, 'Drug Cartels, Street Gangs, and Warlords', in Robert J. Bunker (ed.) *Non-State Threats and Future Wars* (New York: Frank Cass, 2003), p. 40.

21. Linklater, *The Transformation of Political Community* (note 17); Richard Devetak and Richard Higgott, 'Justice Unbound? Globalisation, States, and the Transformation of the Social Bond', CSGR Working Paper No. 29/99 (May), University of Warwick; Jane Kelsey, 'Globalisation, Nationalism, Sovereignty, and Citizenship', University of Auckland School of Law, http://www.pcpd.org.nz/sr/pubs.html.

22. Benedict Anderson, *Imagined Communities: Reflections on the Origins and Spread of Nationalism* (London: Verso, 1983).

23. Robert Jackson, *Quasi-States: Sovereignty, International Relations, and the Third World* (Cambridge: Cambridge University Press, 1990); Nat J. Colletta and Michelle L. Cullen, *Violent Conflict and the Transformation of Social Capital: Lessons from Cambodia, Rwanda, Guatemala and Somalia* (Washington, DC: World Bank, 2000).
24. Anderson, *Imagined Communities* (note 22); see also T.J. Clark, 'In a Pomegranate Chandelier', *London Review of Books*, available at http://www.lrb.co.uk/v28/n18/print/clar05_.html.
25. Mark Granovetter, 'The Strength of Weak Ties', *American Journal of Sociology*, Vol. 78, No. 6 (1973), pp. 1360–80.
26. Much of this owed to the fact that private police were seen as a mainstay of white protection, harkening to the values of Afrikaaner dominance of the past, in the era of political transition in which the new South African Police (SAP) were empowered and legitimized to represent the new South Africa.
27. Diane E. Davis, with Robert C. Davis, Christopher W. Ortiz, Sarah Dadush, Jenny Irish, and Arturo Alvarado, 'The Public Accountability of Private Police: Lessons from New York, Johannesburg, and Mexico City', *Policing and Society*, Vol. 13, No. 2 (June 2003), pp. 197–210.
28. Melvin Webber, 'Order in Diversity: Community without Propinquity', in J. Lowdon Wingo (ed.), *Cities and Space: The Future Use of Urban Land* (Baltimore, MD: Johns Hopkins Press, 1963), pp. 23–54.
29. Craig Calhoun, 'Community Without Propinquity Revisited: Communications Technology and the Transformation of the Urban Public Sphere', *Sociological Inquiry*, Vol. 68, No. 3 (1998), pp. 373–9; Barry Wellman, 'The Network Community: An Introduction', in Barry Wellman (ed.), *Networks in the Global Village* (Boulder, CO: Westview Press, 1999), pp. 1–48.
30. 'Incitan a la deserción militar', *El Mañana*, 14 April 2008, p. 1, available at http://www.elmanana.com.mx/notas.asp?id=51677.
31. Enrique Desmond Arias, 'Faith in Our Neighbors: Networks and Social Order in Three Brazilian Favelas', *Latin American Politics and Society*, Vol. 46, No. 1 (2004), pp. 1–38.
32. 'Exigen un combate neutral ad narco: colocan mantas en el estados', *El Universal*, 26 October 2008, p. 1, available at http://www.vanguardia.com.mx/diario/noticia/seguridad/nacional/exigen_un_combate_neutral_al_narco;_colocan_mantas_en_7_estados/246251
33. As drawn from *Webster's New Collegiate Dictionary* (Boston, MA and New York: Houghton Mifflin, 1995), p. 1056.
34. Arjun Appuradai, 'Sovereignty without Territoriality: Notes for a Postnational Geography', in Setha Low and Denise Lawrence-Zuniga (eds), *The Anthropology of Space and Place: Locating Culture* (Boston, MA: Blackwell Publishing, 2003), pp. 337–49; see also John Agnew, 'Sovereignty Regimes: Territoriality and State Authority in Contemporary World Politics', *Annals of the Association of American Geographers*, Vol. 95, No. 2 (2007), pp. 437–61.
35. Dennis Rogers, 'The State as a Gang: Conceptualizing the Governmentality of Violence in Contemporary Nicaragua', *Critique of Anthropology*, Vol. 26, No. 3 (2006), pp. 315–30.
36. Brennan Kraxberger, 'Strangers, Indigenes, and Settlers: Contested Geographies of Citizenship in Nigeria', *Space and Polity*, Vol. 9, No. 1 (April 2005), pp. 9–27; Ralph A. Litzinger, 'Contested Sovereignties and the Critical Ecosystem Partnership Fund', *PoLAR: Political and Legal Anthropology Review*, Vol. 29, No. 1 (2006), pp. 66–87.
37. Charles Tilly, 'Warmaking and Statemaking as Organized Crime', in Dietrich Rueschemeyer, Peter Evans, and Theda Skocpol (eds), *Bringing the State Back In* (Cambridge: Cambridge University Press, 1985), pp. 169–91.
38. Marika Landau-Wells. 'Capital Cities in Civil Wars: The Locational Dimensions of Sovereign Authority', Occasional Paper 6, Crisis States Research Center, London School of Economics, April 2008.
39. Dennis Rodgers, 'Slum Wars of the 21st Century: The New Geography of Conflict in Central America', Working Paper No. 10, Crisis States Research Centre, London School of Economics, 2007.
40. Diane E. Davis, 'Insecure and Secure Cities: Towards a Reclassification of World Cities in a Global Era', *Sociologia Urbana e Rurale*, Vol. 29, No. 82, (2007), pp. 67–82. (Reprinted in *MITIR: The MIT International Review*, Spring 2008, available at http://web.mit.edu/mitir/2008/spring/insecure.html).
41. Manuel Castells and Alejandro Portes, 'World Underneath: The Origins, Dynamics, and Effects of the Informal Economy', in Manuel Castells, Alejandro Portes and Lauren A. Benton (eds), *The Informal Economy: Studies in Advanced and Less Developed Countries* (Baltimore, MD: Johns Hopkins University Press, 1989).
42. Kees Koonings and Dirk Kruijt (eds), *Fractured Cities: Social Exclusion, Urban Violence, and Contested Spaces in Latin America* (London: Zed Books, 2007).

43. Elizabeth Leeds, 'Parallel Politics in the Brazilian Urban Periphery: Constraints on Local-Level Democracy', *Latin American Research Review*, Vol. 31, No. 3 (2006), pp. 41–83; Teresa Caldeira, *City of Walls: Crime, Segregation and Citizenship in São Paulo* (Berkeley: University of California Press, 2001).

44. Mingardi Guaracy, 'O trabalho da inteligencia no controle do crime organizado', *Estudos Avancados*, Vol. 21, No. 61 (2007), pp. 51–69.

45. Dennis Rodgers, 'Disembedding the City: Crime, Insecurity, and Spatial Organisation in Managua, Nicaragua', *Environment and Urbanization*, Vol. 16, No. 2 (2004), pp. 113–24.

46. Diane E. Davis, 'Conflict, Cooperation, and Convergence: Globalization and the Politics of Downtown Development in Mexico City', *Research in Political Sociology*, Vol. 15 (2006), pp. 143–78.

47. Arif Hasan, 'The Changing Nature of the Informal Sector in Karachi as a Result of Global Restructuring and Liberalization', *Environment & Urbanization*, Vol. 14, No. 1 (2002), pp. 69–78.

48. Elizabeth H. Campbell, 'Economic Globalization from Below: Transnational Refugee Trade Networks in Nairobi', in Martin Murray and Garth Myers (eds), *Cities in Contemporary Africa* (Basingstoke: Palgrave Macmillan, 2006), pp. 125–47.

49. Cathy McIlwaine and Caroline Moser, 'Violence and Social Capital in Urban Poor Communities', *Journal of International Development*, Vol. 13, No. 7 (2001), pp. 965–84.

50. Diane E. Davis, 'Undermining the Rule of Law: Democratization and the Dark Side of Police Reform in Mexico', *Latin American Politics and Society*, Vol. 48, No. 1 (Spring 2006), pp. 55–86.; John Bailey and Roy Godson (eds), *Organized Crime and Democratic Governability: Mexico and the US-Mexican Borderlands* (Pittsburg, PA: University of Pittsburgh Press, 2000).

51. Graham Denyer Willis, 'Deadly Symbiosis? The PCC, the State and Institutionalized Violence in Sao Paulo', in Gareth A. Jones and Dennis Rodgers (eds), *Youth Violence in Latin America* (New York: Palgrave Macmillan, forthcoming).

52. Marc Lacy, 'Officials Say Drug Cartels Infiltrated Mexican Law Unit', *New York Times*, 26 October 2008, p. A9; see also Bailey and Godson, *Organized Crime* (note 50).

53. Susana Rotker, Katherine Goldman, and Jorge Balan (eds), *Citizens of Fear: Urban Violence in Latin America* (Camden, NJ: Rutgers University Press, 2003); Bailey and Godson, *Organized Crime* (note 50); Caldeira, *City of Walls* (note 43).

54. Caroline Moser, 'Urban Violence and Insecurity: An Introductory Roadmap', *Environment & Urbanization*, Vol. 16, No. 2 (2004), pp. 3–16; Mercedes S. Hinton and Tim Newburn (eds) *Policing Developing Democracies* (New York: Routledge, 2009).

55. Philip Oxhorn and Graciela Ducatenzeiler, *What Kind of Democracy? What Kind of Market? Latin America in the Age of Neoliberalism* (University Park, PA: Penn State Press, 1998).

56. David Pratten and Atryee Sen, *Global Vigilantes* (New York: Columbia University Press, 2003); Daniel Goldstein, *The Spectacular City: Violence and Performance and in Urban Bolivia* (Durham, NC: Duke University Press, 2003).

57. Moser, 'Urban Violence and Insecurity' (note 52).

58. Diane E. Davis 'The Political and Economic Origins of Violence and Insecurity in Contemporary Latin America: Past Trajectories and Future Prospects', in Desmond Arias and Daniel Goldstein (eds), *Violent Pluralisms* (Durham NC: Duke University Press, 2008).

59. Pablo Picatto, 'A Historical Perspective on Criminality in Twentieth-Century Mexico', USMEX 2005-04 Working Paper Series, University of California San Diego, 2003.

60. Elizabeth Leeds, 'Rio de Janeiro', pp. 23-35 in Koonings and Kruijt, *Fractured Cities* (note 42), Arias, 'The Dynamics of Criminal Governance' (note 8).

61. Christine Jojarth, *Crime, War, and Global Trafficking: Designing International Coordination* (New York: Cambridge University Press 2009).

62. Kees Koonings and Dirk Krujit, *Armed Actors: Organized Violence and State Failure in Latin America* (London: Zed Books, 2005).

With the State against the State? The Formation of Armed Groups

KLAUS SCHLICHTE

How do armed groups come into being? The perilous acts of organizing a violent subversive group, the refusal of safer alternatives, the danger of being killed – all these risks tend to make the occurrence of armed groups rather unlikely. And while research on motives of recruits has produced various insights, the logic of the formation of armed groups remains somewhat enigmatic.[1]

In this article I will investigate the formation of armed groups by using the concept of figuration that was introduced into political sociology by Norbert Elias.[2] The term shall designate all social settings, groups and less structured collectives that consist of interdependent individuals. In figurations single actors are linked by asymmetrical power balances, as they exchange favours or commodities, as they maintain emotional ties, and even as they fight. This way of conceiving armed groups has the advantage that it goes beyond methodological individualism, which has become the major obstacle to bridge the gap between large-N studies on political violence and field research-based studies of anthropologists or the work of historians. Also, it is open enough not to predetermine the kind of relations between the members of armed groups.

As this contribution argues, there are at least three mechanisms by which armed groups come into being. Based on a statistical overview, on single-case stories, and, most importantly, on systematic comparison, these three mechanisms also allow explanation of many features of the further trajectories of armed groups.[3] First is the *mechanism of repression*. Violent repression exerted by government forces causes political opposition to evolve into armed action. Leaders of these groups are usually not militarily experienced but instead are politicians who have acquired their positions through descent, formal education, and long political activity. Groups that emerge from this mechanism *become* armed.

Second is the *ad hoc mechanism*. It is activated when neo-patrimonial settings experience crises. Individuals who feel excluded from clientelist networks of a political class begin to organize violent actions against state agencies. Groups formed through this mechanism are new creations that can include older modes of organization but have difficulty becoming stable due to the vagaries of war.

The third mechanism is often linked to situations of open political violence. This spin-off mechanism is tied to state policies, but its main characteristic is that the group's activities become free from state control. Originally, the formation of these groups is a state project. In times of war, governments or single-state agencies often employ informal, non-regular armed forces they can deploy for objectives that regular forces are unwilling or unable to achieve. In many cases, these informal troops are initially under government control but later develop a life of their own.

These mechanisms have been generated by systematic comparison between 80 cases described in the database. Although they do not cover all cases with the same precision, it is obvious that they delineate pathways that repeatedly appear in the empirical record. In the form they are presented here, they are similar to Weberian ideal types.[4] In that sense they do not form a classical typology that would sort an empirical manifoldness into a complete list of mutually exclusive types. The claim connected with these three types is to discern three major mechanisms that lead to the creation of armed groups in the period after 1945. This means that there might be more such mechanisms, which could not be detected by the systematic comparison of the accounts of the 80 groups looked at here.

Furthermore, the three mechanisms do not exclude each other in the course of a war. Two or all three can occur within a social conflict at various points in time. Therefore, purpose of the mechanisms presented here is not to explain the entire variety of all cases but to determine those constellations of conditions under which the formation of armed groups is particularly likely to take place.

I will argue that these sets of conditions differ in many regards. But they overlap as well. It is not surprising to observe that the emergence of armed groups in the period under consideration here are closely related to the political dynamics of postcolonial states, especially when shrinking distributional capacities lead to exclusion. Secondly, the formation of an armed group is always a very internationalized process, as the role of exiled personnel and of foreign governments will show. Thirdly and most importantly, all mechanisms show that a decisive element in the process of formation is produced by states themselves. The production of violence expertise, of the capacity to use arms and to organize armed forces, is almost always learned within state institutions.

This last commonality links this article to several ongoing academic discussions. It might relativize the 'newness' of so-called new generations of warfare in which states allegedly play a less important role.[5] And secondly, while these findings confirm the central role of state crises in the outbreak of civil war,[6] it relativizes the 'otherness' of armed groups. To a large extent, political violence revolves around political rule, but it does not necessarily entail the end of stateness as a political form.

In the following presentations emblematic stories will be used to illuminate the causal relations at work in each of them, followed by a short discussion of similar cases in order to outline the consequences of these formative processes for the figuration's life. Depending on the mechanism of formation, organizational features of armed groups begin to differ as they build divergent hierarchies. There is also a relation between methods of funding their activities, and thirdly, practices of violence by armed groups seem to be related to the way they come into being.[7]

Where Leaders and Staff Originate – A Statistical Overview

Nobody rules alone, and only very simple forms of political domination can do without staff. Gerontocracy and primary patriarchal forms are among the only figurations in which specialized personnel is not required, as the rulers themselves suffice to enact and enforce their decisions. But any political setting in which social relations surpass immediate and face-to-face interaction needs some sort of support staff, that is people who reliably acquiesce to general procedures and obey explicit orders of political leaders. The staff is usually augmented by followers and lower ranks. The distinction between leaders, staff, and followers allows the development of rough initial ideas about the foundations and development of these internal relations within armed groups as figurations.

What can be seen from a rough statistical analysis using this distinction is, first, that states are deeply involved in the emergence and logic of armed groups. This becomes apparent when examining the most frequently shared biographical characteristics of leaders and staff. Secondly, the ties between leaders and staff members, with few exceptions, predate the onset of armed violence.

Personal motivations of course play an important role in the formation of armed groups, as they do in any political organization. The chance of financial gain or motives of affection certainly rank high for the explanation of why individual members join such a group. However, if such reasons alone form the motive for political personnel to follow commands, the figuration is rather instable.[8] The core element of Weber's theory of domination calls for stabilization of relations between leaders and staff, and that constitutes the idea of legitimacy.[9] Both within the figuration and in its external relations, insurgencies need to overcome the costs of violence which comprise first and foremost its delegitimizing effects. Armed groups, as I argue, need to develop forms of legitimacy in order to stabilize their organization and in order to survive the vicissitudes of war.

The argument here is not only that all rulers strive to rouse and groom belief in the legitimacy of their rule. For stable rule it is necessary that at least staff members believe in the legitimacy of the respective order. It is by the type of legitimacy that political forms can best be distinguished. This, as I will argue, also holds true for armed groups. Their inner functioning, their internal dynamics, and also their external behaviour can best be understood and explained by the role and quality of legitimization within the figuration. It has often been said that it is extremely difficult to empirically ascertain legitimacy. Empirically, hypocrisy can often be observed in hierarchical relations and might be wrongly taken for legitimacy. Also, personal interest, weakness, or helplessness prompt people to follow a given order. Indeed, all these motives are empirically observable in figurations such as those of armed groups. But no political figuration can endure for long without a certain degree of legitimacy, at least in the eyes of its staff. Furthermore, it is not probable that such weak motivations as indifference or helplessness could explain participation in an armed group in its early, most dangerous phases.

The empirical record shows that many armed groups who were able to fight in civil wars for extended periods had strong forms of inner legitimacy. It is likewise implausible to assume that a group could keep its organization intact through long periods of fighting connected with suffering, hardship, and huge costs in so many regards without such inner bonds.

The formation of an armed group is the process by which the kernel of a figuration is formed. As will be seen in the three mechanisms, this formation always takes place within a context that hands down a minimum of legitimacy to armed groups. There are always rules, relations, and meanings on which the formation's initiators can draw. This does not necessarily imply that the formation will be successful. An uncounted number of armed groups never surpassed their early stages. The pre-existence of these ties, however, means that there is a foundation on which to build first attempts toward legitimization. As will be seen in many examples, this inner legitimacy provides essential cohesiveness for the internal hierarchies of armed groups. Loss of legitimacy leads to a group's ultimate failure.

The form of legitimacy matters not only for the analytical purpose of distinguishing political organizations. It also reveals a great deal about the entire internal logic of any political organization. The main distinction here is between rule-based authority on the one hand and personal authority on the other. Whereas the former can be identified, for example, in bureaucratic forms of rule, the latter either involves charismatic legitimacy – the belief in a specifically exceptional power or qualities of the incumbent, or the belief in the sanctity of old forms and ties, that is on traditional legitimacy. All these forms of legitimacy, rule-based and personal ones, can be found in armed groups, although never in pure forms, but always blended to varying degrees. Nevertheless, the distinction not only allows tracking changes in the inner organization, it is also fundamental to discern varieties of their original formation.

One way to start the investigation of relations within a figuration is to look at numerical distributions of biographical experiences of leaders, staff, and followers. They indicate – of course very tentatively – some features of the processes of armed groups' formation. A first look at leaders of armed groups, for example, shows a surprising number of shared features in their biographies (Table 1).[10]

No specific profile can be deduced from this list. However, one can see that states, in many ways, are involved in the 'production' of the leaders of armed groups. It is supposedly within state institutions that core skills needed for armed rebellion are transmitted. The high percentage of academically educated, for example, suggests that skills such as abstract reasoning and knowledge of bureaucratic and organizational techniques are important preconditions for becoming the leader of an armed group. Also, some degree of military expertise, usually acquired in state

TABLE 1
BIOGRAPHICAL CHARACTERISTICS OF ARMED GROUP LEADERS

Former professional oppositionist	73%
Academic education	61.6%
Former detainee of state prisons	46.6%
Military education	43.8%
Violent oppositional actions	43.6%
Formerly exiled	39.7%
Education abroad	37%
Academic professional	31%
Member of the ruling political class	23.3%
Military professional	16.4%
No sufficient data	8.8%

Notes: n = 80; insufficient data: 8.8 %; multiple selections possible.
Source: MAG database (note 3).

institutions, is a characteristic of the profile of many armed group leaders. And finally, the experience of violence in state prisons and prior political conflicts also suggests a causal relation between encounters with state violence and the resort to arms as a political strategy. The data also leads to the assumption that conflicts in which armed groups are involved are indeed political. This is suggested by the high percentage of those leaders who have been active as political opponents before they became leaders of violent political groups. Furthermore, it is interesting to note that in opposition to what it is often stated in academic as well as the media discourses, few armed group leaders have criminal backgrounds (6.8 per cent) or religious education (9.6 per cent). The 'crook' and the 'mullah' do not rank prominently among those who instigate and organize armed opposition against regimes in power.

Further findings hint at relations between leaders and staff that are not purely instrumental. As indicated above, recent literature suggests that only interest in personal enrichment induces people to participate in armed rebellion. But greed is an insufficient explanation for what drives the formation of an armed group. Much more conclusive evidence about the mechanisms of how armed groups are formed comes from information on shared experiences of leaders and staff.

The empirical record shows that a very high number of staff members share experiences of political battles with their leaders. Many have the same ethnic background, and in an equal number of cases staff members and leaders know each other from attending the same educational institutions. In 50 out of 56 cases in which there is sufficient information on the matter, there is at least one example of ties between staff members and leaders such as a shared political past, a common ethnic background, or socialization at the same school. We know of 28 groups, out of a sample of 80, in which leaders and staff members had been active in the same political organizations before the armed group was formed. In 17 groups of the same sample, leaders and a number of staff members went to the same schools or universities, and there are also many cases in which both share the same ethnic background or even have family ties.[11]

The data discussed here is useful for preliminary speculation on how armed groups come into being. As such, however, they cannot reveal the processes by which formation of armed groups take place. Further evidence is needed for reconstruction of these evolutions. Based on the intense case studies and the comparative discussion of these findings with accounts on additional cases, it is possible to construct the three mechanisms of armed groups' formation discussed in the following.

These mechanisms do not cover all cases of formation. The claim here is that most cases can be explained by one of these mechanisms. The three mechanisms of armed group formation will be elucidated in the following by giving typical stories that will render their causal connections clearer. Evidence from further cases will then bolster the claim that formulation of these mechanisms is not merely an unjustified generalization of single instances.

From Party Politics to War: The Mechanism of Repression

During the 1970s, the years of explosive economic growth in the Philippines, the Muslim Independence Movement (MIM) emerged.[12] The commercialization of agriculture, migration towards cities, and increasing levels of education all fuelled the political dynamics of which the formation of the MIM was a part. At about the same time, foreign actors began to engage with Philippine Muslims. Two hundred young men from the island of Mindanao were given grants by Gamel Abdul Nasser in Egypt, allowing them to study at the famous Al-Azar University in Cairo. However, students who acquired academic degrees, whether in Egypt or the Philippines, could not use them because the old elite was still controlling the access channels and excluded the 'Moros', the Spanish colonial term for Muslim Filipinos. The way up the social ladder was closed. As a consequence a political party was founded whose main goal was autonomy for the Muslim regions of the country. Due to a land shortage in the early 1970s, Christian gangs attacked Muslim farmers, as a consequence of which Muslim gangs formed and took revenge on Christians. The government reacted by declaring a state of martial law. This turned the political party MIM into a guerrilla movement called Moro National Liberation Front (MNLF). Its existing contacts in the Middle East alleviated its situation by quickly beginning to serve as channels for foreign support. Within months, hundreds of thousands fled from rural areas into cities. The war between government forces and the MNLF ended in 1976 when, in the Libyan capital Tripoli, a peace treaty was signed that contained provision for legal autonomy in the Muslim regions.

At the top of the Muslim opposition were men who started out as politicians. Nur Misuari, the first head of the MNLF, had been active in a communist youth group and studied political science. A typical politician turned *guerrillero*, his political skills were useful in the late 1970s for negotiation of a peace agreement. But as the new governor of Mindanao he was unable to prevent dissatisfaction among younger MNLF members and staff persons when implementation of the peace agreements failed.

Salamat Hashkim, the leader of the splinter group Moro Islamic Liberation Front (MILF), had once been Misuari's deputy and belonged to the group of Al-Azhar graduates. After his return he worked as a librarian but was also politically active organizing Muslim cultural circles in his home area. Through these activities in the late 1960s he came into contact with disgruntled Muslim politicians who had lost their status in the clientelist networks of the Philippine oligarchy.

Both leaders proved to be politically apt and able to negotiate complex treaties encompassing the regulations of autonomy for some southern regions of the Philippines. These treaties also encompassed the integration of thousands of fighters into the military and police forces. Despite multiple rounds of negotiations, the conflict was not brought to an end until 2006, partly because defecting factions such as the Abu Sayyaf Group (ASG) disrupted peace agreements and partly because internationalization of the war as a part of the post-9/11 'war on terror' aggravated the conflict and led to further military escalation.

But it is not the possible ways of settling a war that are of interest here. It is rather the MILF's process of formation that reveals typical elements of the mechanism of repression. Governments in societies that have become unstable are overburdened with tasks that result from social change. If they represent an old oligarchy, these regimes lose their legitimacy in a rapidly changing social and political landscape.

In order to preserve their privileged positions, these regimes often resort to violent repression of their opponents. This measure usually has more unforeseen consequences than planned ones. It supports hardliners in oppositional parties and does not encourage attempts to find peaceful solutions. Political activists feel threatened and abstain from political activity or go underground. This renders non-violent politics even less likely, as could be seen in the case of the MIM, which became an armed liberation movement after state repression had begun.

The radicalization of existing parties is alleviated by the fact that state repression is often indiscriminate. As Stathis Kalyvas[13] has convincingly shown, this is always the case when information on opponents is scarce. This typically occurs when government troops are deployed in areas they are not familiar with and thus cannot tightly control. When rebellious forces offer at least partial protection, civilians shift their support towards them. This has been the case in Mindanao too. Indiscriminate government repression made the option of joining the rebellion a more rational alternative than flight and non-action. The young fighters, mostly between the ages of 15 and 25, were largely reporting that they joined the rebellion to defend themselves and their families against the Philippine government.

In contrast to armed groups that emerge as ad hoc formations, the MNLF could draw on pre-existing structures. The earlier political activity of the MIM had secured not only a broad network of politicians, it was also backed locally within the Muslim communities of Mindanao and other islands in the southern Philippines. The political experience of its leaders enabled it to hold a political line throughout the years of war, even if during negotiations and implementation of the agreements these structures proved too unstable to endure internal disputes resulting from disappointments and envy among its leaders and followers.

Armed groups formed by the mechanism of repression do not always fragment like the MNLF. Many succeed in keeping their organizational boundaries and build strong bonds of inner legitimacy. The Liberation Tigers of Tamil Eelam (LTTE) in Sri Lanka is a case in point. Having been formed in much the same manner as the MNLF, the LTTE did not falter but became one of the biggest and best organized armed groups with complex internal organization and strong transcontinental branches.[14] Furthermore, most leftist guerrilla groups in Latin America have been shaped by this mechanism. More often than not they were under oligarchic rule with strong militarist traditions. Similarly, colonial rulers often reacted with repression against what were called at the time 'liberation movements'. The Frente da Libertação de Moçambique (FRELIMO), the beginning of the anti-French Front de Liberation Nationale (FLN) in Algeria, and the foundation of the Viet Minh during Japanese occupation of French Indochina are identical in this regard.

The common features of armed groups formed through the mechanism of repression thus do not extend throughout their entire lifespan. Other mechanisms can alter their fate in many directions. The usual sequence of the repression mechanism of the formation of armed groups can be summarized as follows (Figure 1).[15]

The fate of groups that emerge via this mechanism is not preordained. They seem, however, to be more successful in gaining political power than armed groups on average. This might have its basis in their social ties and organizational forms that

FIGURE 1
SEQUENCE OF THE REPRESSION MECHANISM OF THE FORMATION OF ARMED GROUPS

Rapid social change => overstrained regime => political exclusion =>

organized opposition => repression => radicalization => armed rebellion

---

exist prior to widespread armed conflict. Legitimacy is established before violence sets in. Furthermore, the practices of violence they exert differ from those employed by groups which come about through the two other mechanisms presented below. Also, these groups experience different forms of violence. More often than in the groups of the other two kinds, indiscriminate violent repression such as massacres and collective punishments continuously characterizes the conflicts in which these groups engage. Hence, the last stages of the mechanism are seen repeatedly during wars, constantly producing violent resistance.

The Ad Hoc Mechanism: Initiatives of the Disappointed

The National Patriotic Front of Liberia (NPFL) that pushed this West African country into a civil war, lasting with brief interruptions almost 15 years, was led by a bona fide opportunist.[16] Charles Taylor, born in 1948 in marginal Nimba County, travelled to the United States in 1972 and earned a degree in economics. After returning to Liberia he became a senior official in the regime of Samuel Kanyon Doe. Taylor did not stay long in a government position. Just three years later, he was charged with embezzlement of US$900,000 and escaped to the United States.

Between 1986 and 1989 Taylor travelled throughout West Africa before finding in Blaise Compaoré and Houphouët Boigny, the heads of state of Burkina Faso and Côte d'Ivoire, respectively, two powerful supporters for his plans. They introduced him to Colonel Ghadaffi of Libya who provided training grounds and military expertise to aid formation of the first troops of the NPFL. Taylor also made contacts with businessmen from France and other foreign countries that desired access to Liberia's rich mineral deposits and other valuable natural resources.[17]

The main Liberian support Taylor had for his plans came from exiled politicians, driven out by Doe's tactics designed to protect his own power. This group, however, was not homogenous. Indeed a number of Taylor's early supporters, it became clear, had their own agendas. After a few months this led to the first divisions within the NPFL.

Among these exiled politicians was Moses Duopu, a former minister in Doe's government and main recruiter of the first round of members. Duopu had a joint past with Charles Taylor as student activist. Tom Woewiyu, a long-standing opponent of the Doe regime, was yet another old friend from student days and became the Defense Minister in Taylor's shadow cabinet. Both later challenged Taylor's position. Duopo was killed in June 1990, while Woewiyu survived.

Within six months, the NPFL was split into subgroups and it was only through general mistrust and ruthless internal violence that chains of command could be maintained. Although Taylor's plan had worked as intended in so far as indiscriminate violence by government troops drove thousands of fighters into his ranks, the ties within his ad hoc formation were not strong enough to turn this support into a coherent organization, or to contain the competing interests of its most powerful members.

The formation of the NPFL thus shows in an extreme manner the crucial problem of armed groups formed by the ad hoc mechanism. Typically, they consist of members of the political class who have been driven from power during severe crises in post-colonial regimes. Ad hoc groups are created exclusively for the purpose of taking power by force without relying on existing social or political organizations. They might try to borrow legitimacy from older traditions and to impress external observers by using satellite telephones and press officers, but such tactics cannot disguise their chronic instability.

In Weberian terminology, ad hoc groups are 'voluntary associations based on self-interest' (*Zweckvereine*)[18] that is their inner logic is the shared assumption of its members that military success is necessary to seize the spoils of power. This shared interest is the weak bond holding the initial group together. Only the charisma of the leader would be a viable source of legitimacy that could overcome this fatal weakness. But in Taylor's case it was the intervention of West African states that prevented him from immediately conquering Liberian state power. The ultimate source of warrior charisma, sudden miraculous success, was thus beyond his reach.

Structures of these groups are chronically endangered as any change in the situation might give incentives for members to exit the shaky coalition. This is the primary reason ad hoc groups fragment as frequently as they do. All members who act with strategic views closely observe any change of options. They leave as soon as they have enough supporters to project a chance to get a bigger share through acting independently. Another problem of ad hoc groups is lack of internal control, leading to uncontrolled violence with its de-legitimizing effects on the group as a whole.

This fragility accompanies ad hoc formations from the very beginning. They have sharply limited time frames to organize a wide range of skills in order to take best advantage of their first military strikes. In the case of the NPFL, for example, it seemed vital that they took action without delay as the regime of President Doe was still cut off from official external support. According to unconfirmed reports, the International Monetary Fund and the World Bank were about to resume services to the Liberian regime. Such a step would have increased Doe's options considerably. The most important competencies required to organize this early phase are the ability to raise funds, to organize political support, and to build sufficient military strength. When these competencies cannot be combined in one person, as was the case with the NPFL, centrifugal tendencies are strong from the beginning. Taylor dispensed with the political connections to heads of states of neighbouring countries and had access to the informal business networks that ruled Liberia's economy. But for military expertise he had to rely on others.[19]

The ad hoc mechanism can be summarized as follows: when neo-patrimonial regimes – or any political systems in which clientelist networks structure political life – come under serious strain, members of the political class will be selectively barred from the spoils of power (Figure 2). An increase of export profits or the loss of international monetary credits can lead to this effect.

Those who are excluded tend to organize armed violence when they find propitious conditions, such as sanctuaries offered by neighbouring regimes willing to offer support. If the central figures are able to enlarge their group's competence by the addition of military expertise, the likelihood that exclusion from clientelist rule will eventually lead to armed opposition increases.

Armed groups produced by this mechanism often become structured along patron-client lines themselves. Two reasons account for this. First, their economy does not differ from the political economy of the system in which they operate. William Reno's account of Taylor's predecessor makes this point very clear: the economy of extraversion that underlay Doe's rule, this strategic mix of fees for business concessions and rents from plantations plus mineral exports, development aid, and political loans was and would continue to be the basis for the rule of Taylor or any other president of Liberia. Apart from the political loans, Taylor already had control of such an economy in his para-state, 'Taylorland'.[20] So even when ad hoc groups succeed, they are doomed to replicate the structures they fought against.

This in turn means that their future rule will be threatened by the same dangers they created for their predecessors. Only to the degree the leaders are able to form much deeper and more stable lines of allegiance in their newly conquered territory can they diminish the risk of being overrun by future challengers to their power. The need to create legitimacy first and foremost among the followers does not vanish with the success of these groups' leaders. It is merely postponed.

Furthermore, it is not accidental that ad hoc groups typically develop in settings where systemic change like decolonization has triggered a long-term process of appropriation of inherited institutions, which defines the post-colonial situation. The states of sub-Saharan Africa are one main theatre of these processes. Charles Taylor's NPFL in Liberia and Foday Sankoh's Revolutionary United Front (RUF) in Sierra Leone are not the only salient African cases. Laurent Kabila's Alliance des Forces Démocratiques pour la Libération du Congo (AFDL)[21] follows much the same pattern. Supported by governments of neighbouring states, single particularly ambitious politicians organized exiled members of the political class and enlarged that kernel by including further personnel with military expertise.[22]

FIGURE 2
THE AD HOC MECHANISM OF ARMED REBELLION

Political crisis in neo-patrimonial systems => selective exclusion from political

class => leader initiative => search for military expertise => armed rebellion

---

Intellectuals often play a prominent role in ad hoc groups, but also in armed groups that come about by the mechanism of repression. This has much to do with the close relationship universities maintain with the political field throughout the world. Academic institutions not only reproduce a state-class of bureaucrats and technocrats. Especially in times of political crises and growing social contradictions, they are also hotbeds of political opposition. As Derluguian pointed out,[23] what matters are not only the academic skills, such as the ability to formulate political programs, to address a Western public in a foreign language, or to set up an organization. Of equal importance are the contacts, the social capital, accumulated during the long years in the cultural milieus that are part of the individual's resources. Skills, cultural capital, contacts, and social capital are necessary for successful leaders of armed groups.

In the faltering years of the Soviet Union, such intellectual networks often merged with violent entrepreneurs chasing opportunities in weakened states, and sub-proletarian militancy rendered violent escalation in these situations more likely. That the ad hoc mechanism is not restricted to the post-Cold War period can be seen by a number of further cases in which the mechanism occurred in almost its ideal-typical form. A perfect example is Uganda's National Resistance Movement (NRM), formed by the current president of Uganda, Yoweri Museveni, when he was defeated in contested elections in 1980. The NRM also started with a few dozen fighters in February 1981, who were soon joined by those who were, or feared becoming, victims of indiscriminate repression by government forces. At the end of the year 1981, the NRA already had 1,000 members and began to reject volunteers since they did not possess enough guns. Initially formed as a group of left-wing oppositionists in neighbouring Tanzania, some of the NRA's leading members had learned guerrilla tactics in camps of the FRELIMO, which at the time was fighting Portuguese colonial troops in Mozambique. But apart from a rather rhetorical leftist jargon and some signs of Maoist guerrilla strategy, the NRA was not determined by the usual Cold War tactics of the time.[24]

Armed groups that come into being by the ad hoc mechanism are thus not a product of narrow periods of time. There are structural histories behind their emergence, and these structures extend to the inner workings of these groups. They rely on inter-state rivalries, and they usually appear in patrimonial regimes. For their emergence this institutional setting is causally much more important than the fluctuations of global conflict. The same applies, it seems, to the third mechanism.

Delegated Violence: The Spin-Off Mechanism

One of the most renowned militias of the former Yugoslavia was clearly a state creation. It was the Srpska Dobrovoljačka Garda (SDG, Serbian Volunteer Guard), led by Željko Raznatović, also known as Arkan. Raznatović was born in 1952 as the son of an air force officer. He was a problematic child, and his father had reportedly approached the secret services to request they assume care of his son, who then became a member of secret units of various federal agencies. In the 1970s, Arkan operated mostly abroad and had arrest warrants in several Western European countries. He escaped from prison several times, for example in Belgium and the Netherlands, allegedly with the help of Yugoslavian secret services. Throughout the 1970s and 1980s he was almost certainly under the protection of these secret agencies.

In 1990 Arkan was again arrested, this time by local police forces in Croatia for having smuggled arms into the Krajina region. Once free, he founded his Serbian Volunteers Guard. Much earlier, Arkan had become a member of the fan club Delije (Heroes) of Belgrade's famous soccer club, Red Star. This job was also reportedly undertaken on behalf of the Ministry of the Interior, as the members of this club had become hooligans and were seen as a problem for public order. Arkan, who at the time was officially merely the owner of a bakery, invited fans on tours in other countries whenever Red Star played matches in the European leagues, and thus he soon became a hero among the Heroes. Most members of this fan club seem to have come from the deprived housing areas of Belgrade where the social contradictions of socialist modernization were particularly hard felt. High unemployment rates among youth, declining household incomes, and a constantly deteriorating supply of staple goods marked life in the areas of Novi Beograd. But when the SDG was founded in 1991, recruitment for Arkan's guard was not restricted to socially deprived youths, but included people of all ranges of age and education.[25]

The Serbian Ministry of the Interior provided Arkan's militia a training camp in Erdut in East Slavonia. Certainly with its consent, if not on its order, the SDG participated in the siege and capture of various cities in Slavonia and Bosnia and soon gained a reputation for particularly brutal treatment of non-Serbian civilians[26] as one of the main instruments of the policy of ethnic cleansing. Among Serbian paramilitaries the SDG was well-equipped with light artillery, trucks, and arms from barracks, including tanks according to one source. Although there is divergent information concerning estimates of its size, ranging between three and ten thousand, it seems likely that altogether around 10,0000 men underwent training in Erdut,[27] and that in most cases war participation was not longer than one or two years, while many members stayed only a couple of months.[28]

During the years of war and particularly after the Dayton Agreement in 1995, Arkan had tried to diversify his position. Erdut, the location of the SDG's training camp, became the brand name of a wine company owned by Arkan, and he became the owner of a shipping company, a radio station, and the casino in the Hotel Yugoslavia. His main economic activity, however, developed under the embargo during the war years. Apparently in growing competition with Milosevic's son, Marko, Arkan tried to monopolize the illegal import of petrol and derivatives from Romania and Bulgaria. Other sources also report his activity in further criminal markets, partly in cooperation and partly in competition with Kosovo-Albanian networks.

Arkan increasingly became a political entrepreneur, making efforts to improve his parliamentary career. His Party for Serbian Unity (Stranka srpska jedintsva, SJS), founded in 1992, however, did not fare well, and he failed to gain a seat in the Serbian Parliament after 1993. Three years later Arkan became the owner of Serbia's first league soccer club, FK Obilić. Politically, Arkan had failed, and his erstwhile power base was eroded after the end of war in Bosnia-Herzegovina.

With a pending international arrest warrant and growing competition from rival mafia networks with closer contacts to Serbian authorities, the lives of Arkan and his wife were almost restricted to his fortified house and the lounges of Belgrade's international hotels. In January 2000 he was killed by two men in the foyer of Belgrade's Hotel Intercontinental.

The trajectory of the SDG is typical of armed groups that start out as state militias and become independent of their sponsors. Seemingly, one condition for the fact that many delegated violent organizations develop a life of their own is that the political situation becomes murky, as was the case in Serbia during the 1990s. Another is that leaders of these groups have political ambitions and use the power they assemble as a stepping-stone to an independent political career.[29]

The desire for personal enrichment, whether by legal or illegal means, was definitely a strong character trait. But even Arkan had shown another face. Many of his actions reveal that his ambition was not just to enrich himself and to prove his masculinity in combat. His eagerness to appear in the media, as well as his attempt to build up political support, suggest further motivations. Arkan's political career, however, was not successful, and his appearances as a statesman might have been instrumental for opportunities that were accessible only through public positions. But his desire for public recognition cannot be overlooked. He succeeded in this regard insofar as his image among militaristic nationalist circles comes close to that of a *hajduk*, those outlaws who served, during the long periods of foreign rule in the Balkans, as a positive role model for social bandits.[30]

Whereas spin-off groups such as that of Arkan are not without imprints of local historical traditions and political cultures, the main mechanism that leads to their creation is orchestrated by states. In situations in which governments feel they cannot exclusively rely on their army, they tend to either tolerate or deliberately create other informal armed forces. One reason for this can be that the chain of control is interrupted due to deep political crises and stalemate situations, as was the case in Lebanon in the mid 1970s. Parts of the armed forces then become focal points for the creation of militias.

Another reason, probably more often the case, is the deliberate decision of governments or single state agencies to create a second layer of organized violence because the regular forces are seen as either not sufficiently effective or not trustworthy to undertake missions which are in violation of international ethical standards. Perhaps for this reason, militias and paramilitary troops created in this manner are particularly prone to commit severe human rights violations in civil wars: they feel legitimized to cross moral boundaries since they know they have state backing, and these transgressions are seldom if ever sanctioned.

Very often, regular forces are not trusted to be ruthless enough to commit these deeds, given their ethos as professional soldiers. The creation of paramilitary forces is thus always the result of individuals' ambitions and strategic decisions within state organs. Exactly how these causal moments mix in each case is a question that can only be answered by empirical investigation. Nevertheless, judging from the similarities between cases, the main elements of the spin-off mechanism can be summarized as follows (Figure 3).[31]

FIGURE 3
SPIN-OFF MECHANISM OF GROUP FORMATION

War => informalized state => delegation of violence => own momentum =>

separation

Spin-off groups form in wars or war-like situations. Politically motivated violence is already openly visible, and for individual reasons or in order to support
the official state forces, the commander of the state military delegates the right to
exert violence to newly created groups. When these groups are successful in the
sense that they form, organize, and succeed in combat, their leaders potentially
accumulate enough warrior charisma and resources to sever the chain of command
to official superiors. The newly formed group then gains its own momentum.[32]

Spin-off groups usually encounter several problems not shared with groups emerging through the mechanisms outlined above. Spin-off groups typically do not stand
in an openly hostile relation to state forces, although the relation is never an easy one.
Many officers of the Yugoslavian army (JNA) detested the militias created by the
Serbian Ministry of the Interior.[33] The 'Cossacks' who participated as informal
troops in the short war that led to the separation of the Transdniestrian Republic
from Moldova in 1992 were viewed with contempt by Alexander Lebed, the commanding general of the 14th Army, then stationed in Tiraspol.[34] The uneasy relationship between spin-off groups and formal state forces is somewhat ameliorated by
personal relations and the fact that they share elements of the same military habitus.

Secondly, it is typical for the organizational development of spin-off groups that
they desperately lack popular support. From a sample of nine such groups only one
reportedly enjoyed considerable popular support, whereas for the overall sample of
armed groups popular support was reported to be more than 50 per cent.

Thirdly, spin-off groups are much more inclined to use ruthless violence with
resultant high costs to their legitimacy. This might be related to the fact that their
staff usually includes high numbers of military personnel. Among the nine cases
investigated more closely, six leaders have a military education, whereas the
overall rate for the entire sample is 43 per cent.[35] Also, in six of the nine cases at
least some staff members came directly from positions in state armed forces. In the
entire sample of 80 armed groups, this applies to only one-third of them. Although
spin-off groups become increasingly independent from state control, they might
still feel legitimated by the power originally invested in them by state agencies.

Like the other two mechanisms by which armed groups form, the spin-off mechanism is not inevitable. It can stop at any point if conditions for its unfolding are not
sufficiently developed. Most of these groups do not survive the regime that has
produced them as they are unable to attract sufficient support with their generally
vigilante and nationalist rhetoric. Extreme violent practices characterize them in
comparison to the two other types. Their programs and rhetoric seems to be oversha-
dowed by their violent practices.

Conclusions

The three mechanisms of formation outlined produce slightly different pathways for the future development of the armed figurations they bring about. And although these mechanisms do not determine the odds of these figurations to institutionalize and turn their violent power into domination, the divergence of structural conditions nevertheless accounts for different probabilities.[36]

Groups that suffer excessive violence from repressive regimes seemingly do not suffer noticeably from legitimacy deficits. Repressive states de-legitimize themselves, and in turn, targeted groups can garner popular support, especially if they provide effective protection. These groups also generally benefit from social ties and legitimate forms of organization that precede the outbreak of violence. Given their relatively strong legitimacy base right from the start, groups that come about by the mechanism of repression have much better chances to survive and to be ultimately successful than the two other types.

Ad hoc groups, in contrast, usually have weaker ties at the beginning. They consist of connections that are products of circumstances rather than relations cultivated over time. Consequently, their internal functioning is precarious. Shared interest alone does not suffice to create stable organization, and ad hoc groups are therefore more prone to fragmentation and decay. In propitious settings, such as strong support by other states, they can institutionalize and defeat government armies.

Spin-off groups typically consist of organized kernels, relying on state resources during their beginnings, accompanied by respective organizational capacities. While internal hierarchies initially remain uncontested, spin-off groups have enormous problems overcoming the de-legitimizing effects of the massive violence they often inflict. Their retrogressive discourse is seldom able to raise huge popular support. Their fate depends on the abilities of post-war states to reintegrate them into armed forces. Often they linger on in ambivalent relation to state armed forces.

Despite their differing outcomes, these three mechanisms as processes have many features in common. All three processes of formation of armed groups have a reverse side. They are always to some degree internationalized. Other states are often involved. The experts in violence have partly acquired their skills in remote institutions. Political ideas around which a group's program is centred have a long-standing international history, and even the very act of founding an armed group sometimes takes place on another continent or in another country.

However, the formation of armed groups always takes place in a local arena, as large and far-reaching as the internationalization of these processes might be. While the political project might be connected to events in other states, it is first and foremost aiming at political change in single states. It is, as was shown, not satisfying to point to particular features in the political economy or to material interest to explain the formation of armed groups. The more challenging question is how and under which conditions these groups form. The three mechanisms distinguished share the common feature that these formations often occur in critical situations of post-colonial states, in either a crisis of distribution due to a shortage of resources or in a crisis in which exclusion and political violence already play a role. These situations can be seen as culminating phases of deeper structural change, and through the three mechanisms it is thus possible to say more about the situational and structural background of the formation processes.

It also has become clear that the formation of armed groups is genuine social action in the sense that it has identifiable actors who act intentionally. There is always somebody who makes decisions regarding the creation of armed organizations, be it in reaction to state repression, to being driven from the ruling class, or in a situation perceived as desperate enough to permit the creation of unlawful armed forces. The resort to arms, as legitimate as it may seem to the individuals involved, is always based on a decision. It does not happen without it.

A third commonality concerns expertise in exerting and organizing violence. It is overwhelmingly within state institutions that future insurgents learn how to fight by military means. Rough aggregated data alluded to the state itself as a main source of this capacity. The evidence given in the exemplary stories delivered further evidence for this interpretation. Particularly those armed groups that originate through processes resembling the second or third mechanism sketched above involve personnel who have acquired their knowledge of how to use arms and how to organize armed forces in state institutions.

Fourthly, the formation of armed groups seems to be bound to pre-existing milieus, locales, and micro-arenas. When studying the accounts of various armed groups it is astonishing to see that inevitably there is a structure from which groups develop. Oppositional milieus, universities and armies, prisons and schools appear to be the institutional settings in which focal points crystallize that start the formation of armed groups. The reason for this is certainly the simple organizational requirement that shared interest does not suffice for an organization to emerge. There must be other social ties that allow for the aggregation of interest. This is even more evident when high politics, such as incumbency of power positions, is at stake, and when the outcome is settled by violent means.

Milieus and institutions are necessary as it is within them that focal points occur that serve as the basis of armed groups. At the centre of these figurations are ties that stem from shared experiences such as many years in armies, schools, prisons, or in exile, of having seen the same things and undergone the same or very similar experiences.

These findings might be taken as starting points for further questions. One is to look back at the usual distinction between state armed forces and non-state armed groups. A deeper investigation than the one delivered here might reveal that violent challenges to incumbent regimes in numerous if not most cases are closely related to the failure of regimes to provide enough space for political change. Furthermore, capacities created by states do in numerous regards enhance the chances of armed groups. This applies to soft skills as well as to military expertise and hardware produced by states and used by armed groups. States seem to be confronted with the challenge to control their violent apparatus in the long run: it seems that the very means to counter violent challenges lay at the basis of future formations of armed groups. The dilemma of how to control means of violence without producing even more remains unresolved. But this insight may raise scepticism about current attempts to render the world more secure by creating greater expertise in the exertion of violence.

NOTES

1. Two factors have been highlighted by this research, namely material interest and coercion. This explanation is certainly not covering all relevant forms of motivation that are empirically never pure. Interviews with war veterans always reveal a complex mix of motives and even participation not even based on real decision. The more recent literature is discussed in Scott Gates, 'Recruitment and Allegiance. The Microfoundations of Rebellion', *Journal of Conflict Resolution*, Vol. 46, No. 1 (Spring 2001), pp. 111–30. Macartan Humphreys and Jeremy Weinstein, 'Handling and Manhandling Civilians in Civil War', *American Political Science Review*, Vol. 100, No. 3, (Fall 2006), pp. 429–47, deal with the consequences of recruitment based on material incentives for practices of violence. Paul Richards, *Fighting for the Rain Forest. War, Youth and Resources in Sierra Leone* (London: Heinemann, 1996) has challenged the presupposition of mere material interest, implying that the logics of exclusion matter much more. Thomas McKenna, *Muslim Rulers and Rebels. Everyday Politics and Armed Separatism in the Southern Philippines* (Berkeley: University of California Press, 1999) stressed the role of immediate security needs.
2. Cf. Norbert Elias, *Die höfische Gesellschaft* (Frankfurt am Main: Suhrkamp, 1983).
3. This contribution is based on research that was carried out on a grant from Volkswagen-Foundation between 2001 and 2007 (Project title: 'Nachwuchsgruppe Mikropolitik bewaffneter Gruppen', see www2.rz.hu-berlin.de/mikropolitik). The author is grateful for this support and for the discussions with Astrid Nissen, Katrin Radtke, Jago Salmon, Daria Isachenko, Alex Veit, Stefan Malthaner, and Teresa Koloma Beck on whose research this paper also relies. In this research project in-depth analysis, including field research, was carried out in 14 countries. Hypotheses and theses of these theory-driven studies were tested against a dataset on 80 armed groups, further on referred to as the MAG database. The construction of the mechanisms sketched here has been based on the comparative, reiterative discussion of cases within that research group.
4. See Max Weber, *Gesammelte Aufsätze zur Wissenschaftslehre*, 5th ed. (Tübingen: Mohr, 1988) on the methodology of creating ideal types and their heuristic function, namely to allow for differentiation of empirical observation and to discuss thesis on chains of causalities.
5. On this discussion see Aaron Karp's contribution in this special issue.
6. See the contribution of Diane E. Davis in this issue, and Klaus Schlichte (ed.), *The Dynamics of States. The Formation and Crises of State Domination* (Aldershot: Ashgate, 2005).
7. On these relations to other characteristics of armed groups cf. Klaus Schlichte, *In the Shadow of Violence. The Politics of Armed Groups* (Chicago, IL: Chicago University Press, 2009).
8. 'But custom, personal advantage, purely affectual or ideal motives of solidarity, do not form a sufficiently reliable basis for a given domination. In addition there is normally a further element, the belief in legitimacy'. Max Weber, *Economy and Society. An Outline of Interpretive Sociology* (Berkeley: University of California Press, 1978), Vol. 1, p. 213.
9. Legitimacy is a contested concept in social sciences. I follow here the definition that is fundamental to Weber's political sociology, namely to conceive it as the belief in the 'moral authoritativeness' of a given order. Weber, *Economy and Society*, (note 4), p. 15. On the role of forms of legitimacy in the life of armed groups, especially of 'charismatic ideas', see Schlichte, *In the Shadow of Violence* (note 7), ch. 3.
10. As mentioned above the database from which this information is taken had started with 50 rough sketches of armed groups in order to identify important aspects of actors (leader, staff, follower), organizational aspects (form, agenda, life-story), and practices (funding, violence). Sources for this information have been accounts by eyewitnesses or participants gathered during field research, press reports in several languages and other secondary sources like academic case literature. The most frequently occurring qualities were then systematically investigated in a sample of 80 cases. Although this enlarged sample roughly followed the regional distribution of internal warfare after 1945, preference was given for pragmatic reasons to well-documented cases. For more detail on the database cf. Stefan Malthaner, 'The Armed Groups Database: Aims, Sources and Methodology', 2007, Available at http://www.ipw.ovgu.de/publikationen/inhalt/publikationen_der_mitarbeiter.html (accessed 7 July 2009).
11. MAG database (note 3).
12. The following account largely follows the impressive study of McKenna, *Muslim Rulers and Rebels* (note 1). See also Nikki Rivera Gomez, *Coffee and Dreams on a Late Afternoon: Tales of Despair and Deliverance in Mindanao* (Quezon City: University of the Philippines Press, 2005) and John T. Sidel, *Capital, Coercion and Crime: Bossism in the Philippines* (Palo Alto, CA: Stanford University Press, 1999) on political structures in the Philippines.

13. Stathis Kalyvas, *The Logic of Violence in Civil War* (Cambridge: Cambridge University Press, 2006), ch. 6.
14. Katrin Radke, 'From gift to Taxes. The Mobilization of Tamil and Eritrean Diaspara in Infrastate Warfare', Working Paper *Micropolitics* 2/2006, Humboldt University Berlin, 2006.
15. It is impossible to list all the groups whose emergence follows the pattern of the mechanism of repression rather than the two other patterns. Cases include the National Democratic Front of Bodoland, see Sudhir Jacob George, 'The Bodo Movement in Assam', *Asian Survey*, Vol. 34, No. 10 (October 1994), pp. 878–92; the Sudan Liberation Army in Darfur, see Gerard Prunier, *Darfur. The Ambiguous Genocide* (Ithaca, NY: Cornell University Press, 2005); the Maoist guerrillas in Nepal, see Philippe Ramirez, 'Maoism in Nepal' in Michael Hutt (ed.) *Himalayan 'People's War'. Nepal's Maoist Rebellion* (London: Hurst, 2004), pp. 225–42; the Tigray Movement in Ethiopia, see John Young, *Peasant Revolution in Ethiopia. The Tigray People's Liberation Front 1975–1991* (Cambridge: Cambridge University Press, 1997) and a number of groups in Latin America. The Frente Sandinista de Liberación Nacional (FSLN) in Nicaragua and the Frente Farabundo Martí de Liberación Nacional (FMLN) in El Salvador are classic examples of this, see Cynthia McClintock, *Revolutionary Movements in Latin America. El Salvador's FMLN & Peru's Shining Path* (Washington, DC: United States Institute of Peace Press, 1998).
16. An extensive account of the formation of the NPFL is given in Stephen Ellis, *The Mask of Anarchy. The Destruction of Liberia and the Religious Dimension of an African Civil War* (London: Hurst, 1998). A shorter version can be found in William Reno, *Warlord Politics and African States* (Boulder, CO: Lynne Rienner, 1998), pp. 91–5, laying more stress on Taylor's economic motivations. On the later development of this business network see François Prkic, 'The Phoenix State: War Economy and State Formation in Liberia', in Schlichte, *The Dynamics of States* (note 6).
17. Cf. Prkic, *The Phoenix State* (note 15). The formation of armed groups in such an international space is nothing unusual. The experience of being exiled, apparently, is strongly connected with the emergence of armed groups. Examples abound and evidence is also given by the high percentage of time spent in exile by both leaders and staff. Hypotheses as to why this is so important might be built on lack of integration in host countries, on formal education and politicization abroad, or on social ties growing stronger between fellow countrymen living in a culturally distinctive environment. The formation of first organizational kernels in exile is however not connected to ad hoc groups. The first steps in the formation of Eritrean resistance also took place in Sudan, cf. John Markakis, *National and Class Conflict in the Horn of Africa* (Cambridge: Cambridge University Press, 1987), p. 107.
18. Cf. Weber, *Economy and Society* (note 8), p. 41.
19. In anthropological terminology, these armed groups start out as 'bands', cf. Eugene V. Walter, *Terror and Resistance. A Study of Political Violence* (New York: Oxford University Press, 1969), p. 57. A counter-example to Taylor and a much more successful case is Uganda's current president, Yoweri Museveni, who controlled external political connections at the beginning of the National Resistance Army (NRA)'s rebellion and could also credibly present himself as the military leader of the rebellion. See his own biographical account: Yoweri Museveni, *Sowing the Mustard Seed. The Struggle for Freedom and Democracy in Uganda* (London: Macmillan, 1997).
20. Cf. Reno, *Warlord Politics and African States* (note 16).
21. The history of the RUF and of other armed groups that follow this pattern is given in Christopher Clapham (ed.), *African Guerrillas* (Oxford: Oxford University Press, 1998). On the formation of the AFDL cf. Erik Kennes, *Essai biographique sur Laurent Desiré Kabila* (Paris: L'Harmattan, 2003), pp. 218–21.
22. There are striking similarities with processes that developed in states of the former Soviet Union in the course of its dissolution. Here again, the appropriation of new states included violent confrontations between armed groups that formed almost randomly around certain persons. Many of them did not have sufficient success to receive attention from Western media, as Georgi Derlugian, *Bourdieu's Secret Admirer in the Caucasus. A World-System Biography* (Chicago, IL: Chicago University Press, 2005) and Valery Tishkov, *Chechnya: Life an a War-Torn Society* (Berkeley: University of California Press, 2004) have demonstrated in the Northern Caucasus.
23. Cf. Derlguian, *Bourdieu's Secret Admirer* (note 22), p. 61.
24. On the interpretation of the strategy of the NRA see Museveni, *Sowing the Mustard Seed* (note 19), and Frank Schubert, '"Guerrillas Don't Die Easily': Everyday life in Wartime and the Guerrilla Myth in the National Resistance Army in Uganda, 1981–1986", *International Review for Social History*, Vol. 51, No. 1 (2006), pp. 93–111, and Jeremy Weinstein, *Inside Rebellion: The Politics of Insurgent Violence* (Cambridge: Cambridge University Press, 2007).

25. Author's interviews with war veterans in Belgrade, conducted between March 2003 and October 2005. On the documentation of the veterans of Belgrade's quarter Rakovica see Milislav Sekulic, *Na krilima patriotisma. Borci Rakkovice u ratovima od 1990 do 1999* (Belgrade: self-published, 2001).
26. Laura Silber and Allan Little, *Yugoslavia. The Death of a Nation* (London: Penguin, 1996), pp. 85, 222.
27. In comparative regard, it is one of the particularities of the wars in Yugoslavia that the country had compulsory military service and regular military training so that almost the entire adult male population had intensive military education. The strong militarist tradition relates to the Partisan's war victory as the foundational myth of Yugoslavia and with the security situation of Yugoslavia during the Cold War as it was perceived after the Soviet invasion of Czechoslovakia in 1968. See Robin Alison Remington, 'State Cohesion and the Military' in Melissa K. Bokovoy (ed.), *State-Society Relations in Yugoslavia, 1945–1992*, (New York: St. Martin's Press, 1997), pp. 61–78. This might be seen as another indication for the fuzziness of the state/non-state distinction in the study of armed groups.
28. For more on the trajectories of Serbian paramilitaries see Klaus Schlichte, 'Na krilima patriosma – On the Wings of Patriotism. Delegated and Spin-Off Violence in Serbia', *Armed Forces and Society*, 2009 (forthcoming).
29. The trajectories of militia leaders in Serbia vary however, as they do in other cases. Cf. Jago Salmon, *Militia Politics. The Formation and Organization of Irregular Armed Forces in Sudan and Lebanon*, PhD thesis, Humboldt University Berlin, 2006, (http://edoc.hu-berlin.de/dissertationen/salmon-jago-2006-07-18/PDF/salmon.pdf) and Schlichte, 'Na krilima patriotisma' (note 28).
30. On the role played by the 'Hajduck' image in the politics of militias during the wars of Yugoslavia see John Allcock, *Explaining Yugoslavia* (New York: Columbia University Press, 2000) pp. 390–95. The seminal reading on social bandits is Eric Hobsbawm, *Primitive Rebels. Studies in the Archaic forms of Social Movements in the 19th and 20th Century* (New York: Norton, 1959).
31. I am drawing here again on the comparative study of Salmon, *Militia Politics* (note 29), p. 96.
32. The spin-off groups included in the sample are: the South Lebanese Army (SLA) in Lebanon, see Jürgen Endres, *Wirtschaftliches Handeln im Krieg. Zur Persistenz des Milizsystems im Libanon* (Wiesbaden: VS-Verlag, 2004); Interahamwe in Ruanda, see Gérard Prunier, *Rwanda. History of a Genocide* (London: Hurst, 1998); the Hrvastko vijece obrane (HVO) in Croatia, see Steven L. Burg and Paul S. Shoup, *The War in Bosnia-Herzegovina. Ethnic Conflict and International Intervention* (Armonk, NY: M.E. Sharpe, 1999); the Mchedrioni and the National Guard in Georgia, see Thornike Gordadze, 'Les nouvelles guerres du Caucase (1991–2000) et la formation des Etats post-communistes', in Roland Marchal and Pierre Hassner, *Guerres et sociétés. Etat et violence après la guerre froide* (Paris: Karthala, 2003), pp. 371–402; the Shan United Army (SUA) in Burma, see Alfred W. McCoy, 'Requiem for a Drug Lord: State and Commodity in the Career of Khun Sa', in Josiah McC. Heyman, 8th ed., *States and Illegal Practices* (Oxford: Berg, 1999); and Dostum's militia in Afghanistan, see Antonia Giustozzi, *Respectable Warlords? The Politics of State-Building in post-Taleban Afghanistan* (London: Working Paper Series, Crisis State Programme, LSE, 2003).
33. Interviews with ex-JNA officers in Belgrade March 2003, October 2005.
34. Anatol Lieven, *Chechnya: Tombstone of Russian Power* (New Haven, NJ: Yale University Press, 1999), p. 244.
35. MAG database (note 3).
36. For a comprehensive discussion on these dynamics see Klaus Schlichte, *In the Shadow of Violence. The Politics of Armed Groups* (Frankfurt A.M.: Campus/Chicago: Chicago University Press, 2009, forthcoming).

Grasping the Financing and Mobilization Cost of Armed Groups: A New Perspective on Conflict Dynamics

ACHIM WENNMANN

Introduction

Over the past decade, the economic aspects of armed conflict have received systematic attention in the scholarly and policy world.[1] In academia, contributions on the political economy of conflict and conflict economies provided a wealth of expertise both conceptually and empirically.[2] At the policy level, multilateral and multi-stakeholder initiatives tackling natural resources and terrorist financing placed the economic dimension at the forefront of international politics.[3] Given the wealth of insight produced and the ongoing relevance of policy initiatives, this paper takes stock and explores new perspectives on the financing of non-state armed groups and their implications for conflict dynamics and policy.

While much has been written on conflict financing from the perspective of resource availability (how much money an armed group has available to pay for an armed conflict), there is much less – if not anything – on the cost of organizing an armed conflict. This paper argues that knowledge of revenue sources may not help much in assessing the financing of an armed group if we do not know how much the organization of armed conflict actually costs. In order to estimate the cost of conflict, the paper sketches a costing tool, which is based on recent scholarly work on small arms and ammunitions. The combination of the availability of revenue sources and the cost of conflict in the analysis of conflict financing has much potential. It can be used to define barriers to entry into armed conflict and the cost of competition during armed conflict, and thus inform strategies of conflict management.

The paper conducts its analysis in five parts. The first part reviews the literature on the financing of conflict after the end of the Cold War. The second part charts a tool to estimate the cost of conflict by using parametric cost-estimation techniques. The third part highlights the implications for conflict dynamics, and the fourth part explores the value added of a cost perspective for identifying the effectiveness of conflict-financing methods. The fifth part concludes by elaborating implications for peace processes, peace-building, and policy against conflict financing.

Conflict Financing After the Cold War

After the end of the Cold War, many armed conflict were explained in terms of ethnic and cultural identities, and associated with 'irrational and essentially inexplicably primordial qualities'.[4] However, a focus on ethnic or religious identity as a cause of conflict neither captured the implications of globalization and weak states for armed conflict, nor reflected the economic aspects of armed conflict. This shift led to the creation of an entire research field on the economic aspects of armed conflict.

Armed conflicts after the Cold War were often described as 'New Wars'.[5] These were 'a myriad of transnational connections so that the distinction between internal and external, between aggression (attacks from abroad) and repression (attacks from inside the country), or even between local and global, becomes difficult to sustain'.[6] The increasing globalization of both formal and informal economies transformed war economies through the commercialization of local resources as well as the supply of know-how, manpower, and the material for the conduct of conflict.[7] In this process, conflict economies became increasingly integrated into 'regional conflict complexes' that were characterized by 'the cross-border spill over of violence, the empowerment of borderlands as sanctuaries for combatants and nurseries for recruits and also as centres of shadow economic activities, and the interregional commercial or other connections that make for prolonged and intractable conflicts'.[8]

At the same time, the fragmentation of political authority of the state became a pervasive phenomenon in developing and conflict countries.[9] The weakness of many states helped armed groups to establish de-facto control over specific areas within a state embedded in regional and global economic networks.[10] In addition, after the Cold War, patronage payments were not only reduced for rebel groups, but also for state armies. This contributed to the weakening of the latter, which increased the relative strength of non-state armed groups and their incentives to challenge the state. For rebel groups it meant a lower degree of expected resistance by state armies.[11]

These efforts to understand conflict financing as a consequence of changing economic and political contexts were paralleled by inquiries into the economic causes of armed conflict. The World Bank sponsored an entire research stream on the economic theory of civil war.[12] While this literature became trapped in a polar-izing debate on whether armed conflict was caused by greed or grievance, more recently it shifted to emphasize 'the primacy of feasibility over motivation'.[13] The early literature provoked a wave of responses that exposed methodological problems and situated economic factors of armed conflicts in specific contexts.[14] While academia still remains divided on the use of statistical methods in the analysis of armed conflict, a middle ground suggests that 'the origin of armed conflict cannot be exclusively related to greed or loot seekers' but rather interacts 'with socioeconomic and political grievances, interethnic disputes, and security dilemmas in triggering the outbreak of warfare'.[15] In terms of conflict dynamics 'economic agendas account less for the origins of conflict than the longevity or persistence of violent conflict'.[16]

Yet another strand of literature focused on different methods of conflict financing. Some early studies emphasized the multitude of methods to finance conflict, partly reconnecting to historical work on the financing of interstate war.[17] However, towards the end of the 1990s, much of the literature focused on natural resources, as evidenced by the work on individual commodities such as oil, diamonds, drugs, and timber, conflict goods, and on the link between natural resources and armed conflict.[18] Natural resources were also central to the reports of the United Nations Security Council Sanctions Monitoring Mechanism on Angola, the Democratic Republic of the Congo (DRC), and Sierra Leone. In particular, the role of so-called 'conflict diamonds' in the financing of African conflicts became a key element in multilateral conflict management strategies. These efforts culminated in a multi-stakeholder initiative, the Kimberley Process, in which non-governmental organizations (NGOs) took a leading role in exposing the link between diamonds and armed conflict.[19]

While much of the policy work based on the assumption that the availability of natural resources was a sufficient condition for armed conflict, the scholarly debate developed a more nuanced understanding. Natural resources were held to be important for the financing of some conflicts, but not for others. In most cases, natural resources were just one method of conflict financing. Other methods included, for example, centralized war economies, conflict goods, external assistance and asset transfers from civilians, as well as the printing and forging of money, protection rackets, landing fees, kidnapping, and revenue from portfolio investments and legitimate business ventures.[20]

The following sections attempt to add yet another layer to the way we conceptualize conflict financing. By sketching a tool to estimate the organization cost of armed conflict, this paper combines the availability of revenue sources and the cost of organizing armed conflict in the analysis of conflict financing and dynamics. Such a perspective considers conflict financing as one of the elements of organization in the context of overcoming the problems associated to recruitment, control, governance, and group resilience.[21] Conflict financing is also important in the different phases of the formation of organized armed groups – articulation, mobilization, insurgency, and war – underlining that they have different organizational and financial requirements at different stages.[22]

Estimating the Mobilization Cost of Conflict

The 'cost of conflict' is commonly used to describe two different aspects of armed conflict. The first understanding of 'cost of conflict' refers to the cost of the *effects* of conflict; the second to the cost of *organizing* armed violence. The former is concerned with the collateral economic impact of conflict, including the economic consequences of a war, its effect on civilians and belligerents, and the implications for local, regional or international economies.[23] The latter is concerned with the cost of mobilizing and maintaining a military force or – in other words – the financial aspects of organizing armed violence, including budgeting and fundraising. The following considerations of the 'cost of conflict' are concerned with the latter.

Looking at mobilization costs from the perspective of organization, one must distinguish between yet another two dimensions: the cost of starting and the cost of maintaining armed conflict. The cost of starting armed conflict means having a battle-ready military force with weapons, ammunition, and other equipment, the logistics to deploy them to the battlefield and – in the case of larger formations

– an administration. The second dimension captures the cost of sustaining active combat, including paying, supplying or replacing soldiers, weapons, ammunition, and other materiel during combat.

The main difference between these two dimensions is that the costs of starting a conflict are relatively predictable, while the cost of maintaining a conflict are dynamic depending on the conflict intensity, the rate of replacement for soldiers and materiel, and the development of prices for weapons, ammunition and other items during armed conflict. In this way, the cost of maintaining armed conflict is disproportionately higher than the cost of starting a conflict. In Kosovo, for example, the cost of an AK-47 increased 16.25 times between spring 1997 and autumn 1998.[24]

The wars in Iraq and Afghanistan exemplify the disproportionate cost of the maintenance of combat. The United States' cost of defence activities amounted to $533 billion in the period 2001–2007 and has been projected to cost between $1.2 and $1.7 trillion in the period 2001–2017.[25] The costs of the war in Iraq are extraordinary and exceptional. The high costs are driven by United States' reliance on high-tech equipment and materiel and the need to project military power over large distances. They also occur in the context of a long-term military transformation towards more flexible ground forces and an expanded Marine Corps.[26] Overall, the war in Iraq is an example that the maintenance of armed conflict can be a bottomless pit that is difficult to finance even for one of the world's wealthiest countries.

In contrast to the maintenance of major conventional armed conflict, the maintenance of terrorist activities or asymmetric warfare is relatively inexpensive. The cost of the terror attacks in New York, Madrid, and London illustrate this fact: the 9/11 attacks cost about $500,000, the Madrid train bombings about $10,000.[27] The 7/7 London attacks were estimated by the official inquiry to amount about $15,000 (£8,000) with the main cost elements being overseas trips, bomb-making equipment, rent, car hire, and travel within the United Kingdom.[28] However, one should not underestimate the cost of terrorism because the training and education of suicide bombers, for example, may be relatively small for each individual, but in order to have one successful suicide bomber one may need to train multiple individuals. Thus for each attack, the cost of all trained potential suicide attackers must be considered, which increases the cost of terrorism.[29]

What follows is an attempt to estimate the cost of conflict based on cost estimating relationships (CERs).[30] CERs are formulas that estimate the cost of an item or activity of one or more cost drivers. CERs are commonly used in project budget estimations and inspired by parametric estimating techniques in the sense that they seek to estimate the overall cost of armed conflict by factoring different cost elements into one available data point. [31]

National and insurgent defence budgets are a starting point to identify the main cost drivers in the organization of armed conflict. Table 1 compares the main cost driver of the in military budgets of the United States, Germany, the Kosovo Police Corps (KPC), and the *Fuerzas Armadas Revolucionarias Colombianas* (FARC), and suggests that personnel, operations and maintenance, and procurement are key cost drivers. The centrality of personnel and operating cost is corroborated in an

TABLE 1

MAIN COST DRIVERS IN MILITARY BUDGETS OF THE UNITED STATES, GERMANY, THE
KPC AND FARC (IN PERCENTAGES OF THE RESPECTIVE TOTAL BUDGET)[33]

	USA (2004) (%)	Germany (2005) (%)	KPC (2003) (%)	FARC (2003) (%)
Personnel	24.7	58.9	50.0	n/a
Operations and maintenance	40.3	n/a	33.1	36.5
Procurement	17.6	30.5	11.9	5.3

analysis of developing country defence budgets in the 1980s. In 20 developing country defence budgets operating and personnel costs dominate as cost drivers.[32]

The objective of the estimation is to establish a minimum threshold to set up and maintain an armed group of about 1,000 soldiers for one year. The estimate focuses on an armed group equipped only with firearms, because this type of organized armed group is the most common in contemporary conflict. The identification of a minimum threshold is important because it affects the incentive structure of an armed group to use armed violence. The estimation of mobilization costs therefore only includes conflict drivers which are an absolute necessity for an armed group: personnel, weapons, and ammunition. This estimation can be complemented by costs of a conventional capability and using estimates from arms deals or prices for conventional military equipment.

The estimation of the cost of armed conflict is separated into five CERs (see Table 2). The first two CERs estimate the start-up cost of conflict by using the price of small arms and ammunition to estimate the cost of weapons and ammunition. Start-up costs capture the cost of equipping an armed group *at one point in time*. Maintenance costs capture the expenses for the conduct of armed conflict *over time*. In case an armed group also has a conventional capability, data from secondary sources can be added.

Three CERs estimate the cost of maintaining an armed conflict. Personnel cost are proxied by data for annual average male income compiled by the UNDP Human Development Report. Other costs, such as logistics, alimentation, medication, and clothing are included in the salary estimation. The estimation for salaries captures how much a conflict organizer needs to spend per year to keep one soldier committed to fight by paying a salary as well as food, shelter, and clothes. The CER for weapons during conflict is captured by the rate of weapons replacement and the price of small arms. The CER for ammunition in conflict is related to the Daily Ammunition Expenditure Rate (DAER) and the price of ammunition during conflict. The estimation of maintenance cost is separated into the cost for low, medium, and high intensity conflict.[34] Based on the insights of research on small arms and ammunition it was possible to establish weapon replacement rates and prices, as well as specific multipliers and DAERs.[35] The utility of this tool lies in only needing four data points – the cost of weapons, the cost of ammunitions, the income per soldier, and the number of soldiers – in order to perform an estimation that identifies the lowest threshold to start and maintain armed conflict.

TABLE 2
OVERVIEW OF ESTIMATING THE MOBILIZATION COST OF CONFLICT[38]

Start-up cost		
CER 1: Weapons	1.5 firearms (F) $\times$ Price per firearm (P_F) $\times$ Number of fighters (N)	$\text{CER } 1 = 1.5 \times P_F \times N$
CER 2: Ammunition	1.5 firearms (F) $\times$ 100 rounds of ammunition (A) $\times$ Price per ammunition (P_A) $\times$ Number of fighters (N)	$\text{CER } 2 = 150 \times P_A \times N$
Maintenance cost		
CER 3: Salaries	Annual male income (I) $\times$ Number of fighters (N)	$\text{CER } 3 = I \times N$
Low intensity conflict		
CER_L 4: Weapons	0.33 firearms (F) $\times$ 1 $\times$ Price per firearm (P_F) $\times$ Number of insurgents (N)	$\text{CER}_L\ 4 = 0.33 \times P_F \times N$
CER_L 5: Ammunition	1.5 firearms (F) $\times$ 20 rounds of ammunition (A) $\times$ 90 days of combat $\times$ Price per round (P_A) $\times$ Number of insurgents (N)	$\text{CER}_L\ 5 = 2700 \times P_A \times N$
Medium intensity conflict		
CER_M 4: Weapons	0.45 firearms (F) $\times$ 1.5 $\times$ Price per firearm (P_F) $\times$ Number of insurgents (N)	$\text{CER}_M\ 4 = 0.675 \times P_F \times N$
CER_M 5: Ammunition	1.5 firearms (F) $\times$ 120 rounds of ammunition (A) $\times$ 90 days of combat $\times$ 1.5 $\times$ Price per round (P_A) $\times$ Number of insurgents (N)	$\text{CER}_M\ 5 = 12{,}150 \times P_A \times N$
High intensity conflict		
CER_H 4: Weapons	0.65 firearms (F) $\times$ 3 $\times$ Price per firearm (P_F) $\times$ Number of insurgents (N)	$\text{CER}_H\ 4 = 1.95 \times P_F \times N$
CER_H 5: Ammunition	1.5 firearms (F) $\times$ 60 rounds of ammunition (A) $\times$ 90 days of combat $\times$ 3 $\times$ Price per round (P_A) $\times$ Number of insurgents (N)	$\text{CER}_H\ 5 = 48{,}600 \times P_A \times N$

An experiment for a low, medium, and high cost estimate for starting and maintaining an armed conflict for 1,000 soldiers per year illustrates the mobilization cost of conflict. The cost to start an armed conflict is between \$67,500 and \$450,000 per 1,000 soldiers. The maintenance of a low intensity conflict is between \$2.1 million and \$11.4 million; a medium intensity conflict between \$2.6 million and \$16.2 million; and a high intensity conflict between \$4.5 million and \$34.8 million per

1,000 soldiers per year.[36] The thought experiment also shows that ammunition is one of the key cost drivers during armed conflict. A three-fold increase in ammunition prices during armed conflict increases the total cost of conflict by about one-third. In addition, soldiers' salaries are an important fixed cost that raises the barrier to entry. In low intensity conflicts, salaries account for about 90 per cent and in high intensity conflict about 35 per cent of the total cost of conflict.

Certainly, these figures must be understood in the context of the assumptions built into the CERs.[37] These assumptions include the following:

1. A ratio of 1.5 weapons per soldier;
2. A ratio of 100 rounds of ammunition per soldier;
3. The armed group has no previous arms or ammunition stockpiles;
4. The armed group does not receive arms or ammunition from external backers before the armed conflict;
5. Average annual earned income equals the salary and maintenance cost per soldier;
6. The rates of weapons replacement are 0.33 for low, 0.45 for medium and 0.65 for high intensity armed conflict;
7. Weapons prices rise 1.5 times from a base period for medium and three times for high intensity armed conflict;
8. In one year, 90 days of combat activity take place;
9. No soldier dies in combat;
10. The DAER is 20 rounds per day per soldier for low, 60 for medium and 120 for high intensity armed conflict;
11. Ammunition prices rise 1.5 times from a base period for medium and three times for high intensity armed conflict; and
12. Armed groups do not capture weapons and ammunition from the adversary or receive them from third parties for free during armed conflict.

It is important to specify these assumptions because they can be changed should information from a specific case suggest other ratios or price developments. In this way, the formulas remain flexible if better information becomes available.

New Perspectives on Conflict Dynamics

The inclusion of the cost of conflict into the study of conflict financing opens new perspectives on conflict dynamics. By creating an estimation tool for the cost of conflict it is possible to establish data points for barriers to entry and the cost of competition. Case studies on Angola, Abkhazia, and Kosovo conducted in the framework of a larger study to which the costing tool was applied point out that it is much cheaper to start an armed conflict than to maintain it. The increase in the cost to maintain armed conflict derives from the greater amount of weapons and ammunition as well as the increase in their prices with rising levels of conflict intensity.

By creating data points on the costs of conflict, the estimation tool develops an understanding of barriers to entry and the cost of competition. Given the limited availability of data on military acquisitions of armed groups, the costing tool is a useful heuristic device to estimate the costs involved in the organization of armed conflict. The costing tool helps identifying if a high start-up and maintenance cost can prevent the occurrence and recurrence of armed conflict or limit the escalation of a pre-existing armed conflict. Considering the financing and mobilization cost of armed groups together disproves the assumption that 'rebel groups more than cover their costs during the conflict'[39] and underlines that 'ten thousand dollars and a satellite phone' – as Laurent Kabila in the DRC confessed[40] – are not necessarily sufficient to organize a prolonged armed conflict.

These considerations also highlight that low intensity conflict as the predominant type of contemporary armed conflict may be explained in relation to its mobilization cost. Low intensity conflict occurs frequently because the barrier to entry to armed conflict and cost of competition is low; however, most organized armed groups cannot cover the cost of escalation. As low intensity conflicts become prolonged, the economic agendas of armed groups generate the revenues needed to self-finance a low intensity conflict, but not enough to escalate the conflict to a higher level of intensity.

Combining the availability of revenue sources and mobilization costs also contributes to discussions on the feasibility of armed conflict as a factor in conflict dynamics.[41] It shows that feasibility not only depends on the availability of resources to pay for armed conflict, but also on the cost of organizing armed conflict. In Georgia, for example, government forces were unable to maintain the armed conflict over Abkhazia in 1992 due to a lack of money. As a consequence of the collapse of the Soviet Union and the fighting, the Georgian economy declined sharply and undermined the government's revenue to fight a war. At the same time, Russia entered the conflict in support of Abkhazia and changed the military balance.[42]

In Angola, revenue of the União Nacional para a Independência Total de Angola (UNITA) declined from around $500 million in 1997 to $80 million in 2000. This drop in revenues resulted from government advances into diamond areas and was accompanied by increasing mobilization costs due to multilateral sanctions and longer supply lines.[43] In consequence, UNITA could no longer maintain a conventional military strategy – it became too expensive – and reverted to guerrilla tactics.[44] In the long term, UNITA was unable to diversify revenue sources to pay for another conventional military build-up and match the escalation driven by government forces in 2000. The latter's territorial advances undermined UNITA's centralized structure and heralded its downfall.[45]

El Salvador is another example of how the lack of revenue fostered a change in conflict dynamics, in this case ending the conflict through a negotiated settlement. In 1988, the Soviet Union communicated to the Farabundo Marti National Liberation Front (FMLF) that it would not receive the same level of assistance as in previous years. In 1989, the United States government warned the Salvadorian Army that military assistance would decline over time. The cutting of foreign assistance has therefore been held to influence the parties to the conflict to seek a negotiated settlement.[46]

These examples also underline that conflict financing can influence the type of military strategy used during armed conflict, including guerrilla tactics, conventional military deployments, and foreign intervention.

What Are Effective Methods of Conflict Financing?

The combination of conflict financing and mobilization cost also fosters reflection on the effectiveness of different financing methods to finance major armed conflict. This perspective stands in contrast to associating the risk of armed conflict with the physical concentration of natural resources and dependence on primary commodity exports.[47] Instead, the risk of conflict occurrence and recurrence increases if the method of conflict financing is effective in generating the revenue to pay for the kind of armed conflict needed by an armed group to achieve its objectives.

The cases of Angola, Abkhazia, and Kosovo underline the varying effectiveness of different methods of conflict financing. In Angola, government forces had a strategic advantage because oil revenues generated more revenue sources than diamonds. Moreover, its revenue base was less vulnerable to attack due to its offshore location. UNITA, on the other hand, was unable to maintain the armed conflict because diamonds did not generate enough revenue to escalate the conflict between 1993 and 1999. It was also unable to control alluvial diamond mines once attacked by the government, and with its financial backbone undermined, UNITA's functioning as an armed group was affected.

In Georgia, parallel economies were difficult to control centrally due to the number of stakeholders involved and were part of a governance system in which the control of economic opportunities was devolved to local strongmen in exchange for political support to the centre. After the Rose Revolution, the government centralized state finances, leading to ten-fold increase in the defence budget between 2002 and 2006. However, the threat of Russia's intervention on the side of Abkhazia kept the barrier to entry too high for Georgia to start an armed conflict. The 2008 recurrence of conflict in South Ossetia and the subsequent defeat of Georgia illustrate that the barrier to entry for Georgia to start an armed conflict was relatively low; however, it had neither the revenue sources nor an external backer to respond to Russia's escalation of the conflict.

In Kosovo, favourable conditions for diaspora financing provided sufficient revenue to start but not to maintain the conflict. The Kosovo Liberation Army was in financial and military difficulties at the end of 1998 and was saved by the intervention of the North Atlantic Treaty Organization (NATO). NATO escalated the conflict at a cost of an estimated $4 billion for air operations only.[48] In this case, internationalizing the conflict and finding an external party covering mobilization costs was an effective strategy of conflict financing.

The first starting point of developing a typology for the effectiveness of different methods of conflict financing is to explore what determines effectiveness. A method of conflict financing is effective when revenue sources are controlled centrally and have the potential to generate a high-value revenue stream to cover the costs of a military strategy. Oil, diamonds, drugs, and third-party assistance are therefore effective methods of conflict financing because they are *easy to centralize*, and generate a *high-value* and *immediate* revenue stream.

Conflict financing such as taxation, parallel economies or diaspora financing are less effective because their revenue stream is more difficult to centralize. This is due to the number of intermediaries involved as well as the potential value of revenue they generate to cover the cost of conflict. Nevertheless, they are important because they provide *constant* revenue over time and therefore useful to cover maintenance costs.

Conflict financing using taxation of humanitarian assistance, individual contributions, kidnapping, asset transfers from civilians, landing fees or revenue from portfolio investments are less effective strategies for conflict financing because on their own they are unlikely to finance a major armed conflict. However, they remain significant, not only in terms of their humanitarian impacts, but also by supplementing other revenue sources. In cases in which they contribute to the financing of a low intensity conflict they may even generate enough revenue to keep the conflict going. Thus, they remain important for low intensity conflict as well as providing small groups or gangs with the capabilities to spoil peace processes or peacebuilding.

Table 3 provides an overview of various methods of conflict financing according to different levels of effectiveness. This typology provides a better understanding of conflict financing by showing that methods of conflict financing vary in their effectiveness to provide the means for armed conflict. Very effective strategies are those whose revenue can be centralized easily and is high enough to cover the cost of the military strategy required. In addition, the typology underlines the importance of adopting a comprehensive approach that considers conflict economies as a combination of various methods of conflict financing. In this way, it is possible to identify the financial vulnerability of an armed group and assess how many options it has to diversify revenue if its main sources are cut.

The typology connects with the existing literature on the relationship between natural resources and armed conflict.[49] This literature highlights the importance of the characteristics of natural resources and their geographical occurrence. It complements this literature by highlighting that different natural resources vary in their effectiveness to finance conflict, and that a focus on individual methods of conflict financing is limited if not included in a framework that captures both the multitude of revenue sources and the cost of conflict.

TABLE 3
EFFECTIVENESS OF METHODS OF CONFLICT FINANCING FOR MAJOR ARMED CONFLICT

Effectiveness	Characteristics	Method of Conflict Financing
High	Centralized control relatively easy High-value revenue stream Immediate revenue flow	Oil Diamonds Drugs Third-party assistance
Medium	Centralized control difficult Low-value revenue stream Revenue stream constant over time	Taxation Parallel economies Diaspora financing
Low	Centralized control possible Low-value revenue stream Supplement to larger revenue stream May cover expenses for low intensity conflict	Taxation of humanitarian assistance Contributions of individuals Kidnapping Asset transfers from civilians Landing fees Revenue from portfolio investments

The typology also complements the work on the mobilization of organized armed groups. Weinstein argues that 'patterns of violence are a direct consequence of endowments leaders have at their disposal as they organize'.[50] In contrast to Schlichte,[51] Weinstein highlights that it is the initial resource endowment, rather than the prospect for financial gain of members, that explains the formation of non-state armed groups and the use of violence. Resource-rich groups recruit opportunistic soldiers with coercive strategies; resource poor groups recruit more activist-minded soldiers with participatory strategies.[52] The typology presented above adds the dimension of resource management to Weinstein's argument. It suggests that the initial control of revenue sources is only one aspect in creating a military organization. However, how it is formed depends on the capacity of a leadership to translate revenues into achieving political, military, social or economic objectives. Thus, the available endowment can influence the choices of armed groups as they organize *in one point in time*, however, *over time* their leaderships may change their endowments – by increasing revenues or lowering costs – through innovation and making the most of opportunities deriving from exogenous changes.

Conclusion and Policy Implications

The financing of armed conflict has been a recurring theme in the literature on armed conflict. This paper approached conflict financing as a combination of the revenue sources to armed groups as well as the cost of starting and maintaining armed conflict. What matters is not the total available revenue stream but whether the funds generated meet the armed group's financial requirements to organize the type of armed conflict needed to reach its objectives. Considering revenue and cost together also provides clues about which sources of revenue are effective in financing armed conflict. Such an understanding of conflict financing provides a new platform from which to explore the implications for peace processes and peace-building.

Peace mediators tend to be more concerned with political and military issues and less with economic ones. However, this paper clearly shows that conflict financing is important and can affect the dynamics of conflict. Engaging armed groups only on political or military issues can be counterproductive in terms of conflict resolution if key aspects of a group's organization or motives are not taken into consideration. The value of including a perspective on conflict financing does not lie in material determinism but rather in providing an additional lens. In this way, economic factors – such as conflict financing – can be recognized, related to political and military issues and integrated into a comprehensive conflict resolution strategy.[53]

When starting a peace-building process, the economic transformations taking place during an armed conflict should also be acknowledged. In peace-building terminology there is an emphasis on the 're' as in re-integration and re-habilitation of former combatants, or the re-construction of the economy. However, the notion of reverting to conditions that existed prior to the conflict once a conflict is over may pay insufficient attention to the transformations taking place during armed conflict. Identifying and maximizing the positive unintended consequences of armed conflict may open new opportunities for peace-building strategies. In terms of peace-building, it is therefore important to understand the characteristics of conflict economies and the economic transformations brought about by armed conflict in order to strengthen post-conflict economies for a lasting peace, and prevent high levels of post-conflict violence or the full-scale recurrence of armed conflict.

Combining the cost of conflict with the availability of revenue sources also provides a new conceptual platform from which to revisit policy against conflict financing. First of all, it is important to do away with the notion that contemporary armed conflict is cheap. It is indeed inexpensive to equip a few hundred men with weapons and ammunition and use them for occasional and unstructured attacks. However, as soon as they fire the first bullets (and are shot at), need training and maintenance, and are used as part of a more or less structured military strategy, costs increase and require steady streams of financing. In this context, the financial strength of the adversary and the capacity of an armed group to pay for conflict escalation are important elements in understanding conflict dynamics.

Given the marginal start-up cost for a low intensity conflict – starting at $67,500 for 1,000 soldiers[54] – those who really want to use armed violence (and think they can get what they want with it) will find the funding for it. Cutting off marginal sums of money seems wishful thinking when considering the illicit opportunities for money-making in conflict or post-conflict societies, or in the global illicit market place.[55] In these cases, policy should rest not on cutting financing, but on understanding and changing the motivations behind armed violence. As far as this type of violence can be compared to terrorism, approaching anti-terrorist policy through cutting financing may not be effective as long as terrorists have a high level of commitment.

Policy against conflict financing has greater potential when the financial requirements of the start-up and maintenance are higher. Due to the higher cost, armed groups are more sensitive to variation in the barrier to entry and cost of competition. As far as external actors can engineer changes in the availability of revenue sources and the cost of conflict, there are two potential avenues of engagement to consider (Table 4). The first is to increase revenue and cost disparities in order to support the victory of one armed group over others. This means financing one armed group and targeting the financing of others, as well as lowering the cost of conflict to one belligerent and increasing it for others. The second avenue is to decrease revenue and cost disparities and thereby support a mutually hurting stalemate.[56] This strategy entails providing finances to the weaker party and cutting finances of the stronger armed group(s), as well as lowering the cost of conflict to the weaker party and increasing it for others.

There is some evidence from Angola, Sri Lanka, and El Salvador that these avenues of engagement have been used.[57] Moreover, evidence on why armed groups engage in peace processes suggests that the financial situation of armed groups provides leads as to how predisposed they may be to come to the negotiation table. Armed groups that face revenue constraints are more inclined to engage; armed groups that have multiple revenue sources are less inclined to engage. Third-party pressure on the financial capacity of an armed group has therefore the potential to steer parties towards a more favourable, symmetric environment that favours the resolution of disputes through negotiation.[58]

TABLE 4
ENGAGING ON THE FINANCING AND COST OF CONFLICT

	Victory (increase revenue and cost disparities)			Mutually Hurting Stalemate (decrease revenue and cost disparities)	
	Party A (support)	Party B (target)		Weak party (support)	Strong party (target)
Financing	Increase	Decrease	Financing	Increase	Decrease, or do nothing
Cost	Decrease	Increase	Cost	Decrease	Increase, or do nothing

However, the extent to which leverage can be exerted also depends on the nature of revenue sources. In case of natural resources, the degree of leverage can change according to the occurrence of resources in nature (concentrated or diffuse), the geographical location of resources (proximate or distant from the capital), the characteristics of resources (lootable or obstructable), the means of exploration (labour or capital intensive), and the legal status of the resource (legal or illegal).[59] In general, however, the success of leverage may depend on the effectiveness of a revenues source as a method to finance conflict. If revenue sources can be controlled in a centralized manner and produce a high and immediate revenue stream, it is a most effective method of conflict financing. These characteristics are present in the various financing strategies associated to oil, diamonds, drugs and third parties assistance (see Table 3).

In the final analysis, policy against conflict financing has potential when working on both revenue sources and the cost of conflict. However, it may be little effective if the economic dimension of armed conflict is not embedded in the broader political, military or social dimensions. The challenge is to identify clearly the connections between the economic and other spheres and how they interact in shaping conflict dynamics. Policy against conflict financing should therefore never be delinked from its broader contexts and should be embedded in a strategy that addresses both the material environment and motivations of those organizing armed conflict.

NOTES

1. The author thanks Thomas Biersteker, Oliver Jütersonke, Aaron Karp, Keith Krause, Meghan Pritchard, and three anonymous reviewers for helpful comments.
2. For reviews of this literature see Macartan Humphreys, *Economics and Violent Conflict* (Boston, MA: Harvard University, 2003), http://www.preventconflict.org/portal/economics/Essay.pdf (accessed 1 September 2008); Cynthia Arnson, 'The Political Economy of War: Situating the Debate', in Cynthia Arnson and William Zartman (eds), *Rethinking the Economics of War: The Intersection of Need, Creed and Greed* (Washington, DC: The Johns Hopkins University Press, 2005), pp. 1–22.
3. Karen Ballentine and Heiko Nitzschke (eds), *Profiting from Peace: Managing the Resource Dimension of Civil War* (Boulder, CO: Lynne Rienner, 2005); Thomas Biersteker and Sue Eckert, *Countering the Financing of Terrorism* (London: Routledge, 2007).
4. Michael Pugh and Neil Cooper, *War Economies in a Regional Context: Challenges and Transformations* (Boulder, CO: Lynne Rienner, 2004), p. 97.
5. Mary Kaldor, *New and Old Wars: Organised Violence in a Global Era* (Cambridge: Polity Press, 1999); Mark Duffield, *Global Governance and the New Wars: The Merging of Development and Security* (London: Zed Books, 2001); Herfried Münkler, *Die Neuen Kriege* (Reinbek: Rowohlt, 2002).

6. Kaldor, *New and Old Wars* (note 5), p. 2.
7. Charles King, 'Ending Civil Wars', *Adelphi Papers*, No. 308 (London: International Institute for Strategic Studies, 1997), pp. 37–9.
8. Pugh and Cooper, *War Economies in a Regional Context* (note 4), p. 2.
9. Kalevi J. Holsti, *The State, War, and the State of War* (Cambridge: Cambridge University Press, 1996), pp. 36–40.
10. William Reno, *Warlord Politics and African States* (Boulder, CO: Lynne Rienner, 1998), p. 28.
11. Jeffrey Herbst, 'Economic Incentives, Natural Resources and Conflict in Africa', *Journal of African Economies*, Vol. 9, Vol. 3 (2000), pp. 270–94, at p. 27.
12. Paul Collier, Lani Elliott, Håvard Hegre, Anke Hoeffler, Marta Reynal-Querol, and Nicholas Sambanis, *Breaking the Conflict Trap: Civil War and Development Policy* (Washington, DC: World Bank, 2003); Ian Bannon and Paul Collier (eds), *Natural Resources and Violent Conflict: Options and Actions* (Washington, DC: World Bank, 2003); Paul Collier and Nicholas Sambanis (eds), *Understanding Civil War: Evidence and Analysis* (Washington, DC: World Bank, 2005).
13. Paul Collier, Anke Hoeffler, and Dominic Rohner, 'Beyond Greed and Grievance: Feasibility and Civil War', in *Oxford Economic Papers*, Vol. 61, No. 1 (2008), pp. 1–27, at p. 24.
14. Karen Ballentine and Jake Sherman (eds), *The Political Economy of Armed Conflict: Beyond Greed and Grievance* (Boulder, CO: Lynne Rienner, 2003); Pugh and Cooper, *War Economies in a Regional Context* (note 4); Cynthia Arnson and William Zartman (eds), *Rethinking the Economics of War: The Intersection of Need, Creed and Greed* (Washington, DC: The Johns Hopkins University Press, 2005); Christopher Cramer, *Civil War is Not a Stupid Thing: Accounting for Violence in Developing Countries* (London: Hurst and Company Publishers, 2006).
15. Karen Ballentine, 'Beyond Greed and Grievance: Reconsidering the Economic Dynamics of Armed Conflict', in Ballentine and Sherman, *The Political Economy of Armed Conflict* (note 14), pp. 259–83, at pp. 259–60.
16. Don Hubert, 'Resources, Greed, and the Persistence of Violent Conflict', in Rob McRae and Don Hubert (eds), *Human Security and the New Diplomacy: Protecting People, Promoting Peace* (Montreal: McGill-Queen's University Press, 2001), pp. 178–89, at p. 179.
17. Charles Tilly, *Coercion, Capital and European States, AD 990-1992* (Oxford: Blackwell, 1992); François Jean and Jean-Christophe Rufin (eds), *Economie des guerres civiles* (Paris: Hachette, 1996).
18. For an overview see Michael Renner, *The Anatomy of Resource Wars* (Washington, DC: Worldwatch Institute, 2002).
19. Ian Smillie, 'What Lessons from the Kimberley Process Certification Scheme?', in Ballentine and Nitzschke, *Profiting from Peace* (note 3), pp. 47–67.
20. Achim Wennmann, 'The Political Economy of Conflict Financing: A Comprehensive Approach Beyond Natural Resources', in *Global Governance*, Vol. 13, No. 3 (2007), pp. 427–44, at pp. 432–6.
21. Jeremy Weinstein, *Inside Rebellion: The Politics of Insurgent Violence* (Cambridge: Cambridge University Press, 2007), pp. 39–45.
22. I. William Zartman, 'Dynamics and Constraints in Negotiations in Internal Conflict', in I. William Zartman (ed), *Elusive Peace: Negotiating an End to Civil Wars* (Washington, DC: Brookings Institutions, 1995), pp. 3–29, at pp. 13–16; R. Thomas Naylor, *Wages of Crime: Black Markets, Illegal Finance, and the Underworld Economy* (Ithaca, NY: Cornell University Press, 2002), pp. 45–7.
23. For an overview see Chapter 5 of Geneva Declaration Secretariat, *The Global Burden of Armed Violence Report* (Geneva: Geneva Declaration on Armed Violence and Development, 2008).
24. Small Arms Survey, *Small Arms Survey 2002: Counting the Human Cost* (Oxford: Oxford University Press, 2002), p. 69.
25. Congressional Budget Office, *Estimated Cost of US Operations in Iraq and Afghanistan and of Other Activities Related to the War on Terrorism* (Washington, DC: Congress of the United States of America, 2007), pp. 1–2.
26. International Institute for Strategic Studies, *The Military Balance 2005/2006* (London: Routledge, 2005), pp. 37–8.
27. Michael Buchanan, 'London Bomb Costs Just Hundreds', in *BBC News*, 3 February 2006, http://news.bbc.co.uk/2/hi/uk_news/4576346.stm (accessed 1 September 2008).
28. House of Commons, *Report of the Official Accounts of the Bombings in London on 7th July 2005* (Norwich: The Stationery Office, 2006), http://www.official-documents.gov.uk/document/hc0506/hc10/1087/1087.pdf (accessed 1 September 2008).
29. The author is indebted to Ranan Kuperman, University of Haifa, for this observation.

30. A full elaboration of the costing tool and its application to the armed conflicts of Kosovo, Georgia and Angola is provided in Achim Wennmann, 'Conflict Financing and the Recurrence of Intra-state Armed Conflict: What Can Be Done from the Perspective of Conflict Financing to Prevent the Recurrence of Intra-state Armed Conflict?', PhD dissertation, Graduate Institute of International Studies, University of Geneva, 2007.
31. Department of Defense, *Parametric Estimating Handbook* (Washington, DC: Department of Defense of the United States of America, 1999).
32. Nicole Ball, *Security and Economy in the Third World* (Princeton, NJ: Princeton University Press, 1988), p. 111.
33. All sources and calculations for the figures in Table 1 are presented in Wennmann, 'Conflict Financing and the Recurrence of Intra-state Armed Conflict (note 30), p. 116–20.
34. Conflict intensity refers to the intensity of fighting as measured by the rate of replacement for weapons and DAERs.
35. Small Arms Survey, *Small Arms Survey 2007: Guns in the City* (Cambridge: Cambridge University Press, 2007); Small Arms Survey, *Small Arms Survey 2005: Weapons at War* (Oxford: Oxford University Press, 2005); Small Arms Survey, *Small Arms Survey 2002* (note 24); Small Arms Survey, *Small Arms Survey 2001: Profiling the Problem* (Oxford: Oxford University Press, 2001); Stéphanie Pézard and Holger Anders (eds), *Targeting Ammunition: A Primer* (Geneva: Small Arms Survey, 2006).
36. All figures include ranges for weapons prices between $40 and $250, ammunition prices between $0.05 and $0.50, and income per soldier between $2,000 and $10,000. Wennmann, 'Conflict Financing and the Recurrence of Intra-state Armed Conflict' (note 30), pp. 134–8.
37. Further information provided in ibid., pp. 120–38.
38. For a full explanation see Achim Wennmann, 'Estimating the Start-up and Maintenance Cost of Armed Conflict', Paper presented at the World International Studies Conference, Ljubljana, 23–26 July 2008, available at http://www.wiscnetwork.org/papers/WISC_2008-338.pdf (accessed 30 March 2009).
39. Paul Collier and Anke Hoeffler, 'Greed and Grievance in Civil War', in *Oxford Economic Papers*, Vol. 56, No. 4 (2004), pp. 563–95, at p. 564.
40. Prior to his move to oust Mobutu Sese Seko in 1998, Laurent Kabila was asked by a local journalist what was required to launch a guerrilla struggle: He answered: 'That's easy: Ten thousand dollar and a mobile phone. The cash will buy you a small army. You use the phone to promote yourself to the world.' See Aiden Hartley, 'The Art of Darkness', in *The Spectator*, 27 January 2001, http://findarticles.com/p/articles/mi_qa3724/is_200101/ai_n8941934/ (accessed 1 September 2008).
41. Collier, Hoeffler, and Rohner, 'Beyond Greed and Grievance' (note 13).
42. Achim Wennmann, 'Conflict Financing and the Recurrence of Intra-state Armed Conflict', pp. 238–9 (note 30).
43. Alex Vines, 'Angola: Forty Years of War', in Peter Batchelor and Kees Klingma (eds), *Demilitarisation and Peacebuilding in Southern Africa – Volume II* (Aldershot: Ashgate, 2004), pp. 74–104, at p. 87.
44. Assis Malaquias, 'Angola: How to Lose a Guerrilla War', in Morten Bøås and Kevin C. Dunn (eds), *African Guerrillas: Raging Against the Machine* (Boulder, CO: Lynne Rienner, 2007), pp. 199–220, at pp. 212–15.
45. Wennmann, 'Conflict Financing and the Recurrence of Intra-state Armed Conflict', pp. 203–4 (note 30).
46. Geoff Thale, 'Incentives and the Salvadoran Peace Process', in David Cortright (ed.), *The Price of Peace: Incentives and International Conflict Prevention* (New York: Rowman & Littlefield, 1997), pp. 181–203, at p. 199.
47. Michael T. Klare: *Resource Wars: The New Landscape of Global Conflict* (New York: Henry Holt, 2001), pp. 142, 215–17; Collier and Hoeffler, 'Greed and Grievance in Civil War' (note 39).
48. Taylor B. Seybolt, 'Major Armed Conflicts', in Stockholm International Peace Research Institute, *Yearbook 2000* (Oxford: Oxford University Press, 2000), pp. 15–49, at p. 32. However, $4 billion should be a low-end estimation when considering that NATO flew 38,400 sorties (of which 26,614 were strike sorties) suggesting an average cost per sortie of about $104,200. See Independent International Commission on Kosovo, *Kosovo Report: Conflict, International Response, Lessons Learned* (Oxford: Oxford University Press, 2000), p. 92.
49. Philippe Le Billon, 'The Political Ecology of War: Natural Resources and Armed Conflict', in *Political Geography*, Vol. 20, No. 5 (2001), pp. 561–84; Michael L. Ross, 'Oil, Drugs and Diamonds: The Varying Roles of Natural Resources in Civil War', in Ballentine and Sherman, *The Political Economy of Armed Conflict* (note 14), pp. 47–70; Michael L. Ross, 'How Do Natural Resources Influence Civil War? Evidence from Thirteen Cases', in *International Organization*, Vol. 58, No. 1 (2004), pp. 35–67.

50. Weinstein, *Inside Rebellion* (note 21), p. 20.
51. Klaus Schlichte, 'With the State against the State? The Formation of Armed Groups', *Contemporary Security Policy*, Vol. 30, No. 2 (this issue).
52. Ibid., pp. 171–2, 328–9.
53. Achim Wennmann, 'Money Matters: The Economic Dimensions of Peace Mediation' PSIS Occasional Paper No. 4, Graduate Institute of International Studies, Geneva, http://www.graduateinstitute.ch/webdav/site/ccdp/shared/6305/PSIS-Occasional-Paper-4-Money-Matters.pdf (accessed 1 September 2008), pp. 22–3.
54. With each soldier carrying 1.5 weapons and 100 rounds of ammunition, with weapons costing $40 and a round of ammunition costing $0.05. Wennmann, 'Conflict Financing and the Recurrence of Intra-state Armed Conflict' (note 30), p. 138.
55. Mosés Naím, *Illicit: How Smugglers, Traffickers and Copycats are Hijacking the Global Economy* (London: Arrow Books, 2007).
56. Parties are locked into a mutually hurting stalemate when they lose faith in winning by using force, and thus look for opportunities to cut their losses and exit the conflict. I. William Zartman, *Ripe for Resolution: Conflict and Intervention in Africa* (Oxford: Oxford University Press, 1986), pp. 232–6.
57. Herbst, 'Economic Incentives, Natural Resources and Conflict in Africa' (note 11), p. 271; Rohan Gunaratna, 'Sri Lanka: Feeding the Tamil Tigers', in Ballentine and Sherman, *The Political Economy of Armed Conflict* (note 14), pp. 197–223; Thale, 'Incentives and the Salvadoran Peace Process' (note 46), p. 199. Gunaratna 2003, 210; Thale 1997, p. 199 (note 49).
58. Achim Wennmann, 'Getting Armed Groups to the Table: Peace Processes, the Political Economy of Conflict and the Mediated State', *Third World Quarterly*, Vol. 30, No. 6 (forthcoming 2009).
59. Le Billon, 'The Political Ecology of War?' (note 49); Ross, 'Oil, Drugs and Diamonds' (note 49); Ross, 'How Do Natural Resources Influence Civil War?' (note 49).

From Social Movement to Armed Group: A Case Study from Nigeria

JENNIFER M. HAZEN

Violence has often been a tactic employed at the far end of a spectrum of 'contentious politics'.[1] It is one part of the broader spectrum of political protest actions. Social movement organizations engage in a wide continuum of activities, ranging from letter writing and picketing to street protests and mass marches to violence. The use of violence includes acts such as property destruction, kidnapping, bombings, and clashes with other groups or state security forces. Violence ranges from sporadic use and limited targets to the wider, more systematic and organized use of violence across time and space. Violence, in particular the use of organized military tactics, represents the upper extreme of protest options available to social movement organizations. The majority of social movement groups never engage in violent tactics, and those that do often use limited violent means in a more sporadic manner, rather than opting for a sustained campaign of violence. However, the use of violent tactics does not necessarily equate with the movement away from social protest. The cycle of protest model suggests that this is one logical outgrowth of a social movement.[2]

Many armed groups have their origins in broader social movements.[3] Armed groups have often begun as a smaller subset of individuals within a mainstream social movement who are willing to pursue more radical strategies for political and social change by opting for violent means. Radicalization results from a number of factors: inaction by government to meet popular demands; repressive reactions by government to social protest; an ideology of change that accepts the use of violence as legitimate; threats to the survival of the group; competition for scarce resources from other social movement organizations; and, the perception that other social movement organizations are too weak or timid in their efforts to achieve change. Some groups are extreme splinter groups that represent a small minority of a broader social movement, such as the Revolutionary United Front in Sierra Leone.[4] Other groups have possessed closer ties to a broader social movement, such as the Brigate Rosse in Italy,[5] and the Farabundo Marti National Liberation Front (FMLN) in El Salvador.[6]

Despite pressures for radicalization in situations where attaining group goals is difficult, the decision to pursue violent tactics is a risky one, placing a group in direct confrontation with state security forces. Few groups choose to strike out on their own, breaking with a broader social movement, to engage the state in armed insurrection. Those that do find they must quickly amass sufficient resources to withstand the often violent response by the government. This raises two important questions: why does a group adopt violence as the primary means of protest? And, how does a group sustain itself once it selects a violent trajectory?

This article investigates these two questions through a case study of the Niger Delta People's Volunteer Force (NDPVF) in the Niger Delta region of Nigeria. The analysis provides an assessment of the decision of the NDPVF to break away from a broader, and long active, social movement for development of the Niger Delta and broader political change to pursue its own agenda through the frequent use of violent tactics and the development of an armed group with characteristics more commonly found among militaries. What explains the emergence of the NDPVF from the broader social movement? What explains the NDPVF's selection of violence as a means of political opposition? Once this decision was taken, what enabled the NDPVF to survive as an armed group? The analysis reveals the significant role played by the political democratic transition in Nigeria, the competition for resources among armed groups, the ideology of the NDPVF, and the resource mobilization capacity of the NDPVF as critical factors in the emergence and sustainability of the group.

This article is divided into two main sections. The first section provides a framework for the study through a brief overview of key explanatory variables within social movement theory for the rise of political violence. This is followed by a presentation of the cycle of protest model, which explains why a group passes through the different stages of the cycle and the challenges presented when a group opts for violent tactics. The second section presents the case study of the Niger Delta People's Volunteer Force. Through the use of process tracing, the study identifies key factors that influenced the emergence of the NDPVF, the choice of violent tactics as the primary means of political opposition, and the ability of the NDPVF to sustain itself when it faced repressive tactics. The study also elucidates reasons why the NDPVF, although by many measures successful, faced only two options in 2007: continued fighting or extinction.

Explaining Mobilization, Violence and Persistence

Conflict is common to every society. Arising from competing interests, ideologies, and preferences, social conflict is normal and often seen as a positive force for change when change is pursued and conflicts are resolved through non-violent means. Concern arises when actors respond to conflict in a violent manner. Contentious politics, an important element of conflict, has been defined as any situation in which the involved actors, including the government, make competing claims on one another and any resolution of the situation has an effect on the interests of the involved actors.[7] In other words, resolution of the conflict is likely to have positive effects for some actors and negative effects for others. Contentious politics includes 'wars, revolutions, rebellions, (most) social movements . . . and many more forms of collective struggle',[8] in which violence is seen as a legitimate, but not necessary, means of achieving a group's interests.

Social movements are at the heart of much of non-violent contentious politics. A social *movement* is 'a set of opinions and beliefs in a population which represents preferences for changing some elements of the social structure and/or reward distribution of a society'.[9] A social movement represents a set of broad goals, and it is these goals that attract supporters and prompt the development of groups working to attain these goals. A social movement *organization* is a formally organized group that 'identifies its goals with the preferences of a social movement or a countermovement and attempts to implement these goals'.[10] A social movement consists of several such organized groups that work, at least initially, towards the same goal, which provides the common link between otherwise independent groups. While social movement organizations share a common goal, these groups might also possess additional goals, preferences for specific tactics to achieve their objectives, or different timelines for goal attainment. A wide diversity exists among groups under any given social movement umbrella.

An armed group is a particular type of social movement organization. Armed groups are defined here as any group that is willing to use sustained violent means to achieve articulated political goals.[11] These political goals may range from limited (or specific) changes to public policies to more radical changes in the form of government to advocating the overthrow of the government or secession. The articulation of political goals does not preclude the group from possessing additional goals, for example economic enrichment or an elevation in social status. However, the larger and more numerous the goals, the greater will be the requirement for mobilization of resources and support. All social movement organizations face the challenge of generating resources and support in order to attain their identified aims.

Social movement theory addresses various questions pertaining to the initiation, nature, organization, and evolution of social movements. Building on previous work by scholars,[12] this article uses a process-oriented conceptual framework aimed at capturing the dynamic nature of social movements. The cycle of protest model (introduced in the next section) captures changes over time by assessing which factors influence each stage of the mobilization process of a social movement. The social movement literature suggests a number of important factors. Four variables: political opportunities,[13] framing alignment,[14] resource mobilization,[15] and group competition, have provided the core explanations of political violence and form the basis for the analysis in this article.[16] Each factor is presented below in brief. They are then used in conjunction with the cycle of protest model to analyze the contribution of these factors to the emergence, violence, and evolution of the NDPVF.

The first factor is political opportunity. The political opportunity structure refers to 'the degree to which groups are likely to be able to gain access to power and to manipulate the system'.[17] Common indicators of political opportunity include the degree of repression employed by the state (or the degree of openness to participation), the presence of influential allies, and elite divisions.[18] Opportunities for political action will depend on both the nature of the political system, including both formal and informal channels of power, as well as the position of the group within that system. Authoritarian systems offer far fewer openings for access to the political process due to the elite, hierarchical, and exclusionary nature of the political system as well as the commonly repressive nature of the authoritarian state. Democratic political systems, in theory, provide more opportunities for accessing the political process through elections, political parties, the bureaucracy, and the legislature.[19] Democracies are also less likely to use force to subdue political protest.

The extent to which a group can engage in formal political protest will depend to a large extent on the nature of the democracy. Established democracies are more stable, more open to political debate, and better able to manage political protest non-violently. Countries in the process of democratization, on the other hand, are likely to be at higher risk for violence than either established democracies or authoritarian regimes.[20] The high risk of violence results from the numerous changes taking place during democratization: the changing nature of political power, and the related distribution of goods; the perceived (and real) proliferation of openings for new groups to enter into politics,[21] and competition among old and new groups for a seat at the democratic table. Democracies in transition often entail elements of both democratic and authoritarian regimes, which include the promise of participation along with the real threat of use of force to quell any perceived challenges to the newly formed democratic state. In many transitioning democracies, elitist and exclusionary politics do not change immediately and the vast majority of the population remains outside of the main political power structure.

The second factor is the framing alignment of a social movement, which defines the problem and identifies legitimate solutions. An important element of framing the problem is defining the context in which the group operates. This involves identifying the group's opponent (e.g. another group, the state, particular politicians), the opponent's characteristics, and the group's assessment of its own position vis-à-vis its opponent (e.g. competitor, victim). A second important element of framing is the determination of the legitimacy of using violence as a means of social change. Most social movement organizations pursue political and social change through a range of activities, including public information campaigns, street marches, or public protests in front of government buildings, but they usually stop short of violence. In large part, the refusal to use violent means results from the belief that violence is not a legitimate form of social protest. Armed groups, on the other hand, legitimize the use of violence, either by framing the environment as inherently dangerous and requiring defensive tactics, or presenting violence as the only available means of altering the political landscape. In such cases, violence becomes a legitimate tool of the social movement, and is not simply an outburst of uncontrolled rage or frustration. Rather violence is used selectively for discrete purposes; it is not random aggression.

The third factor is resource mobilization, the level of which determines the support of and constraints on social movement action. 'It examines the variety of resources that must be mobilized, the linkages of social movements to other groups, the dependence of movements upon external support for success, and the tactics used by authorities to control or incorporate movements.'[22] The mobilization of resources – whether in terms of group membership, financial and material resources, or elite political support – requires some level of group organization and capacity to attract supporters. A group must be able to develop some level of popular support in order to garner the resources necessary to maintain this support and to carry out activities to further the action on achieving group goals. In this framework, emphasis is placed on the internal operations of the group: how does it recruit members, how does it keep members (e.g. incentives, ideological motivation), and how does it generate revenue to sustain the group and its activities (e.g. donations of time and money). In the study of social movements, emphasis has often been placed on the voluntary nature of mobilization. The use of resource mobilization in this study relies on an expanded version of this concept to move beyond the voluntary aspect of mobilization to look at the active use of entrepreneurial initiatives to garner resources (e.g. the sale of natural resources),[23] as well as the role of external actors in supporting groups.

The fourth factor is competition. Inter-group competition can contribute to the differentiation of tactics and strategies among groups, and to the escalation of violence. Competition becomes a driving factor of group action when resources are limited. As a social movement develops, groups supporting that movement will multiply. This proliferation of similar groups results in competition for scarce resources (presuming a finite supply of resources). As the number of groups increases, the more competitive the struggle for resources will become. Inter-group competition forces strategic decision making aimed at gaining advantages over other competing groups.[24] The main goal of competition is political influence, not merely political participation. This involves the positioning of a group vis-à-vis other groups to ensure the group has a seat at the political table and that it can access available resources but also benefit from any political or social changes that result from the activities of the social movement as a whole. Competition can also arise between the group and the government. This is particularly true after a group has chosen to pursue a violent course of action that places it in direct confrontation with the government, and government security forces. Violence is a function of political competition, and a strategic tool aimed at winning this competition.[25]

Each of these factors provides a piece of the explanation of mobilization and political violence. No single factor is likely to explain the entire cycle of protest, but neither is there an easy formula for combining factors into a more comprehensive explanation. Furthermore, it is possible that different factors influence the mobilization process at different stages. This suggests the need to take not only a more comprehensive approach to the study of mobilization, but also a more dynamic one. A dynamic assessment of social movements can be captured in the cycle of protest model.

The Cycle of Protest

The cycle of protest model has proven particularly useful in the study of political violence.[26] The model has been used to illustrate the stages of social mobilization (see Figure 1), including the rise, evolution, and demise of social movements.[27] According to the cycle, a social movement often begins as a localized protest of a particular grievance. The likelihood of the local protest expanding to incorporate additional communities depends on how easily the local grievances can be tied to broader popular concerns. If this can be achieved, then expanding popular support for the protest can lead to the formation of social movement organizations and a broadening of the overall social movement to a regional, national, or even international, level. While the broadening of support for the movement provides a positive impetus in sustaining action on the goals of the movement, the multiplication of

FIGURE 1
CYCLE OF PROTEST

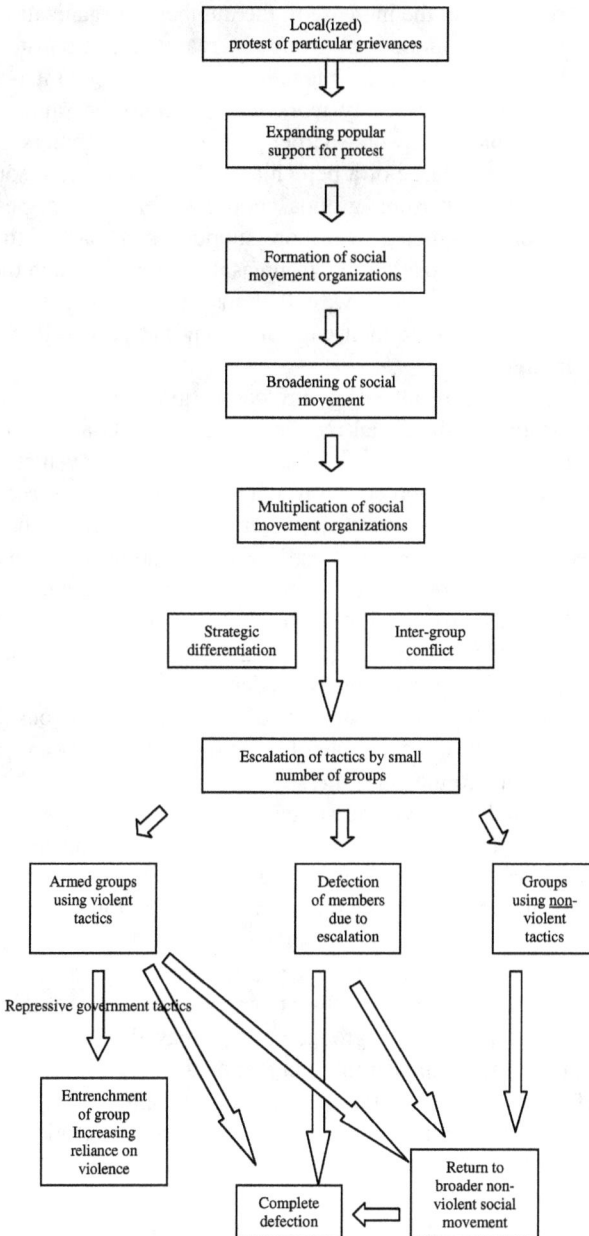

Source: Based on Donatella Della Porta and Sydney Tarrow, 'Unwanted Children: Political Violence and the Cycle of Protest in Italy, 1966–1973', *European Journal of Political Research*, Vol. 14, No. 5–6 (1986), pp. 610–13

organizations involved can impose certain negative costs. The primary negative effect is competition.

Competition results from the increase in the number of organizations involved in a social movement. As the number of groups increases, given constant and limited resources, the struggle for resources intensifies to the point of inter-group conflict between groups that often previously worked together to the same end. Resource competition forces groups to work harder to maintain membership, draw new membership, and garner as large of a percentage of the available resources as possible. In response to this pressure, groups choose different strategies of pursuing resources. This is done in order to win more supporters, as part of the 'advertising image' of the group, and to position the group as the one with which the government must negotiate. Some groups, very few, will choose to escalate tactics to the point of violence in order to differentiate their capacity from that of the other groups and to demonstrate their strength.

Violence occurs as a result of group competition, a repressive government response, or the decline of the social movement. Della Porta and Tarrow argue that violence occurs as a function of competition between social movement organizations over scarce resources, and that violence is a sign of the decline of the social movement, not the broadening of it.[28] However, Tejerina argues that violence 'should be seen as a form of collective action directed towards a mobilization of society'.[29] Violence therefore comes before the decline of a social movement, and can act to galvanize that movement, but it can also lead to a decline in public support for the movement if the violence raises the costs of collective action too high. Violence also results from reversals in political opportunities: when democracy slips back toward authoritarianism, or more specifically, when groups who had enjoyed numerous gains under an opening political system are either cut out of the system or feel they are entitled to even great political power due to the gains already made.[30]

Selecting a more radical or violent strategy can improve the position of the group vis-à-vis the achievement of the goals of the social movement and certainly places the group more visibly on the government's radar, but it also produces negative effects, including the defection of less militant members and the fracturing of social movement organizations into militant and non-violent factions. Violence tends to fracture the broader social movement into non-violent and violent groups due to the high costs imposed by violence. Individuals unwilling to engage in violence may choose to continue agitation with a non-violent group, or they may defect from the movement entirely. The result is a much smaller militant faction than the original social movement organization. The use of violent tactics often prompts a repressive response by government authorities. This is true in both democratic and non-democratic societies, though the latter will have more leeway in terms of using repressive measures. Repressive responses by government authorities can produce two responses: the desistance of the group, or the further mobilization of the group. The choice of response will depend on the nature of the government response, how much pain is inflicted by the government response, and the capacity of the group to absorb the response. Armed groups that survive these initial challenges require the ability to mobilize resources in order to generate the capacity to withstand repressive measures over time.

The following section presents a case study of the Niger Delta People's Volunteer Force (NDPVF) in the Niger Delta region of Nigeria during the time period 1999–2007. The case study uses the four main explanations presented in the previous section to guide the analysis along the cycle of protest model from the emergence of the NDPVF, to its choice to use violence in pursuit of its goals, to determining what enabled the NDPVF to sustain its campaign against the Nigerian government.

The Niger Delta People's Volunteer Force[31]

The Niger Delta People's Volunteer Force (NDPVF) is an ethnic militia purportedly fighting for the rights of the Ijaw population in the Niger Delta of Nigeria. Created in 2003, the NDPVF represented, until 2006, the most visible armed group in the Delta. Its proclaimed goals included increased control over local resources, in particular oil; improved development in the Delta; greater employment opportunities; and, greater self-determination. The NDPVF has largely maintained popular support among communities in the Delta because of its proclaimed goals, but this support has not translated into political support. While many support the goals of the movement, they do not support the violent tactics employed by the group, or the negative consequences felt by the communities affected by the violence. The NDPVF has proven capable of projecting military-level force when necessary, and of engaging in negotiations with the Nigerian government when desired.

By tracing the development of the Niger Delta People's Volunteer Force (NDPVF) over time the changes in the factors influencing the process become more apparent. The following case study demonstrates that different factors proved more important at different times in the evolution of the NDPVF. At the group's initiation, the political opportunity structure, political patrons, and political ideology stood out as important, and often interlinked, factors. The choice of violence was influenced mainly by the political ideology of the group and the competition the NDPVF faced at the time. The ability of the NDPVF to sustain itself and develop into an armed group independent of its political patrons depended heavily on the lack of governance in the Niger Delta, the unwillingness of the Nigerian military to engage in a full civil war against the armed group, and the effectiveness of the group's resource mobilization.

The Rise of the NDPVF

Understanding the origins of the NDPVF requires looking at events in the several years prior to the NDPVF's emergence as an organized group. Important contextual and individual factors played a role in organization and mobilization. The rise of the NDPVF as a militant force can be attributed to a number of factors: democratization in Nigeria, patronage politics, popular support, and an entrepreneurial leader willing to use violent means and able to convince others of the legitimacy of violence.

The political opportunity structure in Nigeria in the post-1999 period is important to explaining the possibilities for social mobilization. Prior to the re-democratization of the country in the 1999 elections, the military government made public protest and social mobilization both difficult and dangerous endeavours. While resistance movements had existed since the 1960s, and activists had been mobilizing in a non-violent fashion in the Niger Delta in the 1990s, the response of the government had always been heavy-handed, and the previous military regimes had proven effective in keeping social movement organizations and militant groups in check. The democratic election of Olusegun Obasanjo in 1999, even though Obasanjo had been among the elite ranks of the military, promised to bring about a substantial change in the political structure of the country and return democracy to the population.

The return to democracy in Nigeria, while far from institutionalized or stable, did provide for an opening of the political space in the country, which had been imposs-ible previously under the military regime. This transition back to democracy did not however involve a large change in the nature of politics. 'Democratic institutions remain[ed] weak and law enforcement structures [we]re prone to manipulation' by politicians and ineffective in providing security to the population.[32] Elite patronage politics remained at the core of the political system in Nigeria, meaning that the vast majority of the population was excluded from politics.[33] Elections, rather than offering a true voice to the public and a mechanism of political control, provided instead an opportunity for the population to practice democracy by voting every four years. Numerous accusations of election rigging in 2003 and again in 2007 pointed to the widespread popular disappointment with the political system. This frustration with democracy never represented a desire for the return of military rule, but instead indicated the mass dissatisfaction with how the current democratic regime functioned.

The Niger Delta represents in many ways a microcosm of Nigerian national politics. Political patronage remains at the core of local governance. The 2003 and 2007 elections demonstrated the strong role of political godfathers in manipulating politics at the local level. While political freedoms exist more broadly in the post-1999 context, access to political power and to the ability to manipulate the political and economic agenda remains severely limited in the hands of a few elites. These elites are part of the ruling political structure, and are the ones with access to money, arms, and private militias that can be used to maintain the political status quo. The elections highlighted the willingness of politicians to use any means necessary to win the election, including the use of violence. The 2003 elections set the tone for the country with the arming of local youth groups and cults by aspiring political candidates who used these groups to intimidate opponents and supporters of opposition candidates.

The distribution of power and resources in Nigeria is the result of political patronage. This explains the intensity with which candidates vie for public positions, including spending vast sums of money on pre-election activities,[34] and engaging in violence and intimidation.[35] Winning an election, in some cases, is not far off from winning the lottery for politicians, even at the local level. Political positions offer great opportunities for wealth. For example, in 2006, the annual budget for Rivers State was estimated to be close to US$1.3 billion.[36] This is a tremendous sum in a country where the vast majority of the population lives on less than two dollars a day. This level of wealth also provides great incentives to politicians to win in a political system where widespread corruption offers the opportunity to access these government coffers for personal gain with little accountability and widespread impunity.

In 2003, political candidates provided arms and cash to cult groups, youth groups, and local gangs in order to create their own personal militias. These private militias provided an important tool for mobilization of supporters and intimidation of opponents. The development of personal militias in the Niger Delta region had a particularly strong impact on the dynamics of political contestation following the elections. Importantly, in the aftermath of the 2003 elections, political candidates failed to retrieve the weapons they had supplied to their private militias, and elected officials failed to fulfil the promises they had made of economic opportunities and benefits to their militant supporters. This left numerous already organized groups armed and disgruntled.

One of the primary groups unhappy with the electoral process was the Ijaw Youth Council (IYC). The IYC was instrumental in mobilizing the Ijaw population as a pressure group on government in the late 1990s. Founded in 1998, the IYC is perhaps most famous for its December 1998 Kaiama Declaration, which demanded that the government return control of the region's resources to the Delta.[37] This declaration served as a rallying call for Ijaw communities, many of which responded with political support for the IYC social movement. The IYC had been working for several years to promote the rights of the Ijaw nation and to seek control of the Delta's resources, but the organization had always remained a non-violent, political social movement.

Mujahid Asari Dokubo won a contested election to become president of the IYC in 2001. Thereafter, Asari strove to implement a more radical agenda, including a willingness to use any means necessary to achieve the goals of the Kaiama Declaration. This change in tenor provoked an internal division within the IYC and prompted efforts by some leaders to oust Asari.[38] Allegations of the ruling party rigging the 2003 elections served as an important impetus for the creation of the NDPVF. The dispute became particularly heated between Asari and Rivers State Governor, Peter Odili, when Asari publicly claimed that the governor, and other politicians, had armed gangs of political thugs in the lead up to the elections. Despite his position as president of the IYC, Asari's increasingly militant stance as well as his confrontation with Odili put him 'at odds with the core leadership of the IYC'.[39] Failing to build widespread support within the IYC for a more militant stance against the government and facing an internal coup by other IYC leaders, Asari left the IYC in late 2003. It was around this time that Asari founded his own armed group, the NDPVF. This marked a clear break with a non-violent path, and began the transition of Asari from a president of a social movement organization to a leader of one of the most notorious armed groups in Nigeria.

Asari became something of a folk hero in the Niger Delta based on his charismatic nature, proclaimed political ideology (e.g. promoting Ijaw rights through demanding control over the Delta's oil resources), and his ability to tap into widespread local grievances. Asari demonstrated an impressive ability to manage the media image of the NDPVF, and of Asari himself, and to utilize this to portray himself as a victim and the NDPVF as the answer to the struggle in the Delta for economic and political rights. Under Asari, the NDPVF initiated not only a military struggle for change but also a powerful propaganda war that captured the sentiments, and support, of many in the Delta. The Delta, despite its wealth in oil and the high revenues this has produced for the national government over the past several decades, remains extremely poor, underdeveloped, and ignored.[40] As a result, the NDPVF has been able to capitalize on these grievances to develop broad popular support and recruit disaffected youth as members. Its position of strength has also enabled it to bring a number of existing cult groups and other armed groups under its umbrella.

Asari's attitude toward the government and the need for armed struggle also contributed significantly to the creation of the NDPVF. However, while Asari as an individual was crucial to the splintering of part of the IYC into a militant faction (i.e. the NDPVF), Asari's charismatic role was necessary but insufficient to the establishment of the NDPVF. The origins of the NDPVF depended heavily on the political opportunity structure at the time in Nigeria and the role of political patrons in the 2003 elections. The political patrons gave many militant groups their start in that year, including the NDPVF. The IYC represents another important element of the existing political opportunity structure. Without the IYC, and in particular his leading role as president, Asari would have lacked the platform for expressing his more radical position and for spreading this message to the broader public.

Asari's rise to power did not come without contention. The creation of the NDPVF marked a clear rejection of the newly elected government and the political structure that enabled its victory. It also identified a drastic change from a previously non-violent political movement to a militarized group. 'The creation of the NDPVF was an effort to achieve through force the demands issued in the Kaiama Declaration' that had not been achieved through non-violent means.[41] The NDPVF offered a platform for change that moved beyond what current groups offered. The NDPVF also stood in direct contrast to the newly elected governor, with whom Asari had had a close relationship, and in direct confrontation with the governor's supporters, namely the cult group, Icelander, headed by Ateke Tom. The clear challenge that the NDPVF posed to the governor, and to the national government, provided the basis for the government to engage in, and legitimize, heavy-handed tactics against the NDPVF.

Choosing Violence as a Means of Political Opposition

Even acknowledging the choice of Asari to leave the IYC and take a different political path to continue to agitate for change, such a choice did not require a militant stance nor did it require the implementation of violent tactics. A key question to answer is why did the NDPVF opt for a militaristic approach instead of continuing the political struggle outside of the IYC framework? An important part of the answer is Asari's ideological convictions and his frustration with the non-violent process. Yet this is not the entire answer. The NDPVF faced stiff competition from other groups, namely the IYC, for resources and for popular support forcing it to distinguish itself as different in order to compete effectively. The NDPVF also faced a serious threat to its survival and to the lives of its leaders from Ateke Tom and the government, which not only stood behind Ateke Tom but also initiated its own efforts to eliminate Asari and disband the NDPVF.

Asari's ideological convictions combined with his perceived ineffectiveness of the non-violent struggle led him to believe that only a military struggle would make the government wake up and take notice.[42] Asari's inability to win electoral contests likely contributed to his hardened stance and his lack of faith in a non-violent political solution. Asari campaigned for a seat in the Rivers State House Assembly in 1992, and then for the chairmanship of the Asari-Toru Local Government Area of Rivers State in 1998, failing both times in his bids for elected office.[43] After failing in the electoral process, Asari joined the IYC, and in 2001 became its president. Asari's rhetoric while president of the IYC provides additional evidence of his preference for and his move towards a more militant stance vis-à-vis the government, as well as his willingness to deploy violence as a means to achieving his goals. This ideological outlook was important to the creation of the NDPVF and the approach the group took to achieving its ends.

The NDPVF at the time of its origins faced stiff competition from other social movement and militant groups. The IYC stood as the main social movement competitor to the NDPVF, and offered a non-violent path to trying to achieve the same end goals. The IYC, whose leadership had not supported Asari's militant stance, in effect competed for the same resources and popular support as Asari's NDPVF. This competition forced the NDPVF to distinguish itself as different from the IYC in order to justify the creation of a new organization and to compete effectively against the IYC. NDPVF clearly marked its differences from the IYC both in its approach to political change and its approach to the population. Rather than trying to mobilize supporters, the NDPVF aimed to radicalize the Delta population as a whole with rhetoric that heightened grievances and justified the use of violent tactics to obtain broader political and economic rights, and to implement the Kaiama Declaration that had received such widespread popular support.

The NDPVF also faced a serious threat to its survival. This threat came from two directions: Ateke Tom as head of the main armed group competitor to the NDPVF, a group called Icelander, and the state and national governments who feared the rise of the NDPVF, the challenge it posed to the local political system, and the threat it represented to oil production in the Delta. Although the threats were distinct, they were also linked. Ateke Tom allegedly received the support and the blessing of the state government to eliminate Asari and rid the Delta of the NDPVF.[44]

Violence in the Delta escalated throughout 2003 and 2004. Much of this violence occurred between the two militant groups: NDPVF and Icelander, in Port Harcourt and the surrounding areas of Rivers State. In part the fighting was territorial – control over the best places to steal oil – but it was also about who had primacy in the region.[45] As Asari expanded the size and strength of the NDPVF, Ateke struggled to do the same.[46] Ateke however lacked the resource mobilization capacity of the NDPVF. Ateke's group is a cult, which is traditionally small in size, localized in its operations, and lacking popular support. The NDPVF, by contrast, is considered by many to be an ethnic militia fighting for the rights of the Ijaw population, the largest ethnic group in the Delta, which enables the NDPVF to garner much wider support and to have a much larger recruitment base. The NDPVF remains popular with the Ijaw population, and with some other groups in the Delta, due to the proclaimed goals of the group, which are widely shared by the Delta population, and the selective targeting of its attacks on other militant groups or the Nigerian military. Although certainly numerous civilians have been displaced, injured, and killed by the clashes between the NDPVF and other groups, the NDPVF has never intentionally targeted the civilian population, which contributes to the group's capacity to maintain popular support.

As the violence escalated and spread it began to impact on oil production, thereby affecting international oil prices and threatening government revenues. By mid 2004 Asari's bases had been repeatedly attacked by military air raids, while NDPVF's allied groups conducted targeted campaigns against Ateke's forces. Governor Odili attempted to initiate a disarmament process in July 2004, but it never moved forward and violence escalated. In September 2004, in response to what he claimed were assassination attempts on his life as well as political backing for Ateke's forces, Asari declared an all-out war against the Nigerian government. This declaration earned him a seat at President Obasanjo's negotiating table, but the negotiations failed to produce a sustainable peace process. By 2005 the violence had begun to escalate once again and Asari and the NDPVF quickly became the focus of military operations in the Delta.

While never a foregone conclusion, numerous factors contributed to the selection of violence as the means by which the NDPVF would conduct its political contestation against government policies. In particular, two factors stand out as important to this decision to choose violent action: an ideology supportive of violence, and the threats facing the NDPVF at its start. Asari, and the other members of the NDPVF, clearly supported the belief that violence was a legitimate means of pressuring the government for change. However, violence was not only perceived of as legitimate (the NDPVF believing it had been attacked first and therefore had a right to defend itself and attack back), it was also seen as the only available option to combat a closed political system and repressive military strategy. The threat to the survival of the NDPVF from both armed groups and the Nigerian military acted to reinforce the belief that military action was the only possible action available.

Survival and Independence: The Evolution of the NDPVF

Once the NDPVF launched its militarized campaign against government forces and competing armed groups in the Delta it required access to significant resources to sustain its activities. The key to the survival of the NDPVF was its impressive resource mobilization capacity, which included recruiting new members, maintaining current members, arming its members, and obtaining the financial means to pay for everything. The second contributing factor to the NDPVF's success was the political opportunity structure in place in the Delta; especially the limited governance capacity and the unwillingness of the national government to engage in full-scale war.

There is very little real governance in the Delta region. Although elected officials do conduct daily business in their localities, the ongoing lack of development in the region suggests that these officials, despite their large annual budgets, are not spending their time addressing local grievances or the needs of their populations. The escalation of violence since 2005 and the inability of the local or national government to gain a handle on the problems in the Delta has led to claims that the region is 'almost ungovernable'.[47] The lack of obvious interest in governing by local officials, as well as the inability of the national government, through the military, to reign in the activities of armed groups offered a small but clear opening in the political dynamics of the region for armed groups to enter into the void. Although armed groups impose de facto rule in certain areas of the Delta by their presence, in particular the riverine areas, they can hardly be called governing structures. However, their ability to act with relative impunity has enhanced their self-perceptions of strength and their expectations that they should play a role in the politics of the region.

The government has stationed a Joint Task Force in the Niger Delta since 2003. This joint team of several thousand military and police officers is headquartered in Warri, Delta State, but operates in Bayelsa and Rivers States as well.[48] Rather than lowering tensions and reducing violence in the region, the task force appears to have had the opposite effect. This is in large part the result of the operations carried out by the military, which have inflicted high levels of damage and injury on local populations in a relatively indiscriminate manner.[49] Police presence is spotty at best, and extrajudicial killings by the security forces are common.[50] The heavy hand used by state security forces has produced additional public support for some armed groups, such as the NDPVF, and reduced support for the state security forces in these areas. These actions have also spurred a violent response by the armed groups, such as NDPVF. Instead of presenting a deterrent to violence, military action has provoked additional violence.

Local government officials and military officers have also proven to be part of the problem, contributing to violence in the region. There are widespread allegations, as well as some substantiated reports, of government officials and military officers being involved in the illegal oil trade or turning a blind eye to the trade in exchange for kickbacks.[51] Local government officials are often involved in the return of hostages in exchange for ransom payments, raising questions about their level of knowledge about the militants' operations as well as their role in hostage negotiations and payments. Evidence also exists of continued support for certain armed groups by politicians; this was especially evident in the lead-up to the 2007 elections, but has also been used as a tool for consolidating politicians' positions, settling old rivalries, and seeking economic gain in non-election periods.

The NDPVF has proven particularly effective in mobilizing resources and establishing sustainable sources of revenue. NDPVF engages in a number of financial endeavours. Importantly, many such endeavours do not involve the procurement of funds through friendly donations, but instead result from the provision of services or the financial transactions of the group.

The NDPVF engages in security services for-hire for local companies in the Delta. In March 2005, Asari claimed he received payments to provide security for the Niger Delta Development Commission and the payments sustained him financially.[52] Oil companies have been known to provide payments to armed groups in order to continue operating in the Delta. For these companies, it is simply another cost of doing business. However, such payments have raised concerns about this money being used to finance militancy and the purchase of arms. The NDPVF has been known to use kidnapping as a form of revenue generation.

Asari has openly admitted to *oil bunkering* (illegally siphoning oil from pipelines) to obtain revenue for purchasing arms and waging his war against the government and rival armed groups. Asari claims he is not stealing the oil, but that the oil belongs to the people of the Delta and therefore it is the right of the population to harvest and sell. While substantiated figures for oil bunkering are not available, many estimate the practice to bring in hundreds of millions of dollars per year. One estimate of oil bunkering in 2004 put the figure at an estimated US$4.49 billion.[53] While all of this amount would not go directly to armed groups, and certainly not to any single group, the large figure does suggest that oil bunkering provides sufficient funds for armed groups to purchase small arms. It also provides a good reason for the intense competition between armed groups for control over oil producing lands.

Evidence suggests the armed groups in the Delta region are well armed. This means that these groups possess powerful weapons and in sufficient supply; it does not indicate that these groups have excess stocks in storage. A survey among militant groups in the Delta region revealed that most groups had relatively small quantities of weapons, ranging in the hundreds, not the thousands.[54] In mid 2004, Asari claimed that he had sufficient access to the small arms trade to supply up to 2,000 men with assault rifles, rocket-propelled grenades, and other firepower.[55] Clashes between the NDPVF and other armed groups and between the NDPVF and the military suggest the NDPVF was well armed. Despite submitting some weapons to the late 2004 disarmament program, the NDPVF seemed little affected by the exercise. On the contrary, it appeared to source new and more sophisticated arms in 2005.[56]

The ongoing struggle of the NDPVF to gain a foothold in the political system through increased political rights in the Delta and control over oil resources (the primary source of economic and political power in the Delta) suggests that the NDPVF is not so much fighting to change the system as it is fighting to have a place within the system, and in particular to control of the oil revenues of the Delta. The problem the NDPVF faces is that it disengaged from the existing political system when it rebelled against Odili, but has not managed either to break into the political system through violent means or to change the political opportunity structure to enable it political access. In fact, the use of violent means to attempt to alter the political system appears to have ensured the NDPVF will never have a seat at the political table. It is simply too weak politically to achieve that goal, and insufficiently strong militarily to force the government to grant it a seat at the table. The NDPVF attempted to influence the political agenda in the lead up to the 2007 elections and to reassert itself as a prominent player in the Delta following Asari's release in June of that year, but has proven ill-equipped for the challenge. The NDPVF now faces a situation of either continued fighting or extinction. If the NDPVF accepts a political deal, it will be sidelined from the broader political process because it is not perceived to be a true political force and has not proven capable of garnering sufficient voter support during elections. Any political deal would be unlikely to change the status quo distribution of power or the political opportunity structure, leaving the NDPVF with few options.

Conclusion

The analysis suggests that the emergence and sustainability of armed groups should be treated as distinct phenomena.[57] The emergence of an armed group in no way guarantees its success. In fact, the decision to choose violence as a primary tactic in a political struggle significantly increases the costs to the group of sustaining its effort. As a result, the ability of the group to sustain itself and its activities requires further conscious action to mobilize resources. Second, the analysis supports the argument that social and economic factors play an important role in the emergence and success of armed groups, suggesting that a focus on political factors (and in particular the political opportunity structure) is insufficient on its own to explain the emergence of armed groups, their choice of violence, or their ability to sustain themselves.[58] Instead, a more comprehensive approach is needed. Broadening the analytical lens to include all four factors – political opportunities, framing alignment, resource mobilization, and group competition – highlights how different factors play a role at each stage of the mobilization process, and underscores the point that not all factors are important at each stage. This has important implications for research and analysis, as well as for the development of government policies aimed at responding to the emergence and challenge of armed groups.

The case study highlights that certain factors proved more important at different stages. The political opportunity structure, political patrons, and political ideology were significant to the emergence of the NDPVF. The choice of violence depended heavily upon the competition the NDPVF faced at the time, but was mainly determined by the political ideology of the group. The ability of the NDPVF to sustain itself depended heavily on the lack of governance in the Niger Delta and the unwillingness of the Nigerian military to engage in a full civil war against the NDPVF. If the military pressure had been more sustained, the NDPVF might have found it difficult to withstand the engagement, and it would have required significantly more resources for the NDPVF to continue the fight. The key to the NDPVF developing into an armed group independent of its political patrons, however, was the effectiveness of the group's resource mobilization through the sale of bunkered oil.

The case study also raises a number of additional factors that need to be considered in future analysis of armed groups. These include: the role of charismatic leaders, the nature of resource mobilization (and in particular the use of natural resource sales), the use of violence as a strategic tool, and the effects of violence on the opportunity structure that in fact lead to the parties getting 'stuck' in violence.

The NDPVF case study highlights the importance of having a charismatic leader at the head of an armed group. Charismatic leaders play an important role in framing the issues and the position of the group. Those who are able to pitch their cause to followers, recruit new members, and sustain existing membership will be more successful. They are also more likely to and garner public support. Asari remains widely perceived as a hero and a rallying point for the Delta fight against the government.

However, having a charismatic leader produces both positive and negative effects. While a charismatic leader can act as a leading force to guide an armed group, mobilize a population, and hold together a movement, the disappearance of such a leader (either through death or jail) tends to decapitate the group and leave it directionless. The NDPVF became largely defunct while Asari was in jail, with many members shifting to more active groups. This proved difficult for Asari to remedy upon his release from prison, and he faced intense competition from other armed groups, which gained power during his internment.

Two aspects of resource mobilization deserve to be highlighted: the proactive support of political patrons and the entrepreneurial opportunities for raising material support for an armed group. Political patrons can provide economic resources to militant groups in the form of monetary support, military logistics and equipment, and access routes to arms purchases and sales of natural resources. However, this support often comes with strings attached. Political patrons are neither benign nor altruistic; their support results from their own strategic interests and these may not coincide with the goals of the armed group. This can impose constraints on the actions of the armed group, or make patron support capricious. Armed groups increasingly have alternatives to patron support. The domestic harvesting of natural resources (e.g. diamonds, timber, and oil) and their sale on the international market provide one source of financial resources. This has been well documented in the literature. Additional sources of income include the sale of security services and the imposition of 'security' taxes on communities by armed groups. An important element of sustainability for an armed group is the development of an effective and reliable system of resource mobilization, and one that is not entirely dependent on the whims of political patrons.

Violence is an important strategic tool for armed groups when they can use it wisely and if they can control it. Allowing members to act violently on their own (e.g. loot for their salary) results in a reduction in popular support and increased resistance by communities. This alters the opportunity structure and raises the operational costs of the group. However, targeting violence at the primary opponent (whether another armed group or government forces) can produce positive dividends by demonstrating the commitment of the group to the cause, reinforcing the framing of the problem by clearly identifying 'the enemy', and making it clear that the group aims to protect the community. It can also reduce the operational costs by enabling the armed group to only engage in violent tactics when necessary. However, once the choice for violence is made, this in itself can reframe the opportunity structure and inhibit the achievement of the group's political goals.

Violence often produces an escalatory cycle of tit-for-tat measures wherein it becomes difficult to de-escalate the violence and enter into political negotiations. Violence can also de-legitimize the group in the eyes of the government; offering the government an easy way of marking the group as a threat to the state, and therefore a target of military action, not a viable negotiating partner or a legitimate political actor. Violence can therefore place constraints on negotiations and the future political options of the armed group. While violence can provide a useful tool for getting the government's attention and a seat at the negotiating table, the use of violence crosses the threshold of legitimacy in many societies, posing difficulties for negotiations, and raising an important question of how a government can back down in the face of violent attacks without losing legitimacy itself. While some armed groups have successfully transitioned into political parties, many have not.

The NDPVF survived and developed into a formidable militant group capable of relatively efficient and sophisticated military organization, yet ultimately it failed as a social movement because it was inherently weak politically. The strength of the group lies in its capacity to wreak havoc on oil production and thereby hold the local and national government hostage. However, it is incapable (and perhaps unwilling) to ratchet up its attacks into a national military movement. In fact, the pursuit of its limited goals – development of the Niger Delta and a redistribution of oil monies – militates against such a national movement. However, the NDPVF, despite its relative popularity, has failed to develop a political basis in the region, leaving it with limited options in its political struggle. Given its weak political position, the group faces two options: continue its low-intensity insurgency in order to stay on the nation's radar, or seek a political solution in which the group faces extinction because it cannot garner sufficient popular support to earn itself a seat at the political table.

ACKNOWLEDGEMENTS

The author would like to thank Keith Krause for his comments on earlier versions of this paper and the participants of the conference on Transnational and Non-State Armed Groups for their comments during the conference.

NOTES

1. Doug McAdam, Sidney Tarrow, and Charles Tilly, 'Toward an Integrated Perspective on Social Movements and Revolution', in Mark Irving Lichbach and Alan S. Zuckerman (eds), *Comparative Politics: Rationality, Culture, and Structure* (Cambridge: Cambridge University Press, 1997), p. 142.
2. For a discussion of terrorism and political violence through a social movement lens see Colin J. Beck, 'The Contribution of Social Movement Theory to Understanding Terrorism', *Sociology Compass*, Vol. 2, No. 5 (2008), pp. 1565–81.
3. Donatella Della Porta in a review of research on social movements and political violence argues that the study of political violence has been discontinuous. See Della Porta, 'Research on Social Movements and Political Violence', *Qualitative Sociology*, Vol. 31, No. 3 (2008), p. 229.
4. See Ibrahim Abdullah, 'Bush Path to Destruction: The Origin and Character of the Revolutionary United Front/Sierra Leone', *Journal of Modern African Studies*, Vol. 36, No. 2 (1998), pp. 203–13.
5. See Vincenzo Ruggiero, 'Brigate Rosse: Political Violence, Criminology and Social Movement Theory', *Crime, Law & Social Change*, Vol. 43, No. 4–5 (2005), pp. 292–7.
6. See Elizabeth Jean Wood, *Insurgent Collective Action and Civil War in El Salvador* (Cambridge: Cambridge University Press, 2003).
7. McAdam, Tarrow, and Tilly, 'Toward an Integrated Perspective', p. 143 (note 1).
8. Ibid.
9. Mayer N. Zald and John D. McCarthy, 'Social Movement Industries: Competition and Cooperation Among Movement Organizations,' CRSO Working Paper No. 201, Center for Research on Social Organization, University of Michigan, 1979, p. 2.
10. Ibid.
11. This does not include groups that use violent means to attain purely economic goals.
12. See, for example, McAdam, Tarrow, and Tilly, 'Toward an Integrated Perspective' (note 1); and James Ron, 'Ideology in Context: Explaining Sendero Luminoso's Tactical Escalation', *Journal of Peace Research*, Vol. 38, No. 5 (2001), pp. 569–92.

13. McAdam, Tarrow, and Tilly, 'Toward an Integrated Perspective', p. 155–7 (note 1).
14. Ibid., p. 157; Ruggiero, 'Brigate Rosse' (note 5), pp. 298–302.
15. See John D. McCarthy and Mayer N. Zald, 'Resource Mobilization and Social Movements: A Partial Theory', *The American Journal of Sociology*, Vol. 82, No. 6 (May 1997), pp. 1212–1241.
16. Della Porta, 'Research on Social Movements' (note 3).
17. Peter Eisinger, 'The Conditions of Protest Behavior in American Cities', *American Political Science Review*, Vol. 67, No. 1 (1973), p. 25.
18. Kurt Schock, 'People Power and Political Opportunities: Social Movement Mobilization and Outcomes in the Philippines and Burma', *Social Problems*, Vol. 46, No. 3 (1999), p. 361; Benjamin Tejerina, 'Protest Cycle, Political Violence and Social Movements in the Basque Country,' *Nations and Nationalism*, Vol. 7, No. 1 (2001), p. 48.
19. Kurt Schock, 'People Power and Political Opportunities' (note 18), p. 361.
20. Havard Hegre, Tanja Ellingsen, Scott Gates, and Nils Petter Gleditsch, 'Toward a Democratic Civil Peace? Democracy, Political Change, and Civil War, 1816–1992', *American Political Science Review*, Vol. 95, No. 1 (March 2001), p. 33.
21. Ron, 'Ideology in Context' (note 12), p. 579.
22. McCarthy and Zald, 'Resource Mobilization' (note 15), p. 1213.
23. Ibid., p. 1236.
24. Ron, 'Ideology in Context' (note 12), p. 581.
25. Donatella Della Porta and Sydney Tarrow, 'Unwanted Children: Political Violence and the Cycle of Protest in Italy, 1966–1973', *European Journal of Political Research*, Vol. 14, No. 5–6 (1986), p. 607.
26. Della Porta, 'Research on Social Movements' (note 3), p. 222.
27. For a discussion of the cycle of protest see Sidney Tarrow, *Democracy and Disorder: Protest and Politics in Italy 1965–1975* (Oxford: Clarendon Press, 1989).
28. Della Porta and Tarrow, 'Unwanted Children' (note 25), p. 607.
29. Tejerina, 'Protest Cycle' (note 18), p. 40.
30. Jack A. Goldstone, 'More Social Movements or Fewer? Beyond Political Opportunity Structures to Relational Fields', *Theory and Society*, Vol. 33, No. 3–4 (2004), p. 345.
31. This case study is based on previous research by the author. For a discussion of the research methods used see Jennifer M. Hazen, *Small Arms, Armed Violence, and Insecurity in Nigeria: The Niger Delta in Perspective*, Occasional Paper No. 20, Small Arms Survey, Geneva, 2007.
32. International Crisis Group, *Fuelling the Niger Delta Crisis*, Africa Report No. 118, September 2006, p. 1.
33. Darren Kew, 'Seeking Peace in the Niger Delta,' *New England Journal of Public Policy*, Vol. 21, No. 2 (June 2007), p. 161.
34. Ibid., p. 158.
35. International Crisis Group, *Nigeria: Want in the Midst of Plenty*, Africa Report No. 113, July 2006, p. 27.
36. Human Rights Watch, *Chop Fine: The Human Rights Impact of Local Government Corruption and Mismanagement in Rivers State, Nigeria*, Human Rights Watch Report, Vol. 19, No. 2 (January 2007), p.76.
37. Erich Marquardt, 'Nigerian Militants Influencing Election Campaign', *Terrorism Focus*, Vol. 4, No. 5 (March 2007), The Jamestown Foundation, p. 2.
38. International Crisis Group, 'Fuelling the Niger Delta Crisis' (note 32), p. 4.
39. Marquardt, 'Nigerian Militants' (note 37), p. 2.
40. Hazen, 'Small Arms' (note 31), pp. 22–3.
41. Marquardt, 'Nigerian Militants' (note 37), p. 2.
42. Ike Okonta, *Behind the Mask: Explaining the Emergence of the MEND Militia in Nigeria's Oil-Bearing Niger Delta*, Niger Delta Economies of Violence Working Papers No. 11, University of California, Berkeley, 2006, p. 12.
43. Erich Marquardt, 'Mujahid Dokubo-Asari: The Niger Delta's Ijaw Leader', *Terrorism Focus*, Vol. 5, No. 15, (August 2007), The Jamestown Foundation, p. 2.
44. Marquardt, 'Mujahid Dokubo-Asari' (note 43), p. 3.
45. International Crisis Group, 'Fuelling the Niger Delta Crisis' (note 32), p. 4.
46. Simon Lewis, 'Illegal Arms Importation', Unpublished Niger Delta Peace and Security Working Group background paper, June 2006, p. 52.
47. Michael Watts, 'Crisis in Nigeria: Oil Inferno', *CounterPunch*, January 2007.
48. International Crisis Group, *The Swamps of Insurgency: Nigeria's Delta Unrest*, Africa Report No. 115, August 2006, p. 9.

49. Hazen, 'Small Arms' (note 31), pp. 98–9.
50. International Crisis Group, 'The Swamps of Insurgency' (note 48), p. 5.
51. Stephen Davis, Dimieari Von Kemedi, and Mark Drennan, 'Illegal Oil Bunkering in the Niger Delta', Unpublished Niger Delta Peace and Security Working Group background paper, June 2006, p. 40.
52. International Crisis Group, 'The Swamps of Insurgency' (note 48), p.10.
53. Davis, Von Kemedi, and Drennan, 'Illegal Oil Bunkering' (note 51), p. 31.
54. Academic Associates PeaceWorks, 'Armed Groups in the Niger Delta', Unpublished survey, 2006.
55. Stephen Davis and Dimieari Von Kemedi, 'The Current Stability and Future Prospects for Peace and Security in the Niger Delta', Unpublished Niger Delta Peace and Security Working Group background paper, June 2006, p. 19.
56. Ibid., p. 19.
57. Goldstone, 'More Social Movements' (note 30), p. 347.
58. Tejerina, 'Protest Cycle' (note 18), p. 50.

Gangs as Non-State Armed Groups: The Central American Case

DENNIS RODGERS AND ROBERT MUGGAH

Gangs are routinely excluded from theoretical and policy debates on 'non-state armed groups' or NSAGs. Rather, the acronym tends to be reserved to clusters of individuals who comprise rebel opposition groups, guerrillas, localized militia, or civil defence and paramilitary forces. In other words, discussions of NSAGs are narrowly confined to groups operating in opposition to the state – often impelled to action by 'greed' or 'grievance'[1] – and generally with a view to taking it over.[2] Conceptualizations are thus embedded in a state-centric framework wherein the state is not just a key referent, but according to Alston, 'the indispensable and pivotal one around which all other entities revolve'.[3] Consequently, efforts to engage and contain NSAGs tend to focus on their (il)legitimacy and the extent to which they can be made to comply to the prescribed norms and rules of state action.

At the same time, however, as other authors in this special issue make clear, significant ambiguity persists concerning the conceptual parameters of the concept. Interpretations are frequently dependent as much on the circumstances and motivations of the observer as the (actual) interests and characteristics of the observed. Tellingly, human rights scholars such as Clapham advocate for as broad a definition as possible including 'every entity apart from states'.[4] Likewise, Alston includes a host of entities ranging from rebel groups and terrorist organizations to religious associations, militant civil society organizations, private corporations and businesses and even some international agencies.[5] Certain researchers have also focused on the environment(s) in which non-state armed groups operate, or their attributed or imputed motives, in order to articulate coherent forms of classification.

While it is recognized that the 'types' of NSAGs are dynamic and fluid, there is nevertheless a tendency in the literature to focus primarily on their manifestations in war or post-war contexts.[6] This is largely due to the centrality attributed by international relations scholars and policymakers to (liberal) state-building and the consolidation of the monopoly over violence in fragile post-war settings. NSAGs are thus frequently cast as explicit threats, spoilers, and a 'cause of instability around the globe'.[7] Yet an increasing number of studies reveal that such groups also originate and thrive in non-war situations.[8] Moreover, they can also be understood as alternative and legitimate nodes of authority to the state, particularly when the latter is perceived to be ineffectual and/or repressive.[9] Indeed, gangs provide a compelling example of both of these observations, as is well evidenced by the contemporary Central American context.

This article provides a descriptive overview of the regional gang panorama in Central America, in order to highlight its underlying logic and dynamics. It seeks to broaden the theoretical debate on NSAGs beyond a narrow treatment of guerrilla and rebel groups fighting to purposefully assume control of the state. In particular, it seeks to account for non-state armed groups that despite perhaps undermining the state by virtue of their violence, are not consciously seeking direct control over all (or even any) of its institutions. It also reveals a complex dialectic shaping gang-state relations – including the instrumental 'criminalization' of the former by the latter as a means of concealing more fundamental social and economic injustices and disparities. The article is divided into three sections, beginning with a brief overview of violence in contemporary Central America, before then characterising the differentiated origins and dynamics of gangs operating in the region. It concludes with an assessment of state-led policy response to Central American gangs and related implications for future scholarship on non-state armed groups.

Violence in Contemporary Central America

Violence is on the upswing in Central America,[10] with the region currently exhibiting amongst the highest rates of reported homicide and criminal victimization in Latin America and, indeed, the world.[11] While the annual global homicide rate was estimated by the World Health Organization (WHO) to be approximately eight per 100,000, in the Americas the figure was over 20 per 100,000, and in Central America above 30 per 100,000.[12] Homicidal violence is described by policymakers and public health researchers as one of the primary population health issues facing societies across the region,[13] with perpetration and victimization of violence particularly concentrated amongst young males between 15 and 34 years of age.

There are many determinants shaping the temporal, demographic, and spatial dynamics of violence. The World Bank, for example, attributes the rise in Central American violence to 'a complex set of factors, including rapid urbanization, persistent poverty and inequality, social exclusion, political violence, organized crime, post-conflict cultures, the emergence of illegal drug use and trafficking and authoritarian family structures'.[14] The United Nations Office on Drugs and Crime (UNODC) also emphasizes the role of geography and weak institutions; with an estimated 90 per cent of the cocaine supplies destined for the US passing through Central American states from Andean production centres, organized crime and violence are both enmeshed and entrenched.[15]

One of the most visible faces of the new Central American panorama of violence is the gang phenomenon. Gangs are by no means an uncommon social phenomena. They can be observed in most societies around the world, although the vast majority of what are identified as 'gangs' are often little more than ephemeral groups of youth who gather on street corners and engage in behaviour that is frequently labelled 'antisocial'. Gangs in the proper sense of the term are much more definite social organizations that display an institutional continuity independent of their membership. They have fixed conventions and rules, which can include initiation rituals, a ranking system, rites of passage, and rules of conduct that make the gang a primary source of identity for members. Gang codes often demand particular behaviour patterns from members, such as adopting characteristic dress, tattoos, graffiti, hand signs, and slang, as well as regular involvement in illicit and violent activities. Such gangs are also often – but not always – associated with a particular territory, and their relationship with local communities can be either oppressive or protective (indeed, this can change from one to the other over time). Central American gangs clearly correspond to this second type of institution.

Although gangs have long featured in Central American societies, certainly well before the wars of the 1980s and early 1990s, they have experienced unprecedented growth and attention in the past two decades. Estimates of the total proportion of contemporary regional violence attributable to gangs vary wildly from 10 to 60 per cent,[16] while they have been accused of a whole slew of crimes and delinquency, ranging from mugging, theft, and intimidation, to rape, assault, and organized/ petty drug dealing. More recently, there have even been attempts to link gangs to incipient revolution and global terrorism. A 2005 US Army War College publication contends that Central American gangs constitute a 'new urban insurgency' that had as an ultimate objective 'to depose or control the governments of targeted countries' through '*coups d'street*' [sic], for example.[17] Similarly, Anne Aguilera, the head of the Central America office of the International Narcotics and Law Enforcement Affairs branch of the US State Department recently asserted that gangs were 'the greatest problem for national security at this time in Central America'.[18] Although gangs are unquestionably a significant security concern, such obviously sensationalist pronouncements suggest that they remain profoundly misunderstood and betray a profound lack of understanding of their underlying logic.[19]

The Gangs of Central America

Reliable information on the scale, dynamics, and demographics of Central American gangs is scarce. Official statistics are especially problematic owing to chronic under-reporting, deficient data collection, and issues of political interference.[20] Publicly available figures indicate that there are some 70,000 gang members operating in Central America. By way of contrast, a host of NGOs and academics contend that the number is likely much higher, as many as 200,000, while the UNODC provides a range that goes up to as many as 500,000 gang members.[21] Even a lower estimate suggests that the numbers of gang members rivals the armed forces of most countries in Central America: Nicaragua and Honduras have armies of about 12,000 soldiers each, El Salvador 13,000 soldiers, and Guatemala 27,000.[22] While there is compara-tively limited reliable quantitative data available on gangs, there are an increasing number of qualitative studies suggesting that gangs constitute primary actors within the contemporary regional panorama of violence.[23]

Qualitative studies also reveal considerable diversity amongst gangs in and between countries in the Central American region. Specifically, El Salvador, Guate-mala, and Honduras are currently experiencing more severe levels of gang violence than Nicaragua, for example (although violence in this latter country is much higher than generally reported)[24] – while the problem is of a completely different- and lower- order of magnitude in Costa Rica and Panama. Likewise, the distribution of violence within these countries varies greatly, even if the overwhelming majority of gang violence can definitely be said to occur in urban areas, particularly in capital cities (which are often primate settlements within the national context). This is not entirely surprising. Gangs are very much urban manifestations since a critical demographic mass of youth in inevitably necessary for a gang to emerge.

There is in fact a strong correlation between violence-affected urban spaces and gang consolidation, size and distribution. Certain studies have reported that up to 15 per cent of youth within gang-affected communities may ultimately join a gang. Other assessments suggest that on average, the figure is likely closer to 3 to 5 per cent. Gangs tend to register between 15 and 100 members, although the average size is approximately 20–25 members.[25] Moreover, gangs are not evenly distributed within cities. Although the association between poverty and gang violent is neither causal nor systematic, gangs are more likely to emerge in poorer and marginal sections of the urban landscape. There are of course many exceptions to the rule: a study in Guatemala's capital found that neighbourhoods falling within the metropolis's bottom quartile in terms of impoverishment suffered from comparatively less gang-related crime than neighbourhoods falling within the second-to-last quartile.[26]

The vast majority of real and potential gang members are male youth.[27] There is also evidence of all-female gangs operating in Nicaragua and Guatemala.[28] The age range of gang members can be highly varied, although a 2001 study based on some 1,000 interviews with gang members conducted by researchers at the *Instituto Universitario de Opinión Pública* (IUDOP) in El Salvador found that the average gang member in the country was 20 years old, with a mean age of entry into the gang of 15 years of age. Nicaraguan gang members have been found to fall between seven and 23 years old, while the age of Guatemalan and Honduran gang members ranges from 12 to 30 years of age.

Most studies of Central American gangs have highlighted the difficulties of systematically pinpointing specific factors explaining gang membership. Stereotypical 'determinants' such as family fragmentation, domestic abuse, or a particular psychological make-up are not consistently significant, and the only factor that has been reported as systematically affecting gang membership is religion, insofar as evangelical Protestant youths in Nicaragua tend not to join gangs.[29] The IUDOP assessment found that some 40 per cent of respondents claimed to join gangs in order to 'hang out', 21 per cent because they had gang member friends, and 21 per cent in order to avoid from family problems. The study also found a partial correlation between youth unemployment and gang membership: 17 per cent of gang members were employed, and 66 per cent actively characterized themselves as 'unemployed'.[30]

The emergence and spread of gangs are commonly linked to structural factors, including the pervasive *machismo* that characterizes Central American societies (many gang codes are clearly expressions of a heightened masculinity). Other influencing factors include high levels of social exclusion and inequality, the long history of war and its aftermath in several countries,[31] the unregulated availability of weapons (it is estimated that there are over two million unregistered small arms in Central America),[32] as well as the widespread absence of the state and concomitant 'local governance voids' that gangs seek to fill as 'micro-political' social forms.[33] Considering that these factors affect Central American youth universally, but not all youth become gang members, they must be seen more as contextual variables than determinants, however.

A more significant variable shaping the formation and consolidation of gangs is migration. Even if there is frequently a tendency to talk about Central American gangs generically, a distinction must be made between '*maras*' on the one hand, and '*pandillas*' on the other. *Maras* are a phenomenon with transnational roots, while *pandillas* are more localized, homegrown entities that are the direct inheritors of the youth gangs that have long been a historic feature of Central American societies. *Pandillas* were initially present in certain countries emerging from war during the 1990s, but are now only significantly visible in Nicaragua – and to a lesser extent in Costa Rica (where they are often called '*chapulines*') – having been almost completely supplanted by *maras* in El Salvador, Guatemala, and Honduras.

The contemporary manifestation of the *pandilla* phenomenon finds its origins during the transition from war to peace in the late 1980s and early 1990s. During this period, demobilized combatant youth in Nicaragua, El Salvador, and Guatemala returned to their home communities and faced situations of heightened uncertainty, insecurity, and socio-economic flux within a broader context of state crisis and fragility. Drawing on what was effectively a traditional organizational vehicle for youth collective action, some of these young men formed localized vigilante-style self-defence groups in an attempt to provide a measure of order and predictability both for themselves and their local communities, with many community members embracing these early gangs as the sole predictable source of order and authority. From these relatively fluid and organic beginnings, *pandillas* rapidly began to develop particular behaviour patterns, which included engaging in semi-ritualized forms of gang warfare that were regulated by strict codes and expectations, including in particular protecting local territories and residents.[34]

Clear parallels can be made with past gangs insofar as these often emerged as informal defence organizations in illegal squatter settlements. The *pandillas* of the mid and late 1990s were however much more numerous and also more violent than their predecessors, partly due to the legacy of war and insurrection which provided youth with unprecedented martial skills.[35] They also became much more institutionalized than past gangs – which tended to be generationally ephemeral – giving themselves names – examples from Nicaragua include *los Dragones, los Rampleros*, or *los Comemuertos* ('Eaters of the Dead') – and developing hierarchies and rules that persisted over time, irrespective of gang member turnover.[36] Thus, to interpret *pandillas* solely as a form of post-conflict violence would be rather limiting, insofar as contemporary gang members were often born after the war in Nicaragua ended. Ultimately, *pandillas* can best be interpreted as localized institutional responses to the circumstances of insecurity, exclusion, and uncertainty that affected many Central American countries during the 1990s and 2000s, even if there are significant variations both between and within different societies.

The *maras*, on the other hand, are groups that can be directly linked to specific migratory patterns. Formally, there are just two *maras*, the *Dieciocho* (18) and the *Salvatrucha* (MS). They are present only in El Salvador, Guatemala, and Honduras within the Central American region, although they have reportedly begun to extend into Southern Mexico as well. The origins of the *maras* reside in the 18th Street gang in Los Angeles, a gang founded by Mexican immigrants in the Rampart section of the city in the 1960s, although it rapidly began to accept Hispanics indiscriminately. The 18th Street gang grew significantly during the late 1970s and early 1980s as a result of the influx of mainly Salvadoran and Guatemalan refugees, who sought to incorporate into the gang in order to feel included as outsiders in the US. In the latter half of the 1980s, a rival – possibly splinter – group founded by a second wave of Salvadoran refugees emerged, known as the '*Mara Salvatrucha*' (a combination of 'Salvadoreño' and 'trucha', meaning 'quick-thinking' or 'shrewd' in Salvadoran slang).[37] The *Dieciocho* and the *Salvatrucha* rapidly became bitter rivals, and frequently fought each other on the streets of Los Angeles.

The two groups were also heavily involved in the violence and looting that accompanied the 1992 Rodney King riots. As a result, the State of California subsequently implemented strict anti-gang laws and prosecutors charged young gang members as adults instead of minors, sending hundreds to jail for felonies and other serious crimes. By 1996, the US Congress established the Illegal Immigration Reform and Immigrant Responsibility Act which ensured that non-US citizens sentenced to a year or more in prison were to be repatriated to their countries of origin. Even foreign-born US naturalized felons could be stripped of their citizenship and expelled once they served out their prison terms. As a result, between 1998 and 2005 the US deported almost 46,000 convicts to Central America, in addition to 160,000 illegal immigrants caught without their requisite permits.[38]

Central America's northern triangle – El Salvador, Guatemala, and Honduras – received over 90 per cent of the deportations from the US.[39] Many of these deportees were members of the 18th Street and *Salvatrucha* gangs who had arrived in the US as toddlers but had never secured legal residency or citizenship. Many had joined gangs as a way to feel socially included in a receiving country that routinely impeded their integration. Owing to their sense of exclusion from the US and following their arrival in countries of 'origin' that they seldom knew, it is unsurprising that they reproduced the structures and behaviour patterns that had provided them with support and security during their time in the US. Deportees rapidly began to found local '*clikas*', or chapters, of their gang in their communities of origin, which in turn rapidly began to attract local youth and either supplanted or absorbed local *pandillas*.[40]

Each *clika* is explicitly affiliated with either the *Mara Dieciocho* (as the 18th Street gang is known in Central America) or the *Mara Salvatrucha*. But while *clikas* from different neighbourhoods affiliated with the same *mara* will often join together to fight other groupings claiming allegiance to the opposing *mara*, neither gang is a real federal structure, and much less a transnational one. Neither the *Dieciocho* nor the *Salvatrucha* gangs answer to a single chain of command, and their 'umbrella' nature is more symbolic of a particular historical origin than demonstrative of any real organizational unity, be it of leadership or action.

In many ways, the federated nature of the *maras* is more of an imagined social morphology than an actually occurring phenomenon, based on the fact that the steady flows of deportees from the US share a common language and reference points. To this extent, although the *maras* can be conceived as (very loose) networks of localized gangs, these do not necessarily communicate or coordinate either within or between countries. Certainly, there is little evidence of any cooperation between *maras* in El Salvador, Guatemala, or Honduras, and even less with the original putative 'mother gangs' in Los Angeles. Rather, the ties that exist are more akin to a common sense of social identity, founded organically on individuals' experiences of gangsterism in the US, deportation, and stigmatization in Central America.

The migratory origin of the *maras* is a crucial factor explaining why Nicaragua does not have *maras*. Not only does Nicaragua register a very low deportation rate from the US – less than three per cent of all Central American deportees are Nicaraguan – but Nicaraguans who have emigrated to the US have mainly settled in Miami. According to US census data, only 12 per cent have settled in Los Angeles, where they account for just four per cent of Central Americans in the city, while in Miami they represent 47 per cent – where contrarily to the more 'open' gangs of LA, the local gang scene is dominated by highly exclusive African-American and Cuban-American gangs which do not let Nicaraguans join them.[41] This is also a potentially important factor explaining why Nicaraguan *pandillas* are not as violent as *maras*, and by extension why El Salvador, Guatemala, and Honduras are more violent than Nicaragua. The transnational transposition of US gang culture in the northern three Central American countries has arguably had much more brutal results due to the fact that it is clearly less embedded within a local institutional context than traditional Central American *pandilla* culture, and therefore less rule-bound and constrained. At the same time, it is important to note that the *mara* phenomenon is not simply a foreign problem imported by deportees, but rather has evolved and grown in response to domestic factors and conditions.

In contrast to sensationalist accounts linking Central American gangs to migrant trafficking, kidnapping, and international organized crime, it seems that both *pandillas* and *maras* are mainly involved in small-scale, localized crime and delinquency such as petty theft and muggings.[42] These activities are frequently carried out on an individual basis, although the *maras* in El Salvador, Guatemala, and Honduras are also increasingly collectively involved in the extortion of protection money from local businesses and the racketeering of buses and taxis as they pass through the territories they control. Both *pandillas* and *maras* however make use of military-style weaponry such as AK-47s and explosives such as fragmentation grenades. The 2001 IUDOP survey of Salvadoran gang members mentioned above for example found that 25 per cent of those questioned admitted to having committed a murder in the past year, while 25 per cent refused to answer the question.[43] Even so, most *pandilla* and *mara* violence is circumscribed, occurring as it does in the poorer, local communities from which the gangs emerge rather than wealthier neighbourhoods. The majority of gang violence in fact tends to be directed against rival gangs, as was for example starkly illustrated by the occurrence of tit-for-tat prison warfare between rival incarcerated gang members in Guatemala.[44]

Nevertheless, both *pandillas* and *maras* have become increasingly involved in narcotics trafficking and dealing over the past decade.[45] It is worth recalling that the consumption of drugs has long been associated with the gang lifestyle, as well as the fact that Central America has become a transit point for most cocaine traffic between the Andean countries and North America.[46] Drug trafficking in Central America tends to be decentralized, however, with shipments passing from small local cartels to other local cartels, members of whom extract a profit before narcotics are then passed on to the more organized Mexican cartels. The role that gangs – both *maras* and *pandillas* – serve is principally as the local security apparatus of the smaller cartels, or as modest street vendors connected to larger players on an informal basis. Gangs on their own are neither involved in the large-scale, transnational movement of drugs nor in wholesaling, although certain studies suggest that the leaders of these small, local cartels are often ex-gang members who have 'graduated'. At the same time, there is compelling evidence that involvement in drug trafficking and dealing is leading to the elaboration of more violent behavioural patterns among both categories of gangs.[47]

This can however also be linked to the fact that increasingly large swathes of the urban poor in Central America are finding themselves able to access fewer and fewer licit economic opportunities. Having to survive as best they can outside the formal ambit of the state, they generally do so based on 'ruthless Darwinian competition', with competition 'for the same informal scraps, ensur[ing] self-consuming communal violence as yet the highest form of urban involution'.[48] Such processes are reinforced by the new patterns of segregation and exclusion that have emergence in Central American cities as a result of their market-led urban re-modelling, for example through the proliferation of gated communities and closed condominiums, as well as the transformation of transport networks.[49] Such patterns of segregation and exclusion are also related to the emergence of new forms of (repressive) state governance. On the urban plane this has involved patterns of regular police patrolling in wealthier areas of the city and on the new roads on the one hand, and the unpredictable, arbitrary, and violent patrolling of slums and poor neighbourhoods on the other.[50] This has served to precipitate localized conditions of terror and to symbolically demonstrate the power of the elite-captured state.[51] The most visible facet of this new approach is the implementation of a 'war on gangs' by Central American states over the past five years.[52]

Mano Dura: *The War on Gangs*

The opening salvo of the veritable 'war on gangs' currently raging in Central America was El Salvador's adoption of a *Mano Dura* (Iron Fist) policy in July 2003. The directive advocated the immediate imprisonment of gang member for having gang-related tattoos or flashing gang signs in public, a crime punishable by two to five years in jail and applicable to gang members from the age of 12 and older. Between July 2003 and August 2004, approximately 20,000 *pandilleros* were arrested, although 95 per cent of them were eventually released without charge when the *Mano Dura* law was declared unconstitutional by the Salvadoran Supreme Court for violating the United Nations Convention on the Rights of the Child (UNCRC). A new *Mano Super Dura* package of anti-gang reforms was rapidly approved, which respected the provisions of the UNCRC but stiffened the penalties for gang membership to up to five years in prison for ordinary gang members, and nine years for gang leaders. Although under the new law the police are required to demonstrate proof of active delinquent behaviour in order to arrest an individual, El Salvador's prison population has doubled over the past five years, from 6,000 to 12,000, 40 per cent of which are gang members.[53]

Honduras implemented a comparable policy called *Cero Tolerancia* (Zero Tolerance) almost simultaneously in August 2003, which was also partly inspired by Rudy Giuliani's eponymous policy in New York. Among the measures that this package promoted was the reform of the penal code and the adoption of legislation that established a maximum 12-year prison sentence for gang membership, a penalty which was later stiffened to 30 years, as well as provisions for better collaboration between the police and the Honduran army in urban patrolling. Guatemala likewise adopted its *Plan Escoba* (Operation Broomsweep) in January 2004 which, although not as draconian as the Salvadoran *Mano Dura* and the Honduran *Cero Tolerancia*, still contained new provisions allowing minors to be treated as adults, and the deployment of 4,000 reserve army troops in troubled neighbourhoods in Guatemala City. Nicaragua similarly regularly implemented a range of anti-gang initiatives from 1999 onwards, although these were of a significantly 'softer' nature.[54] Although these crackdowns have been very popular with the general public in all the Central American countries, they have also been vigorously opposed by human rights groups who are concerned with the potential abuse of gang suspects. More ominously, organizations such as Human Rights Watch and Amnesty International have presented evidence – corroborated by the US State Department in 2005 – of the existence of paramilitary death squads in Honduras and El Salvador that are deliberately targeting gang members, and often youth more generally, in collusion with state authorities.[55]

Central American states have also initiated unprecedented regional cooperation in order to deal with gangs. During a September 2003 summit of heads of state, gangs were declared to be 'a destabilising menace, more immediate than any conventional war or guerrilla'. By January 2004, El Salvador, Guatemala, Honduras, and Nicaragua agreed to lift legal barriers to the cross-country prosecution of gang members, whatever their nationality. In March 2005, Presidents Saca of El Salvador and Berger of Guatemala agreed to establish a joint security force to patrol gang activity along their common border.

Central American states have also sought to involve the US. Although initially resistant to participate in anti-gang initiatives, the US position changed in June 2004 after the Honduran Minister of Security, claimed that a suspected Saudi member of Al Qaeda, Yafar Al-Taya, had arrived in Salvador in order to meet with gang leaders. Although this was an unfounded and likely spurious assertion, by December 2004 the Federal Bureau of Investigation (FBI) had created a special task force focusing on Central American gangs. In February 2005 it announced the creation of a liaison office in San Salvador to coordinate regional information-sharing and anti-gang efforts. Following a new (and no less ludicrous) claim by the Honduran Minister of Security to have thwarted a Colombian FARC-*mara* plot to kill President Maduro in April 2005, Central American military leaders formally called on the US Southern Command for assistance in the creation of a multinational force to tackle organized crime and youth gangs, although this has yet to be implemented. Likewise, the Merida Initiative, in coordination with the US, also emphasizes security provision enhancement in Central America and Mexico,[56] with the objective to counter the trade in drugs, reduce weapons-trafficking and confront gangs and organized crime.[57]

Such heavy-handed policies have clearly been widely supported,[58] partly due to the visibility they afford political leaders and their constituencies, but also because in many ways they mimic the principle kind of response that states plagued by NSAGs have adopted around the world. As such they arguably serve a classificatory function, by drawing implicit parallels between gangs and other violent organizations that they are not necessarily equivalent to, even if they can be said to belong to the same spectrum. Having said that, although there are some reports that different anti-gang initiatives have reduced crime significantly, there is evidence that these interventions have generated significant changes in gang dynamics, with increasing reports that the widespread heavy-handed repression of gangs is leading to their becoming more organized and more violent.[59]

This is something that was well illustrated by the tit-for-tat violence that certain *maras* engaged in with the Honduran authorities following the implementation of *Mano Dura*. Specifically, on 30 August 2003, one month after the promulgation of the new anti-gang legislation, gang members attacked a bus in the Northern city of San Pedro Sula in broad daylight, killing 14, and leaving 18 wounded, as well as a note to President Maduro ordering him to withdraw the law. The following month, in the town of Puerto Cortes, a young woman's head was found in a plastic bag with a note addressed to President Maduro saying that this was a response to the extrajudicial assassination of a gang member by the police. Over the course of the following year, more than 10 decapitated corpses were left in various cities with messages from gang members to the Honduras president, each time in response to a putative extrajudicial killing. On 23 December 2004, in Chamalecon, gang members again attacked a bus and killed 28, once again leaving a message claiming revenge for the May 2004 death of 105 gang members in a prison following a suspect fire. Similarly gruesome events have been reported in El Salvador and Guatemala.

The 'war on gangs' has reportedly also led to *maras* changing their behaviour patterns in less violent but nonetheless insidious ways. For one, gangs are attempting to become less conspicuous. For example, gang members in El Salvador have begun to use less obvious signs and symbols, including, in particular, getting rid of tattoos and no longer keeping their hair in the short-trimmed *rapado* style, in order to avoid being arrested. They have also become more mobile, with the emigration of *maras* into Southern Mexico widely attributed to the repression.[60] While this might be interpreted as gangs losing ground vis-à-vis Central American states, their underlying evolutionary trajectory suggests otherwise. The transformation of Nicaraguan *pandillas* between the 1990s and the 2000s is a case in point. These moved from being institutions that attempted to create localized forms of social order and belonging to organizations promoting parochial forms of drug dealing instead. Rather than protecting local neighbourhood inhabitants, gangs acted to ensure the proper functioning of

local drug economies solely in the interests of their members and associated local
dealers – more often than not ex-gang members – through the imposition of localized regimes of terror based on fear, threats, and widespread acts of arbitrary violence.[61] By 2007, however, *pandillas* in Nicaragua seemed to be disappearing, as
most gang members were 'retiring' and not being replaced by a new generation,
with a small minority joining more professional and de-territorialized criminal organizations that emerged around drug trafficking.[62] This professionalization is ominous,
insofar as the corrosive role that organized crime can play in developing contexts is
well-known,[63] and clearly has much more wide-ranging consequences than youth
gangsterism.

While a tendency toward heavy-handed responses persists in Central American
countries, there recently appears to be an increasing evolution from 'first' to
'second-generation' policies.[64] First-generation initiatives such as *Mano Dura* can
be characterized as *enforcement-first*, combining aggressive crackdown operations
with increased penalties to deter gang membership. Interventions are executed by
the state security apparatus together with reforms on the judicial and penal
systems, as well as, in many cases, extra-judicially.[65] Rehabilitation is seldom integrated into such strategies, which can therefore contribute to the stigmatization of
gang members and prevent their reform and ultimately reintegration into society.
In the wake of the significant criticism that such activities have generated,
Mano Dura programmes are being increasingly complemented – although not
necessarily replaced – by *Mano Amiga* (friendly hand) and *Mano Extendida*
(extended hand) interventions focused on incentivizing demobilization from gangs.
These second-generation activities are typically more *compliance and voluntary-
oriented* and combine carrots with sticks to address the risks and symptoms of
gang violence.[66]

The question remains, however, to what extent such second-generation initiatives
truly represent a transformation in Central American policy culture. In a detailed study
mapping out the incentives governing the institutional and organizational framework
regarding youth violence reduction in Nicaragua, José Luis Rocha traces how the government's promotion of second-generation policies is in many ways highly cosmetic,
and principally aimed at pleasing potential donors and raising international funds. On
the ground, government action remains much more 'first generation' in nature.[67]
Similar dynamics are evident in other Central American countries, underscored by
the fact that there is little empirical evidence that second-generation approaches are
actually achieving major changes on the ground.[68] What this ultimately suggests is
that there may well be ulterior motives on the part of Central American states to continue to stigmatize and treat gangs in a way that associates them with insurgents and
other 'classic' NSAGs. Ultimately social policy choices inevitably reflect the political
and economic dynamics underlying any given society, and seen from this perspective,
perhaps the biggest obstacles to the coherent application of 'second-generation' gang
violence-reduction politics in Central America is the deeply entrenched oligarchic
nature of the societies in question, and the hugely unequal political economies that
they display,[69] but which are obscured by discourses laying the blame on gangs that
must be cracked down upon at all costs.

Conclusion

Gangs constitute a very real but much misunderstood feature of the Central American panorama of violence. There is no doubt that a significant proportion of regional violence is attributable to the phenomenon. Even so, gangs constitute in the main a local-level security challenge rather than the transnational threat that the media and some policy outlets make them out to be. Although they are clearly linked to an array of deep-rooted factors such as the long legacy of war, *machismo*, and the availability of small arms in the region, they are also an immediate symptom of growing inequality and exclusion, and as such a reflection of deeply iniquitous social processes. Most research on gang formation emphasizes the role of social and economic variables such as marginalization, rapid and unregulated social change, and lack of meaningful opportunities. Moreover, both a careful appraisal of the origins of gangs, as well as their evolution over time suggests that although they may well often emerge in post-conflict contexts, these are not necessarily determining their emergence.

The contemporary Central American landscape of violence clearly suggests that gangs can be conceived as important non-state armed groups despite the fact that they lack ambition to overthrow the state. Gang violence tends only to indirectly erode or undermine the state, often emerging instead as a result of state weakness, as gangs seek to potentially fill in for the absence of certain state functions. But the dialectical relationship between gangs and state institutions must be carefully interrogated. The proposition that gangs can be seen as NSAGs is clearly supported by the fact that the presence of gangs more often than not leads to a violent state reaction, which effectively treats them as an enemy 'other' in a manner very similar to its treatment of more conventional rebels or insurgent organizations. This more often than not leads to an upsurge of collective and inter-personal violence, however, as the case of *mara* violence following the implementation of *Mano Dura* in Honduras dramatically illustrates, and can lead to a transformation in the nature of gang violence.

The repressive approach adopted by Central American governments has in many cases exacerbated the problem, precipitating a tit-for-tat spiral of violence and radicalising the gangs. Repression simply does not remedy the underlying factors that contributed to gang formation and consolidation in the first place, and is leading to the rise of more organized crime. Although second-generation initiatives have been promoted, these have yielded few concrete results, largely because the form of social policy within any given social context will ultimately inevitably reflect to a greater or lesser degree the political dispensation and economic dynamics of a given society. As such, arguably one of the biggest obstacles to developing a coherent approach to gang violence in Central America is the region's deeply entrenched oligarchic nature, and the hugely unequal political economies of its societies.[70]

This of course takes us beyond the relatively straightforward dilemmas associated with policy paralysis and raises the question of why some Central American governments are undertaking visible and widely publicized crackdowns on gangs. In many ways, they divert attention from the fact that states are otherwise doing little to remedy to the admittedly much more tricky issues of exclusion, inequality, and the lack of meaningful employment creation. Put another way, gangs have become convenient scapegoats. They allow certain actors to avoid addressing basic social and economic challenges and allow those in power attempt to maintain an unequal *status quo*. This is a potentially important insight in relation to NSAGs, insofar as they are rarely considered from this perspective, in terms of the functions that their classification as NSAGs plays in relation to the wider political economy of both intra- and inter-state relations. It also suggests that the tensions and conflicts that lead to the emergence of NSAGs are very much systemic, and cannot be understood solely in terms of narrowly conceived impulses linked to simplistic rational utility frameworks.[71]

NOTES

1. P. Collier and A. Hoeffler, 'Greed and Grievance in Civil War', *Oxford Economic Papers, Oxford University Press*, Vol. 56, No. 4 (October 2004), pp. 563–95.
2. See, for example, S. Kalyvas, *The Sociology of Civil Wars: Warfare and Armed Groups* (New Haven, CT: Yale mimeo, 2003). See also R. Shultz, D. Farah, and L. Itamara, 'Armed Groups: A Tier-One Security Priority', INSS Occasional Paper 57, USAF Institute for National Security Studies, 2004. According to the Trans-national and Non-State Armed Groups project of Harvard University and the Graduate Institute of International and Development Studies, for example, the 'expression "non-state armed groups" ... is used generically to describe armed groups – both transnational and national – that have the capacity to challenge the state's monopoly of legitimate force'. See http://www.armed-groups.org/home.aspx.
3. P. Alston, *Non-State Actors and Human Rights* (New York: Oxford University Press, 2005), p. 3.
4. A. Clapham, 'Non-State Actors', in V. Chetail (ed), *Post-Conflict Peacebuilding: A Lexicon* (Oxford: Oxford University Press, 2009), forthcoming.
5. Ibid.
6. There are some rare exceptions, however, including recent studies on heavily armed gangs in the Delta region of Nigeria who appear to be threatening the country's oil production and supply routes. See, for example, K. Oruwari, 'Youth in Urban Violence in Nigeria: A Case Study of Urban Gangs from Port Harcourt', Niger Delta Economies of Violence project, Working Paper No. 14, Institute of International Studies, University of California, Berkeley, 2006, http://geography.berkeley.edu/ProjectsResources/ND%20Website/NigerDelta/WP/14-Oruwari.pdf.
7. Richard Shultz, Douglas Farah, and Itamara Lochard 'Armed Groups: A Tier-One Security Priority', INSS Occasional Paper 57, USAF Institute for National Security Studies, Colorado, 2004, pp. x.
8. Carolyn Moser and Dennis Rodgers 'Change, Violence and Insecurity in Non-Conflict Situations', ODI Working Paper No. 245, Overseas Development Institute, London, 2005.
9. David Keen, *Conflict and Collusion in Sierra Leone* (Oxford: James Currey, 2005). As Carolyn Holmqvist rightly cautions, 'an emphasis on the "positive" functions served by membership of an armed group should not be seen as giving licence to such group's existence: but a more subtle understanding of reasons for their longevity is fundamental for devising effective strategies to counter their existence'. Carolyn Holmqvist, 'Engaging Armed Non-State Actors in Post-Conflict Settings', in Andrew Bryden and Hans Hanggi (eds), *Security Governance in Post-Conflict Peacebuilding* (Munster: Lit Verlag, 2005), pp. 45–68.
10. For the purposes of this research, Central America consists of the geographical isthmus that includes Panama, Costa Rica, Nicaragua, Honduras, El Salvador, and Guatemala.
11. Geneva Declaration, *The Global Burden of Armed Violence* (Geneva: Geneva Declaration and Small Arms Survey, 2008).
12. See WHO, *Violence*, 2008, available online at: http://www.who.int/topics/violence/en/ (accessed 10 June 2008).
13. See R. Briceno-Leon, 'Urban Violence and Public Health in Latin America: A Sociological Explanatory Framework', *Cadernos Saude Pública*, Vol. 21, No. 6 (2005), pp. 1629; Jennifer Hazen and Chris Stevenson, *Public Health Interventions* (Geneva: Small Arms Survey, 2008).
14. World Bank, *Urban Crime and Violence in LAC: Status Report on Activities, Sustainable Development Department, Latin American and Caribbean Region* (Washington, DC: World Bank, 2008), p. 3.

15. See UNODC, *Annual Report 2008: Covering Activities in 2007* (Vienna: United Nations Office on Drugs and Crime, 2008), p. 38, available online at: http://www.unodc.org/documents/about-unodc/AR08_WEB.pdf.

16. UNODC, *Crime and Development in Central America: Caught in the Crossfire* (Vienna: United Nations Publications, 2007), p. 64.

17. See M.G. Manwaring, *Street Gangs: The New Urban Insurgency* (Carlisle, PA: Strategic Studies Institute, US Army War College, 2005); M.G. Manwaring, 'Gangs and Coups D'streets in the New World Disorder: Protean Insurgents in Post-Modern War', *Global Crime*, Vol. 7, No. 3–4 (2006), pp. 505–43. A follow-up report by the same author published in 2008 further contended that gang violence consti-tuted 'another kind of war (conflict) within the context of a "clash of civilizations"' . . . being waged . . . around the world'. M.G. Manwaring, *A Contemporary Challenge to State Sovereignty: Gangs and Other Illicit Transnational Criminal Organizations (TCOs) in Central America, El Salvador, Mexico, Jamaica, and Brazil* (Carlisle, PA: Strategic Studies Institute, US Army War College, 2008), p. 1.

18. See T.C. Bruneau, 'The Maras and National Security in Central America', *Strategic Insights*, Vol. 4, No. 5 (2005), available online at: http://www.ccc.nps.navy.mil/si/2005/May/bruneauMay05.asp (taken from Salvadoran newspaper *La Prensa Gráfica*, 8 April 2005). See also H. D. Schultz, D. Farah, and L. V. Itamara, 'Armed Groups: A Tier-One Security Priority', INSS Occasional Paper 57, USAF Institute for National Security Studies, Colorado, 2004, available online at http://www.usafa.af.mil/df/inss/OCP/ocp57.pdf.

19. See S. Huhn, A. Oettler, and P. Peetz, *Exploding Crime? Topic Management in Central American News-papers*, GIGA Working Paper No. 33, German Institute of Global and Area Studies, Hamburg, 2006.

20. S. Huhn, A. Oettler, and P. Peetz, 'Construyendo inseguridades: aproximaciones a la violencia en centroamérica desde el análisis del discurso', GIGA Working Paper No. 34, German Institute of Global and Area Studies, Hamburg, 2006, pp. 8–13.

21. UNDOC, *Crime and Development in Central America* (note 15), p. 60.

22. R.L. Millett and O.J. Perez, 'New Threats and Old Dilemmas: Central America's Armed Forces in the 21st Century', *Journal of Political and Military Sociology*, Vol. 31, No. 1 (2005), p. 59.

23. For an overview, see Huhn, Oettler and Peetz, 'Construyendo inseguridades' (note 19), pp. 8–13; as well as M. Liebel, 'Pandillas juveniles en Centroamérica o la difícil búsqueda de justicia en una soci-edad violenta', *Desacatos*, No. 14 (2004), pp. 85–104. The most comprehensive general study is undoubtedly that reported on in the three volumes produced by a conglomerate of Central American research institutes: ERIC, IDESO, IDIES, and IUDOP, *Maras y Pandillas en Centroamérica*, Vol. 1, (Managua: UCA Publicaciones, 2001); ERIC, IDESO, IDIES, and IUDOP, *Maras y Pandillas en Centroamérica: Pandillas y Capital Social*, Vol. 2 (San Salvador: UCA Publicaciones, 2004); ERIC, IDIES, IUDOP, NITLAPAN, DIRINPRO, *Maras y Pandillas en Centroamérica: Políticas juveniles y rehabilitación*, Vol. 3 (Managua: UCA Publicaciones, 2004). Three further overview studies have also been published recently: USAID, *Central America and Mexico Gangs Assessment* (Washington, DC: United States Agency for International Development, 2006); Demoscopía, *Maras y pandillas, comunidad y policía en Centroamérica* (San José: Demoscopía, 2007); and the work of the 'Pandillas juveniles transnacionales en Centroamérica, México y Estados Unidos' project coordi-nated by the Instituto Tecnológico Autónomo de México's (ITAM) Centro de Estudios y Programas Interamericanos (CEPI), whose output is available online at: http://interamericanos.itam.mx/ maras/index.html. The country that has been studied in greatest depth is Nicaragua: J.-L. Rocha, 'Pan-dilleros: la mano que empuña el mortero', *Envío*, No. 216 (2000), pp. 17–25, J.-L Rocha, 'Pandillas: una cárcel cultural', *Envío*, No. 219 (2000), pp. 13–22; J.-L. Rocha, 'Tatuajes de pandilleros: estigma, identidad y arte', *Envío*, No. 258 (2003), pp. 42–50; J.-L. Rocha, 'El traido: clave de la continuidad de las pandillas', *Envío*, No. 280 (2005), pp. 35–41; J.-L. Rocha, 'Pandilleros del siglo XXI: con hambre de alucinaciones y de transnacionalismo', *Envío*, No. 294 (2006), pp. 25–34; J.-L. Rocha, 'Mareros y pandilleros: ¿Nuevos insurgentes, criminales?', *Envío*, No. 293 (2006), pp. 39–51; J.-L. Rocha, *Lan-zando piedras, fumando 'piedras'. Evolución de las pandillas en Nicaragua 1997–2006*, Cuaderno de Investigación No. 23, (Managua: UCA Publicaciones, 2007); J.-L. Rocha, 'Del telescopio al microsco-pio: Hablan tres pandilleros', *Envío* No. 303 (2007), pp. 23–30; J.-L. Rocha, 'Mapping the Labyrinth from Within: The Political Economy of Nicaraguan Youth Policy Concerning Violence', *Bulletin of Latin American Research*, Vol. 26, No. 4 (2007), pp. 533–49; J.-L. Rocha and D. Rodgers, *Bróderes Descobijados y Vagos Alucinados: Una Década con las Pandillas Nicaragüenses, 1997–2007* (Managua: Envío, 2008); D. Rodgers, 'Un antropólogo-pandillero en un barrio de Managua', *Envío*, No. 184 (1997), pp. 10–16; D. Rodgers, 'Living in the Shadow of Death: Violence, Pandillas, and Social Disintegration in Contemporary Urban Nicaragua', unpublished PhD dissertation, Department

of Social Anthropology, University of Cambridge, 2000; D. Rodgers, 'Living in the Shadow of Death: Gangs, Violence, and Social Order in Urban Nicaragua, 1996–2002', *Journal of Latin American Studies*, Vol. 38, No. 2 (2006), pp. 267–92; D. Rodgers, 'The State as a Gang: Conceptualising the Governmentality of Violence in Contemporary Nicaragua', *Critique of Anthropology*, Vol. 26, No. 3 (2006), pp. 315–30; D. Rodgers, 'Managua', in K. Koonings and D. Kruijt (eds), *Fractured Cities: Social Exclusion, Urban Violence and Contested Spaces in Latin America* (London: Zed, 2007; D. Rodgers, 'When Vigilantes Turn Bad: Gangs, Violence, and Social Change in Urban Nicaragua', in D. Pratten and A. Sen (eds), *Global Vigilantes* (London: Hurst, 2007); and D. Rodgers, 'Joining the Gang and Becoming a Broder: The Violence of Ethnography in Contemporary Nicaragua', *Bulletin of Latin American Research*, Vol. 26, No. 4 (2207), pp. 444–61.
24. Rodgers, 'The State as a Gang' (note 22).
25. ERIC, IDESO, IDIES, and IUDOP, *Maras y Pandillas en Centroamérica* (note 22); and Rodgers, 'Living in the Shadow of Death: Gangs, Violence, and Social Order in Urban Nicaragua (note 22).
26. PNUD (Programa de las Naciones Unidas para el Desarrollo – United Nations Development Programme), *Informe Estadístico de la Violencia en Guatemala* (Guatemala: PNUD, 2007).
27. The fact that most gang members are young men, and that Central America suffers the highest male youth homicide rates in the world. See P.S. Pinheiro, *World Report on Violence against Children* (Geneva: United Nations, 2006), p. 357 – indirectly supports the notion that gangs are an important factor within the regional panorama of violence, even though they are by no means the only vector of violence in Central America.
28. See Rodgers, 'Living in the Shadow of Death: Gangs, Violence, and Social Order in Urban Nicaragua, 1996–2002' (note 22); and A. Winton, 'Using "Participatory" Methods with Young People in Contexts of Violence: Reflections from Guatemala', *Bulletin of Latin American Research*, Vol. 26, No. 4 (2007), pp. 497–515.
29. Rodgers, 'Living in the Shadow of Death: Gangs, Violence, and Social Order in Urban Nicaragua, 1996–2002', (note 22). It can be speculated that this is perhaps because the totalizing nature of evangelical Protestantism is such that churches constitute a complete organizational framework for their members that is institutionally equivalent to that provided by the gang.
30. M. Santacruz Giralt and A. Concha-Eastman, *Barrio Adentro: La Solidaridad Violenta de las Pandillas* (San Salvador: Instituto Universitario de Opinión Pública (IUDOP), 2001).
31. Despite the introduction of disarmament, demobilization, and reintegration (DDR) programmes in the wake of various peace agreements, large numbers of ex-soldiers and militia were only partially integrated back into civilian life. See, for example, Robert Muggah, *Securing Protections: Dealing with Fighters in the Aftermath of War* (New York: Routledge, forthcoming), for a review of DDR programmes. In many ways, however, demobilization-related gang violence can be seen less as a function of war than of the return to peace.
32. See W. Godnick, R. Muggah, and C. Waszink, 'Stray Bullets: The Impact of Small Arms Misuse in Central America', Small Arms Survey Occasional Paper No. 5, Geneva, Small Arms Survey, 2003 for a description of arms collection activities throughout the region.
33. Rodgers, 'Living in the Shadow of Death: Gangs, Violence, and Social Order in Urban Nicaragua, 1996–2002' (note 22). K. Koonings and D. Kruijt, *Societies of Fear: The Legacy of Civil War, Violence and Terror in Latin America* (London: Zed Books, 1999); K. Koonings and D. Kruijt, *Armed Actors: Organized Violence and State Failure in Latin America* (London: Zed, 2004).
34. Rodgers, 'Living in the Shadow of Death: Gangs, Violence, and Social Order in Urban Nicaragua, 1996–2002' (note 22).
35. Ibid.
36. 'Maturing out' is a universal feature of youth gangs; as *pandilleros* in Nicaragua put it, 'there are no old gang members'. Rodgers, 'Living in the Shadow of Death: Violence, Pandillas, and Social Disintegration in Contemporary Urban Nicaragua' (note 22). There is evidence to suggest that this is not quite as clear-cut in the case of *maras*, which are widely reported to have gang members ranging up to 30 years old, and from which it is said to be very difficult to 'retire'. See Demoscopía, *Maras y pandillas, comunidad y policía en Centroamérica* (note 22); International Human Rights Clinic, *No Place to Hide: Gang, State, and Clandestine Violence in El Salvador* (Cambridge, MA: Human Rights Program, Harvard Law School, 2007).
37. The origins of the word '*mara*' are unclear. It has been widely suggested that it is derived from the word '*marabunta*', a term used to describe a particularly vicious species of ants in certain South American countries. The fact that this does not include El Salvador, Guatemala, or Honduras makes it an unlikely proposition, although considering the US origins of the *maras*, it might be speculated that the term derives from the classic US horror film 'The Naked Jungle' (1954), in which an army

of *marabunta* ants devastate a plantation in Brazil despite the best efforts of Charlton Heston, which was remade for television in the early 1980s. This is purely speculative, although it is interesting to note that this putative link was also mentioned in the first study of gangs ever carried out in Central America (D. Levenson et al., 'Por sí mismos: Un estudio preliminar des las "maras" en la ciudad de Guatemala', Cuaderno de Investigación no. 4, Asociación para el Avance de las Ciencias Sociales en Guatemala, Guatemala, 1988).

38. USAID, *Central America and Mexico Gangs Assessment*, (Washington, DC: United States Agency for International Development, 2006), pp. 18–19.

39. Ibid.

40. This seems to have occurred almost universally in El Salvador and Honduras, but there still exist more localized *maras* in Guatemala, whose origins go back to the mid-1980s, and who are arguably closer in nature to *pandillas*. See D. Levenson et al., 'Por sí mismos' (note 36); E.C. Ranum, 'Diagnóstico Nacional Guatemala', Proyecto 'Pandillas juveniles transnacionales en Centroamérica, México y Estados Unidos', Centro de Estudios y Programas Interamericanos (CEPI) del Instituto Tecnológico Autónomo de México (ITAM), 2006, available online at: http://interamericanos.itam.mx/maras/docs/Diagnostico_Guatemala.pdf. The general trend, however, is for these to be increasingly absorbed within *Dieciocho* and *Salvatrucha mara* structures. See D. DeCesare, 'The Story of Edgar Bolaños', in L. Kontos, D. C. Brotherton, and L. Barrios (eds), *Gangs and Society: Alternative Perspectives* (New York: Columbia University Press, 2003). According to Demoscopía, *Maras y pandillas, comunidad y policía en Centroamérica* (note 22), p. 49, deportee gang members are becoming a minority as the rate of deportation from the US declines, and are taking on more 'veteran' roles, influencing *mara* behaviour through their prestige rather than actually taking part in gang activities.

41. Rocha, 'Pandilleros del siglo XXI' (note 22).

42. According to C.M. Ribando, 'Report for Congress: Gangs in Central America', *Congressional Research Service*, Report RL34112, 2 August (2007), pp. 1–2: 'Gangs are generally considered to be distinct from organized criminal organizations because they typically lack the hierarchical leadership structure, capital, and manpower required to run a sophisticated criminal enterprise. Gangs are generally more horizontally organized, with lots of small subgroups and no central leadership setting strategy and enforcing discipline. Although some gangs are involved in the street-level distribution of drugs, few gangs or gang members are involved in higher-level criminal drug distribution enterprises run by drug cartels, syndicates, or other sophisticated criminal organizations.' As Geoff Thale, the Research Director of the Washington Office on Latin America (WOLA), has testified before the US Congress, gangs are just one example of a whole spectrum of violence in Central America, which also includes intra-familial violence, street crime, politically motivated crimes, drug-related violence, traditional organized crime, state violence, and human rights violations (cited in Ribando, 'Report for Congress', p. 3).

43. M. Santacruz Giralt and A. Concha-Eastman, *Barrio Adentro* (note 29).

44. On 15 August 2005, newly imprisoned members of the *Dieciocho mara* attacked members of the *Mara Salvatrucha* in El Hoyon prison near Guatemala City, killing 30 and leaving more than twice that number seriously wounded. A retaliatory attack by members of the *Salvatrucha* in the San José Pinula juvenile detention centre on 19 September 2005 killed at least 12 and wounded another ten.

45. International Human Rights Clinic, *No Place to Hide* (note 35); Rodgers, 'Living in the Shadow of Death: Gangs, Violence, and Social Order in Urban Nicaragua, 1996–2002' (note 22); Rocha, *Lanzando piedras, fumando 'piedras'* (note 22).

46. See UNODC, *Crime and Development in Central America* (note 15).

47. See J. Aguilar, 'Los efectos contraproducentes de los Planes Mano Dura', *Quorum*, No. 16 (Winter 2006), pp. 81–94, International Human Rights Clinic, *No Place to Hide* (note 35); Rodgers, 'Living in the Shadow of Death: Gangs, Violence, and Social Order in Urban Nicaragua, 1996–2002' (note 22); D. Rodgers, 'When Vigilantes Turn Bad' (note 22).

48. M. Davis, 'Planet of Slums: Urban Involution and the Informal Proletariat', *New Left Review*, No. 26 (2004), p. 28. See also Rodgers, 'The State as a Gang' (note 22), pp. 315–30; and D. Rodgers, 'Slum Wars of the 21st Century: Gangs, *Mano Dura*, and the New Geography of Conflict in Central America', *Development and Change* (forthcoming).

49. Managua's notoriously abysmal road infrastructure, for example, was transformed in the space of just three years through a massive concentrated investment in the constitution of a highly selective network of good quality, high-speed roads that connect the spaces of the rich – the international airport, the presidential palace, the gated communities, the malls – and have no traffic lights but only roundabouts, meaning that those in cars avoid having to stop – and risk being carjacked – but those on foot risk their lives whenever they try to cross a road. See D. Rodgers, 'Disembedding the City: Crime, Insecurity,

and Spatial Organization in Managua, Nicaragua', *Environment and Urbanization*, No. 16, No. 2 (2004), pp. 113–24; D. Rodgers, 'A Symptom called Managua', *New Left Review*, No. 49 (January–February 2008), pp. 103–20.

50. See E. Pieterse, *City Futures: Confronting the Crisis of Urban Development* (London: Zed Books, 2008), and Rodgers, 'Slum Wars of the 21st Century (note 47).

51. See Rodgers, 'The State as a Gang' (note 22).

52. See Aguilar, 'Los efectos contraproducentes de los Planes Mano Dura' (note 46); M. Hume, 'Mano Dura: El Salvador Responds to Gangs', *Development in Practice*, Vol. 17, No. 6 (2007), pp. 739–51; and Rodgers, 'Slum Wars of the 21st Century (note 47).

53. Hume, 'Mano Dura' (note 51).

54. Although Nicaragua has gained a reputation for focusing on 'preventative' rather than 'repressive' anti-gang policies, the evidence of its practices on the ground tends to belie this. See Rocha, 'Mapping the Labyrinth from Within' (note 22). Overall, the police response to gangs has not been as violent as in other Central American countries, partly because of the less violent nature of the *pandillas* compared to the *maras*.

55. See F. Faux, *Les Maras, Gangs d'Enfants: Violences urbaines en Amérique Centrale* (Paris: Autrement, 2006).

56. The Merida Initiative was launched following US President George W. Bush's trip to Latin America in March 2007, where security was emphasized by Mexico and Central American leaders.

57. US Department of State, *The Merida Initiative Fact Sheet* (Washington, DC: Bureau of Public Affairs, 2008), available online at: http://www.state.gov/r/pa/scp/2008/103374.htm (accessed 19 June 2008).

58. See, for example, A. Forter, 'Youth Gangs and Human Rights in Central America: A Comparative Study on Policy and Law', Paper presented to the University of Chicago Human Rights program workshop, Winter 2005, which surveyed citizens in El Salvador, Honduras, and Guatemala.

59. J. Aguilar and L. Miranda, 'Entre la articulación y la competencia: Las respuestas de la sociedad civil organizada a las pandillas en El Salvador', in J.M. Cruz (ed.), *Maras y Pandillas en Centroamérica: Las respuestas de la sociedad civil organizada* (San Salvador: UCA Editores, 2006), p. 42. The Central American Coalition for the Prevention of Youth Violence (CCPVJ) has shown that *Mano Dura* policies can be linked to a dramatic surge in youth violence in Guatemala, El Salvador, and Honduras – up to 40 per cent in the first three years of implementation. R. Gutiérrez, 'Central America: Harsher Measures Don't Cut Crime', *Inter Press Service News Agency (IPS News)*, 1 November 2006, available online at: http://ipsnews.net/news.asp?idnews=35337.

60. Aguilar and Miranda, 'Entre la articulación y la competencia' (note 58), p. 49.

61. See Rodgers, 'Living in the Shadow of Death: Gangs, Violence, and Social Order in Urban Nicaragua' (note 22); D. Rodgers, 'Managua' (note 22); D. Rodgers, 'When Vigilantes Turn Bad' (note 22).

62. Rodgers, unpublished research. Another reason for the decline in *pandillerismo* is that the rise of these criminal organizations has left no sociological 'space' for youth gangs.

63. See M. Glenny, *McMafia: Crime Without Frontiers* (London: Random House, 2008).

64. See, for example, N. Colletta and R. Muggah, 'Rethinking Post-War Security Promotion', *Journal of Security Sector Management*, Vol. 7, No. 1 (Winter 2009), pp. 1–25, for a review of first- and second-generation policies.

65. In Honduras, organizations such as the London-based Amnesty International and Casa Alianza have also reported that death squads are killing youngsters suspected of belonging to gangs, often merely because they sport tattoos. The NGO Casa Alianza has documented 2,778 murders of young people below the age of 23 between 1998 and July 2008. Most of the victims were members of *maras*. Because these murders are usually not investigated, the perpetrators enjoy total impunity.

66. See D. Rodgers, R. Muggah, and C. Stevenson, 'Gangs of Central America: Causes, Costs, and Interventions', Small Arms Survey Working Paper, Geneva, 2009.

67. Rocha, 'Mapping the Labyrinth from Within' (note 22).

68. Certainly, the few studies that exist are notable for their lack of evidence for successful large-scale interventions. See for example N. Barnes, 'Resumen Ejecutivo', Proyecto 'Pandillas juveniles transnacionales en Centroamérica, México y los Estados Unidos', Centro de Estudios y Programas Interamericanos (CEPI) del Instituto Tecnológico Autónomo de México (ITAM), 2007, p. 9, available online at: http://interamericanos.itam.mx/maras/docs/Resumen_Ejecutivo_Espanol.pdf.

69. See Rodgers, 'A Symptom Called Managua' (note 48).

70. Ibid.

71. See P. Collier and A. Hoeffler, 'Greed and Grievance in Civil War' (note 1).

The Role of Non-State Actors in 'Community-Based Policing' – An Exploration of the *Arbakai* (Tribal Police) in South-Eastern Afghanistan

SUSANNE SCHMEIDL AND MASOOD KAROKHAIL

Despite the ousting of the Taliban and a subsequent peace agreement reached at the end of 2001,[1] Afghanistan continues to struggle with insecurity and an increase in insurgent activity and violent incidents.[2] The Afghan state is currently unable to fulfill its role as security provider[3] and faces a fundamental crisis of governance.[4] An informal poll among civil society groups by the Afghan Civil Society Forum in 2006 showed that merely ten per cent of all Afghans feel protected by international security forces and only about 30 per cent by the Afghan government.[5] A 2007 report by the International Crisis Group observed that 'Afghanistan's citizens often view the police more as a source of fear than of security'.[6]

In many countries around the world where a fledgling state struggles for legitimacy and lacks capacity to fulfil fundamental functions, such as the provision of security, (armed) non-state actors (ANSA) often address these deficiencies.[7] Schneckener observes that 'in extreme cases they may even replace the state and its security apparatus'.[8] ANSA are therefore often viewed as challenging states[9] and spoiling state and peace-building efforts.[10] This view, however, does not only ignore the diversity of ANSA and their goals but also their complex relationships with the state[11] on the one hand, and communities on the other. Research in Africa, for example, illustrates that especially in the area of policing, non-state actors (armed and unarmed) offer 'localized protection of various levels of legality, effectiveness, availability, cost, methods and services'.[12] While this 'multilateralization'[13] of policing or 'pluralization of security'[14] functions at times quite independent of the state, it does not always need to be perceived as a challenge to it.[15]

Afghanistan is a country with a complex reality in light of its long history of war and wide array of ANSA (e.g., strongmen militia, Neo-Taliban insurgency, terrorist groups, criminal organizations, and community and customary structures). Some of these ANSA have historically and are currently challenging the state; some have functioned quite independently of it; others have established 'para-state structures' that 'usually act on behalf of, or are at least tolerated by, a given regime',[16] and some are hedging their bets. Thus, as Krause and Milliken caution in the introduction to this special edition,[17] we need to nuance our thinking about the role and function of ANSA, and not focus our attention exclusively on those able to challenge the state's monopoly over the legitimate force.

An increased understanding of the particularities of ANSA is especially crucial when contemplating the use of ANSA to advance interests of states[18] and making them part of the solution of state consolidation.[19] In Afghanistan, for example, there is a move to create or reinvent ANSA to help the state overcome its security deficit. This includes calls for a 'community defence initiative' proposed by the newly established Independent Directorate for Local Governance (IDLG), 'neighbourhood defence teams' for village-level security proposed by the British,[20] or a more general proposal of the Americans to arm (tribal) militias to assist in the war against the Taliban.[21]

Literature considering the engagement with ANSAs in general, unfortunately, tends to focus exclusively on those that challenge states, leaving more context-specific and unique customary structures such as the *arbakai* in Afghanistan out of their analysis.[22] Advocates of creating new para-state ANSAs in Afghanistan often seem to demonstrate only a superficial understanding of their diversity and uncritically lump militia of all kind into the same category as customary structures such as the *arbakai* (community-based policing) or the *lashkar* (tribal army).[23] Possible unintended consequences of attempting to duplicate such context-specific ANSA or present them with tasks outside their scope of influence are rarely discussed.[24] The uniqueness of the *arbakai* in terms of legitimacy and accountability structure[25] on the one hand and a mixed record of community policing elsewhere is also overlooked.[26] Yet without a 'thorough understanding of their [ANSA] characteristics and the context in which they are embedded',[27] engagement with ANSA is not only difficult, but potentially dangerous. Afghanistan's history here bears witness to miscalculated policies regarding the use of ANSA, when President Najibullah enlisted the help of pro-government militia to fight against the *mujahideen* resistance in the late 1980s. Once the Soviet Union collapsed and support for the communist government, and its associated para-state actors, dried up, these actors turned their attention elsewhere and ultimately contributed to its overthrow.[28]

This article attempts to contribute to the on-going debate of the use of ANSA for security provision in Afghanistan by presenting original research on the *arbakai* in south-eastern Afghanistan between 2004 and 2008.[29] As suggested by Krause and Milliken in the introduction to this special edition,[30] the article aims to broaden the scope of inquiry of ANSA by analysing the *arbakai* along the following criteria:[31] motivation and function, purpose and mandate, strength and scope (of influence), funding sources, organizational structure and recruitment procedures, and relationship with state authorities. Due to a frequent equating of *arbakai* with other ANSA, especially (tribal) militia,[32] the article presents some basic differences between these groups, without claiming to present a detailed account of ANSA in Afghan history. The contrast with other ANSA also serves to enhance the understanding of the *arbakai*.

One of the main aims of this article is to enrich the debate by presenting an example of an ANSA (the *arbakai* in Afghanistan) that has tried to fill gaps in state security provision and since 2001 has never challenged the state. Thus, in agreement with Krause and Milliken and others, we conclude that it is important to understand the context-specificity of ANSA before drawing overarching conclusions or policies.[33] Furthermore, it is crucial to understand the dimensions of ANSA before promoting nation-wide policies such as advocating a transferability of the *arbakai* outside their unique cultural and regional context. We caution the use of ANSA beyond their capacities (specifically counter-insurgency activities), such as *arbakai* or similar structures for anything but community-based policing.

Lastly, drawing on Baker's work on community-based policing in Africa,[34] we suggest that Afghanistan and its international supporters consider a security policy that embraces plurality of security provision, without necessarily embracing each and every ANSA. It might be best to cooperate with those community-based security providers that focus on complementing state deficits rather than fundamentally replacing and challenging the state. Key for such engagement, however, is to define clearly exact parameters for what kind of ANSA to engage with and develop formal mechanisms on how such a formalized relationship between ANSA and the Afghan government may look like, and monitor compliance.[35] Lessons can be drawn from government-*arbakai* cooperation during the 2004 and 2005 Afghan elections.

Who Are the *Arbakai*?

The *arbakai* are best described as a community-based customary policing structure[36] with a central focus on keeping law and order and stopping fighting within tribal communities. *Arbakai* means 'guardian' in Pashtu.[37] Though different from the 'tribal army' (*lashkar*), *arbakai* means army in Arabic, which possibly explains the frequent confusion between these two related yet distinct ANSA. The *arbakai* historically has existed (and still does) only in the south-eastern region of Afghanistan and remains anchored in the very cohesive structure of the Pashtun communities of Loya Paktia (Greater Paktia).[38] As history is passed down orally among Pashtuns, it is hard to confirm when the *arbakai* were first used, and if they have changed over time, but it is safe to say it is a very old tradition among the Pashtuns of south-eastern Afghanistan, likely as old as their governing structures (*jirga*) and customary law (*pashtunwali*).

The re-emergence of the *arbakai* in post-2001 Paktia (and later neighbouring Khost) was linked to the power vacuum after the fall of the Taliban, which local strongmen were eager to fill (such as Pasha Khan Zadran).[39] Three days after the Taliban government crumbled, different communities in Paktia called a *jirga* (community gathering) in Gardez, which comprised leaders from all major *wandas* (sub-community level).[40] This *jirga* aimed at fulfilling government functions until a new state administration was able to emerge. Shortly thereafter, each community created an *arbakai* force with the Ahmadzai, Zazee (Jaji), Tutakhail, and especially Mangal tribes being among the first. The size of these individual *arbakai* varied depending on the opposition encountered from small-scale commanders and unwanted criminal elements.

Motivation and Function

The fundamental focus of the *arbakai* on making peace rather than defending the interest of the tribe against an outside threat must be emphasized. The latter is the task of the *lashkar* (tribal army), such as dealing with threats to tribal territory or resources or to assist the Afghan state in cases of internal uprisings or foreign invasions. A recent example of the use of a *lashkar* in Loya Paktia was during a mid 2004 conflict between the Mangal and Tutakhail communities. The Mangal community retaliated against the extortion of Mangals passing through Tutakhail territory. The Mangal only withdrew their *lashkar* when the Afghan government intervened and asked local mediators to help solve the dispute.

The *arbakai* are linked to the customary governance mechanism (*jirga*) of the Pashtun tribes[41] governed by the communal law (tribal code) of the Pashtuns called the *pashtunwali*.[42] This customary codex of honour passed down orally over history among community leaders has co-existed with state structures. It consists of two parts: A codex of social behaviour still widely used by Pashtuns[43] in Afghanistan and neighbouring Pakistan, and an accumulation of laws used for decision-making by all communal institutions such as *jirgas* (tribal gathering), *shuras* (tribal/community council), and the *arbakai*.[44] While there are regional variations (likely also temporal ones due to the oral nature of the law) in the *pashtunwali*, such as between the different Pashtun confederations (Durrani, Ghilzai, and Karlyani), the main underlying values influencing all interpretations of the *pashtunwali* tend to be the same: that all Pashtun (men) have an equal status (especially in front of the law) and that no one should possess more rights and power than others.[45] This idea of equality characterizes the design of tribal institutions such as the *jirga* as well as the socioeconomic distribution of land. Land ownership remains an important characteristic of being a Pashtun today as it expresses the autonomy of the tribesmen.[46]

There are two important and inter-connected particularities that need to be understood about the *pashtunwali*. First it is based on a communal/collective rights approach, where peace between communities is more important than the rights of individuals.[47] It strongly emphasizes the notions of equity and community consensus for sentences.[48] Second, instead of focusing on retributive justice as formal systems in the West do, it emphasizes restorative justice that is based on local conceptions of fairness in order to reconcile conflict parties and restore harmony to the community.[49] 'Rather than being sent to prison for a wrong committed, the wrongdoer is asked to pay *poar*, or blood money, to the victim and to ask for forgiveness [*nanawati*].'[50] It is important to note, however, that an *arbakai* that is mandated under the *pashtunwali* to secure an area or implement a decision is exempt from *poar* in the case it comes to killings.

The main traditional decision-making body in Pashtun Afghanistan applying the *pashtunwali* is the *jirga*.[51] Steul argues that a *jirga* contains elements of legislative (being able to pass new regulations), judiciary (being able to sentence), and also executive authority (albeit the latter is often passed on to others, such as the *arbakai*).[52] It is a temporary and ad hoc body created mainly for the resolution of disputes between extended family groups (*quam*), clans (*wands*), sub-tribes and tribes, but also between the government and the tribes.

After the *jirga* reaches a decision it is usually dissolved and only revived if the decision is not accepted or if a new conflict or dispute arises. The form and composition of a *jirga* depends on the dispute considered (as participants are required to hold knowledge of the case considered), but generally it includes *marakachian*, *rishsafidian/spin giri* (the white-beard elders, notables, tribal leaders etc.), and in some areas, such as the South, also religious figures (*sayyeds, mawlawis* and *mullahs*)[53] and since the Afghan wars also commanders. The only common feature is that it is comprised exclusively of adult males and governed by a patriarchal egalitarian ideology, which in reality is marked by inequality of access and participation (especially by women and youth). A *jirga* decision is binding for the entire community. During the Afghan wars a more permanent decision-making body of community dignitaries called *shura* emerged, which are now frequently used for more basic community decision-making, at times also overseeing the *arbakai*.[54]

If the *jirga* (and *shura*) can be compared mainly to the legislative and judicial authority among the Pashtuns, then their executive arm is the *arbakai*. We find Baker's definition of 'community-based policing' that is 'authorized and provided by the community (or part of it) and for the community (or part of it)'[55] as a fitting description for the *arbakai*. While the *arbakai* can be created by a group of elders from a sub-community (*quam/wand*) through a *jirga*, and subsequently is managed by a *shura*, the tribal army (*lashkar*) can only be created by an agreement of the entire tribal leadership. In sum, both the *arbakai* and *lashkar* are an alternative form of governance, fulfilling functions that are normally the responsibility of a state.[56]

Purpose and Mandate

Arbakai are raised for specific purposes all within the interest of community security or protection of community resources. The *arbakai* is generally called into life for three main reasons: to enforce and implement the decisions of a *jirga/shura*, to 'maintain law and order' (general policing), and 'to protect borders and boundaries of the tribe or community'.[57] The last function overlaps somewhat with the *lashkar* mandate of defending tribal boundaries. The difference in mandate might be best explained as the task of an army to defend a country vs. that of the border police to control boundaries.

The maintaining of law and order can include conflict de-escalation and protecting natural resources (forest, agricultural land, common mountains), roads or designated territory (e.g., district area; often in collaboration with the Afghan National Police, ANP). As such, the *arbakai* operate on specific and ad hoc mandates, lasting from a few days to several years. The *arbakai* never were (and still are not) envisioned as a permanent body.

While the *arbakai* usually necessitates a *jirga* or *shura* decision and can take up to seven days to be established, it also acts in emergency situations and is called to action by the beating of a 'scream' drum (*cheghay dol*).[58] The *arbakai* then almost functions as a rapid-reaction force, mobilizing 'reservists' – but it still takes at least a day, as community elders (in an ad hoc *shura*) need to sanction the operation. In rare occasions it can take up to 30 days to establish an *arbakai*, mostly when the mandate necessitates more thorough discussion (such as is the case with multi-tribal *arbakai*). Operations depend on seasonal weather conditions and mandates, but duties are expected, at least formally, to be 24 hours per day.

Arbakai mandates often supplement main mandates with smaller sub-tasks. At the time of the initial survey in 2004, a total of 42 *arbakai* forces could be identified in Paktia, tasked with 63 different operations since 2002. The majority of all operations (37 per cent) were short-term (mere days; such as election security), followed by operations lasting a few months (28 per cent). Some of the longest operations dealt with general district security coupled with road and forest protection (forests being a scarce resource with a lot of illegal logging). Most Mangal and Zadran *arbakai* were engaged in lengthier operations due to insecurity in their areas.

In terms of mandate, most operations (41 per cent) focused on providing district security, with some operations including forest security, narcotics, water, and election security. The next biggest mandate included road security (32 per cent), at times combined with election, district, area, and forest security. The last primary mandate focused on forest security (27 per cent) with some operations also working on border security. All tribes were engaged during 2004 with securing polling sites of the presidential elections and again during 2005 for parliamentary elections. In recent years, the *arbakai* operations have become rare due to reduced need on the one hand, and increased threats from the insurgency on the other. Only three districts in Paktia had *arbakai* in early 2008: Ahmad Aba (60 *arbakai* guards to protect the Machalgho dam project), Jani Khail/Mangal (22 *arbakai* guards to protect the forests), and the border district of Dand wa Patan (12 *arbakai* guards paid by the Ministry of Interior, MoI). By the end of 2008, the only *arbakai* that remained active was in the Machalgho area of northern Ahmad Aba district.

Strength and Scope

It is hard to make a generic statement about the size of an *arbakai* force as it depends on the mandate to be fulfilled and the overall geographic area to be secured (village, district, province, tribal territory). The upper limit of an *arbakai* is the number of suitable males eligible to be recruited within each community. Thus, figures can fluctuate greatly, but due to the localized and ad-hoc nature, most *arbakai* operations tend to be rather small in size. The range of the individual *arbakai* forces surveyed was between eight to 150 individual guards with the average *arbakai* comprising 65 men. Some exceptions do exist, for example the *arbakai* of the Mangal tribe created in 2002 had grown to be 400-men strong by 2004. Due to the size of the force, the principal Mangal *shura* of 18 elders grew to 50 people via inclusion of Mangal sub-tribes to assist in manpower provision for the expanded force. This demonstrates that when more *arbakai* guards are needed, the decision-making body overseeing the *arbakai* is also increased in order to become more inclusive and representative. Other main tribes in Paktia, including the Ahmadzai, Zadran, and Zazee (Jaji), subsequently followed the Mangal precedent.

Despite the fact that an individual *arbakai* force is never very big, its combined force can overshadow state security providers. For example, in 2005 when *arbakai* operations peaked in Paktia the combined number of all *arbakai* guards was estimated at approximately 1,950 men, compared to some 660 provincial and district government police at that time. The ratio of about one *arbakai* guard for every

1,200 residents compared to one ANP for every 3,500 residents illustrates the limited reach of formal security mechanisms to remote (rural) areas.

The geographic scope of influence of the *arbakai* is quite narrow. As noted earlier, they can only be found in the south-eastern provinces of Afghanistan incorporating the provinces of Paktia, Khost, and Paktika, and some districts of Ghazni. The *arbakai* are most prevalent in Paktia and Khost and much weaker in Paktika and Ghazni. This can be explained by the fact that Paktika (and southern districts of Ghazni) broke away from Loya Paktia in 1978, while Khost became a separate province more recently. All four provinces (except the Hazara part of Ghazni) share overlapping tribal and religious relations and leadership, but the later split of Khost from Paktia makes the two provinces more similar. The only use of *arbakai* outside Loya Paktia has been reported in Afghan refugee camps in Pakistan, where south-eastern communities re-created their known community-based police in exile.[59]

Secondly, their jurisdiction is limited to the territory governed by the respective *jirga/shura* they are mandated by. This means, that if a villages raises an *arbakai* it cannot work anywhere else (this creates parallels to neighbourhood watch committees). Similarly, an *arbakai* comprised of villagers closest to the sites secures remote areas such as mountains and forests. If a tribe raises an *arbakai* it is only authorised to work within tribal boundaries. Even in the rare cases of multi-tribal *arbakai*, each individual force only has jurisdiction over its tribal territory. *Arbakai* guards automatically re-integrate into their communities when their task is completed.

Funding Sources

Traditionally, each community is responsible for supporting its *arbakai*, with contributions being clearly stipulated by the *jirga* invoking the force. Families unable to provide a capable man to the *arbakai* (contribution in kind) usually provide some other contribution to the functioning of the force (such as food or other consumable/exchangeable items), although poor families may be exempt altogether until they are able to provide a guard. As there is usually a rotation of serving men, there is enough room for everybody in a community to contribute eventually.

The Afghan government has occasionally paid for the *arbakai* to perform certain services such as contributing to district or election security. Since 2001 this was done through discretionary funds given to Provincial Governors by the MoI with payment (or other benefits) channelled via the community leadership. The closest collaboration occurred during the 2004 and 2005 presidential and parliamentary/provincial elections, when donors through the United Nations Assistance Mission in Afghanistan (UNAMA) and the provincial governors paid the *arbakai*.

Organizational Structure and Recruitment Procedures

In theory the structure of the *arbakai* is quite hierarchical as the example of a 60-men strong *arbakai* force of the Ahmadzai tribe in Ahmad Aba district in Paktia illustrated in Figure 1 shows. This strict structure, however, needs to be understood as an ideal type, which may function somewhat more decentralized in practice. Furthermore, as

FIGURE 1
EXAMPLE OF TRADITIONAL *ARBAKAI* STRUCTURE

```
                        ┌──────────────────┐
                        │   jirga/shura    │
                        └──────────────────┘
                                 ↕
                        ┌──────────────────┐
                        │     arbakai      │
                        │  commander (mir) │
                        └──────────────────┘
         ┌───────────────┬──────────┴──────────┬───────────────┐
   ┌───────────┐  ┌───────────┐        ┌───────────┐   ┌───────────┐
   │ Deputy mir│  │ Deputy mir│        │ Deputy mir│   │ Deputy mir│
   └───────────┘  └───────────┘        └───────────┘   └───────────┘
         ↓              ↓                    ↓                ↓
   ┌───────────┐  ┌───────────┐        ┌───────────┐   ┌───────────┐
   │15 arbakai │  │15 arbakai │        │15 arbakai │   │15 arbakai │
   │  guards   │  │  guards   │        │  guards   │   │  guards   │
   └───────────┘  └───────────┘        └───────────┘   └───────────┘
```

illustrated later, *arbakai* have adapted their organizational structure when collaborating with Afghan government actors.

Each *arbakai* has a commanding officer (the *mir*) that has deputies managing a small number of *arbakai* guards if an *arbakai* is larger than 15–20 men (although no clear regulations exist). The number of *mirs* (and their deputies) varies depending on the size of the *arbakai* and the geographical terrain it must cover. The *mir* is authorized and accountable to the *jirga* that initiated the *arbakai* and supervised by a *shura* specifically set up for this purpose. In rare cases of multi-tribal *arbakai*, each tribe has its own *mir* appointed by a multi-tribal *shura* (deputy *mirs* often do not exist in this set up).

The *arbakai* are made up from male community members whose elders called the force into action. If requested, every family *must* contribute one man for the *arbakai* service, or if unable they must pay compensation to the value of the *arbakai's* salary. While *arbakai* guards are given on the basis of voluntarism, the decision is not individual but based on collective community/family decision-making. Exemptions from service are sometimes made if the family is poor and unable to provide a person for service, or provides a financial compensation. As *arbakai* forces are usually small, appointment to the *arbakai* may rotate among families within a community, each family eventually getting their turn to serve their community. While the *arbakai* usually involves only the needed number of men to accomplish the task at hand, the *lashkar* calls upon all male community members of fighting age to join.

Some vetting does seem to apply as anecdotal evidence suggest that young men are not recruited if they are seen as unsuitable due to poor physical condition or 'dubious' moral character (e.g., a criminal or impolite person). Ideal candidates are described as young men who are brave, honest, and vigilant, have experience with weapons, and are sufficiently fit to undertake the often-arduous patrolling tasks associated with the *arbakai* service. Nevertheless, *arbakai* members can be as old as 40 years of age, especially in leadership positions, where more experienced individuals are required.

Relationships with State Authorities

The *arbakai* have to be understood within the context of Afghan history and the complex relationship between the Afghan state at the centre and communities at the periphery. Afghanistan shares with many African nations a situation where there is a dual legitimacy between an emerging and weak (modern) state and strong customary structures (such as *shuras* and *jirgas*). As the Afghan state historically was largely restricted to cities,[60] vast rural areas were under the control of communities and their governance structures, including customary security providers. Most Afghan rulers, especially during periods of state consolidation, were only able to rule by providing communities with a certain level of autonomy to govern their spaces; in return communities assisted the state when needed (that is, in the face of a foreign threat or internal uprisings). Thus, power-sharing agreements existed between communities and the emerging Afghan state (including the use of *arbakai* in the Southeast). This precarious balance broke down during the Afghan wars, was shortly re-established during the Taliban regime, and is currently defined on a provincial basis.

Despite more informal relations with Afghan rulers, communities tend to respect the jurisdiction of the Afghan state, and once the Afghan government managed to set-up a strong governorship and local administrative structures in Paktia in 2002, communities adapted their framework of reference of the *jirgas* and *shuras* commanding the *arbakai* from the tribal to the district level (hence from customary to state) in order to cooperate with the new local administrative order. While the territory of some communities coincided with the district boundaries, in other districts the *jirga or shura* and subsequently the *arbakai* became multi-community. This shift in the reference point of *arbakai* operation shows the willingness of communities to collaborate with the Afghan government, something that was proven further when *arbakai* collaborated with the ANP in providing security for polling stations during the presidential (2004) and parliamentary/provincial (2005) elections.

The greater capacity of communities to mobilize *arbakai* guards compared to available ANP, which was already illustrated earlier, is also visible in Figure 2. Even in Ghazni with traditionally less active *arbakai*, there were more available

FIGURE 2
POLLING SECURITY IN THE SOUTHEAST: ARBAKAI VS. POLICE

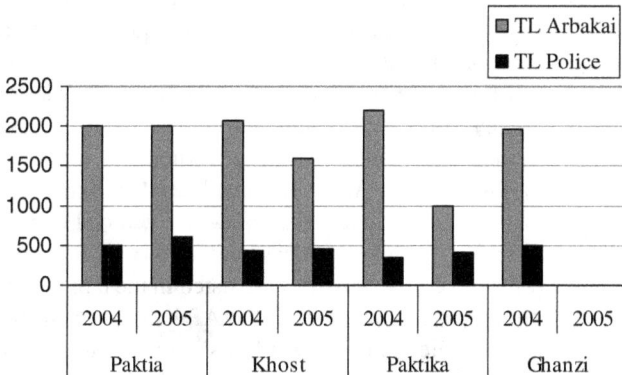

Source: Data supplied by Head of Office, UNAMA Southeast Region, July 2008.

arbakai guards than ANP. In the four provinces, the combined *arbakai* was 10,000 guards as compared to fewer than 2,000 police.[61] Using estimated population figures from the Central Statistics Office,[62] and election data, the following population-police/*arbakai* ratio can be established: one *arbakai* guard for about every 235 people in Khost and Paktia compared to one policeman for every 1,000 people in these provinces. While the *arbakai* size in Paktia stayed the same, it decreased by about 23 per cent in Khost and over 50 per cent in Paktika between 2004 and 2005.

   In 2007, the Governors of Khost and Paktia decided to put the *arbakai* more permanently on the government payroll for one year. At that time each district was to have between 20–40 *arbakai* guards responsible for law and order. This temporarily changed the non-state character of the *arbakai* to an armed para-state actor, emphasizing the difficulty of placing certain ANSA into definite categories. This relationship ceased in 2008 for financial reasons and changes in governorship, with only one *arbakai* currently remaining in Paktia. Furthermore, the mode of payment (provincial governors to district councils/*shuras* to *arbakai*) and the slow flow of resources to the governors' offices led to allegations of corruption. The overall lack of transparency has created tensions between community and government and *arbakai* guards and their leadership when payment was lower than expected or not received at all. *Arbakai* were paid anywhere from 1,500 to 3,500 Afghani (US$30–50) per month, with the latter being comparable of the pay of a regular Afghan policemen. This illustrates difficulties in trying to merge community-based policing structures into state security arrangements.

What Distinguishes the *Arbakai* from other ANSA in Afghanistan?

It is not unusual for a country like Afghanistan with a long history of war and difficulties to stabilize its territory to have weak state security forces.[63] Baker's description of African governments inability 'to enforce law' because they are struggling 'to establish order' is therefore very fitting for the Afghan context.[64] As noted in the introduction, the existing security deficit is currently being filled by a variety of ANSA with various levels of legitimacy and effectiveness in the type of governance and security provided. Table 1 presents a simplified overview of the main ANSA currently active in Afghanistan in order to highlight the uniqueness of the *arbakai* and other community-based policing structures.

   The categories in Table 1 are in many ways ideal types that are in reality not mutually exclusive. Many commanders and individual 'fighters' have reinvented themselves by becoming state actors (e.g., governors, ministers, Parliament), joining state security bodies (the ANP, Afghan National Army – ANA),[65] or private security companies;[66] some function as para-state actors. Despite this blurring between categories, Table 1 illustrates the complex reality of security providers in Afghanistan. While private security providers are listed in the table for completeness, they are excluded from the discussion here, as the Afghan government has begun to regulate their activities in late 2008.[67] 'Warlords' are subsumed under the first category of strongmen, as there are currently many debates about the accuracy of the term in the Afghan context, which go beyond the scope of this paper.

TABLE 1
OVERVIEW OF MAIN ARMED NON-STATE ACTORS IN AFGHANISTAN

Non-state actor group	Authorizer/ legitimacy	Key security functions	Relationship with state security bodies	Funding	Recruitment
Strongmen[68] militia (both pro-government, anti-government)	Individuals or families	Security for strongman and their clientele, which can be a (tribal/ethnic) community in a defined territory	Informal via individual government actors; sometimes contracted as para-state actor	Individual strongmen, extortion, criminal activities (smuggling)	Kinship and clan ties, individual
Mafia-like and criminal networks[69]	Individuals or families	Drug convoy security, security for drug lord, security for clientele	Informal through individual government actors	Drug revenue or protection money, criminal activities, extortion	Kinship and clan ties, individual, or rolling over of existing militia
Private security contractors (local/international)[70]	Client, recent government regulation	Static and mobile security services for clients only; training, etc.	Regulated through Afghan government, sometimes contracted to perform specific services to Afghan state and security forces	Clients, criminal activities, smuggling, extortion	Individual, kinship and clan ties, or rolling over of existing militia
(Neo)-Taliban insurgency[71]	Individual leadership, sometimes communities	General security in area they control (albeit not always even), *sharia* court-like system, drug convoy security	Informal 'co-existence' arrangements with local government officials	External funding, local tax levy on opium poppy cultivation; opium mafia, communities (often extortion)	Individual, *madrassas*, kinship and clan ties
Terrorist groups (mainly Al Qaeda)	Individuals, international leadership	Likely only for own group and clientele		External	Individual, *madrassas*, kinship and clan ties
arbakai/lashkar	Customary governance mechanism of communities (*jirga, shura*)	Enforce and implement the decisions of a *jirga/shura*, maintain law and order, to defend and protect borders and boundaries of the community	Individual Afghan government actors (e.g., governors), often informal, sometimes contracted as para-state actor	Community; government	Community, customary governance structures
Other community-based policing structures	Community governance mechanisms	Maintain law and order, to defend and protect borders and boundaries of the community	Individual Afghan government actors (e.g., governors), often informal, sometimes contracted as para-state actor	Community, government	Community, customary governance structures

Table 1 illustrates the similarities and differences between *arbakai* and other ANSA in Afghanistan. The *arbakai*, like other ANSA have had at least an informal relationship with the Afghan state; terrorist groups may form an exception here. This relationship was formalized when ANSA became (temporary) para-state actors. Despite this history of interaction and cooperation, Afghanistan still lacks a clear policy on how to engage with ANSA or para-state actors, with the 2004 Afghan constitution granting the monopoly of the legitimate use of force to the state only, something that is reiterated in the 2005 police law.

In terms of security functions provided, most ANSA in Afghanistan tend to serve specific communities, clientele within patronage networks. The *arbakai* is no exception here. In contrast to other ANSA, the *arbakai* tend to respond to very specific mandates provided to them, all within the interest of community security or protection of community resources, and all defensive in nature. *Arbakai* are thus a strictly 'internal security body', and function in areas with strong and cohesive community structures, while militia and other ANSA in principle can function outside a specific territory (e.g., transnational terrorist networks or foreign 'Taliban' fighting in Afghanistan). Other ANSA, while also including security mandates of their clientele, often diversify their engagements, and may also engage in criminal activities and/or offensive actions.

Over time, many ANSA have added commercial aims to their repertoire and become self-serving structures for their leadership. Here the *arbakai*, similar to other community-based policing structures that have existed in Afghanistan throughout the years and are currently re-emerging due to the security deficit, are most distinct from other ANSA. An example of an *arbakai*-like structure that still serves their community and individuals is the 40-person community-based police of the Hazara ethnic group in Gizab district of Uruzgan.[72] The police is mandated and maintained by a 20-person community council, including representatives of all six Hazara tribes in the district as well as prominent religious figures. In addition to the police force, the council maintains a district jail and *mullah*-headed court that adjudicates communal disputes on the basis of *sharia*. Similar to the *arbakai*, the police force is only mandated to maintain law, order, and security within the community, and enforce council decisions. It has thus far not engaged insurgents.

Another difference between the *arbakai* and most ANSA in Afghanistan is the growing permanence of the latter. The *arbakai* never were (and still are not) a permanent body. Much like other community-based policing structures, they tend to emerge when communities feel that the state is unable to provide for local security. Other ANSA, in contrast, become much more permanent and function even after their initial aims are reached. For example, many *mujahideen* factions that emerged during the Afghan resistance continued to exist even after the communist government was defeated.[73] Mafia and criminal networks also have a tendency to be around for the long-term, unless rooted out by force.

The fact that militia, while keeping their command structures intact, have been able to integrate or reinvented themselves into state security forces or as private security contractors illustrates their longevity.[74] Many ANSA, especially militia, continue until the death of a commander or internal power-struggle leads to its disintegration. While many militias disappeared during the Taliban rule, except for the areas controlled by the Northern Alliance, they resurfaced after 2001 and began to play a more official role in Afghan politics.[75] The 2001 Bonn Conference prompted a reorganization and formal recognition of some militias (known collectively as the Afghan Military Forces [AMF]) placing them under the authority of the Ministry of Defence and targeting them for disarmament. Some of those not disarmed rolled over into the MoI and ANP,[76] while others stayed outside the state security apparatus, engaging in privatized security or criminal activities.

The reason for size differentials between *arbakai* and other ANSA is worth exploring. The size of the *arbakai* (and other community-based policing structures) is determined by its mandate and the geographic area that needs to be covered. While also linked to the task at hand, other available resources and the influence of the individual commander in charge more often than not determine the size of other ANSA. Recruitment practises also influence the size of ANSA forces. As described earlier, the *arbakai* and other community-based policing forces are made up of community members provided voluntarily and not through coercion. As noted, the upper limit of any *arbakai* would be the size of capable male community members, as no outside recruiting is permitted. Fewer rules seem to apply for recruitment into militia or other ANSA. While some militia are also drawn from a specific community, there are examples of multi-community, and even multi-ethnic militia, especially during the Afghan wars.[77] Even in the rare event of multi-community *arbakai*, each community has its respective *arbakai* force and command-chain, loosely connected only through a multi-community *shura* or outside entity (such as the Afghan government). No outside community (or individual *mir*) can interfere with the territory of other communities. This makes the *arbakai* and the earlier described Hazara community-based police force in Gizab district of Uruzgan very homogeneous in nature (an 'inside' vs. 'outside' security force). While other ANSA may also be drawn from one community, or at least ethnic group, they may also recruit externally and thus become more heterogeneous.[78]

There are also stark differences how *arbakai* and other community-based policing structures access funds. As noted earlier, the *arbakai* are funded by the communities they serve. Similarly, the Hazara community-based police in Gizab are financed through community taxes. Only if the *arbakai* is raised on behalf of the government will the state provide resources. Similarly, in Gizab the Hazara community council has engaged in discussions with the governor for funding. Funding for other ANSA, in contrast, tends to be more diverse, depending on whom they provide security for or what activities they engage in (that is, extractive and criminal activities). Thus it can range from some contributions from the Afghan government such as through the Ministries of Interior and Defence (such as payment for the Dostum militia during the Najibullah government), over external sources (specifically, the support of the *mujahideen* factions by Pakistan and US in the 1980s and support for the Neo-Taliban from various sources), to war booty and commercial income (for example, when militia provide private security services).

Today, the financing of most ANSA in Afghanistan tends to be linked to their commander, even if they roll over into private security firms or ANP.[79] Thus, individual members of ANSA tend to be loyal foremost to a person (immediate commander), and accountability is linked to a 'personality-cult'[80] and not to a collective customary 'institution' as in the case of the *arbakai* (or the Hazara community-based police force). When the leader dies and there is no clear command structure to follow, militias can disintegrate, and individual soldiers may join another militia or form their own. It also happens that militias break up when commanders disagree. This may lead to violent clashes among and within militias linked to power struggles. There are no known records of different *arbakai* forces fighting one another; however, this can occur with the tribal army (*lashkar*).

Loyalties within militia, however, are not just linked to charismatic leadership. Larger factional militia commanders maintain the loyalty of mid- and lower-level commanders through protection and extension of resources. Thus, in order to maintain loyalty, benefits have to be extended to the militias (or insurgency or criminal networks) in order to maintain allegiance. In many ways the structure of a militia and similar ANSA can be erratic and unpredictable, especially when leaders are removed (usually through imprisonment or capture).[81] This reflects the opportunistic behaviour and strategies of violent entrepreneurs such as strongmen who operate in a 'market of violence'.

The biggest difference between the *arbakai* (and similar community-based policing efforts) and other ANSA, however, is likely that it maintains a level of accountability through its link to a customary justice system. This is not the case even for militias that share all other characteristics of the *arbakai* (homogeneity, drawn from the same community, size, and purpose). Most ANSA in Afghanistan have very weak or nonexistent links to customary governance systems. Even though pro-government militias have existed (and still do) in Afghanistan, they tend to operate outside the law and rule through coercion by instilling fear in the population. While leaders of ANSA usually can act at will, neither the *arbakai mir*, nor his deputy or individual *arbakai* guard are permitted to make their own decisions in political matters. Everything has to be sanctioned and approved by the *jirga/shura*. Transgressions are punished by disciplinary measures not just against the individual *arbakai* guard but his entire family in severe cases (such as the burning of houses and expulsion from the community).

The Potential and Limits of Working with the *Arbakai* and Similar Community-Based Police Structures in Afghanistan

It is important to consider carefully not just possibilities, but also limitations of existing community-based security structures to avoid unintended consequences or ultimately failure by overburdening them with unrealistic expectations,[82] especially in the context of a weak state struggling for legitimacy. The article so far has emphasized the strong elements of the *arbakai*: link to a customary structure, mobilisation from within communities it polices, limited jurisdiction on 'home territory', and willingness to cooperate with the Afghan government. We discuss now three areas of limitations: its very specific socio-cultural context, how to engage with the Afghan government and possibilities to export it outside.

Internal Limitations of the Arbakai System

Despite the acknowledgement that customary structures have been quite efficient in dealing with the resolution of conflict across Afghanistan,[83] it is important to re-emphasize that these systems tend to rest on their own set of laws – such as the *pashtunwali* for the *arbakai* – which conflicts in some areas with international human rights and the Afghan state, especially in the area of individual and women's rights.[84] The fact that enforcement is often unnecessary due to the communities' adherence to shared values and principles does not change this point. While the ANP has not received a very good report sheet in terms of guaranteeing adequate human security or establishing law and order, at least in theory it is linked to a legal body in line with international law and a national rule of law framework.[85]

Linked to this point is the limited experience of the *arbakai* with what we may consider state policing, as they are ad hoc and called into action during crisis and function generally with limited mandates (spatial and temporal). One critical voice argues: 'one striking phenomenon is that village institutions do not readily fit into patterns that would neatly correspond to the interest of the government and international agencies...[as they are] immediate, spontaneous and of limited reach'.[86] However, it might be unrealistic to judge the *arbakai* against the same standards as state police structures or fit them within a modern state-building project. A better approach might be to see the utility of the *arbakai* simply for what it is – community-based policing with limited reach and mandates and develop policies accordingly rather than making the *arbakai* what they are not or cannot be.

Furthermore, as the *arbakai* concept rests on protecting the interests of communities, including their assets (resource-rich areas such as agricultural lands, mountain areas, and forests), and enforces *jirga* decisions, they may actually get involved in fuelling conflicts further or reinforcing injustice in case there are unresolved disagreements.[87] Depending on how intact customary structures remain, certain elders (if strong) could try to dominate and manipulate the *arbakai* for their own purpose (through blood feud, or to settle rivalries or resource competition). For example, in Khost, some of the settled communities have created *arbakai* in order to restrict the access of Kuchi (Afghan nomads) to contested territory (often communal pasture land). In another case, the border between Ahmad Aba and Sayed Karam in Paktia, the Esa Khail Ahmadzai have put up a permanent *arbakai* outpost to deter possible infiltration from a Tutakhail strongman that has been involved in bloody clashes since 2002.

A major limitation of any *arbakai*, however, is that of a police force in general. The reduction of the *arbakai* in the Southeast are not only linked to a lack of resources, but also to an increasing level of insurgent activity. The areas where the *arbakai* so far have fared worse are those where the insurgency is in control. For example, in Loya Paktia districts inhabited by the Zadran tribe (specifically, Gerda Serrai, Waza, and Shwak), very strong insurgency networks (Haqqani) have managed to co-opt the community and weaken customary structures. The experience of Pashtun tribes in the Federally Administered Tribal Areas (FATA) in Pakistan has long demonstrated the powerlessness of tribal actors against the growing

Neo-Taliban. The insurgency has been only too keen to manipulate and exploit community difference and engage community security forces.

It is worth remembering that the *arbakai* sets out to address very specific and generally small-scale problems within tribes. While there are precedents in Paktia, where *arbakai* have successfully defeated smaller-level commanders, they have failed with bigger strongmen such as Pasha Khan Zadran. Just as state police may be able to tackle criminal elements, they can never substitute for an army when it comes to a larger-scale insurgency. It has been an ongoing problem in Afghanistan that the police are too often used for counter-insurgency purposes.[88] Wilder highlighted this dilemma already for the ANP that 'are paying a very heavy price for performing tasks for which ANA soldiers are much better prepared and equipped'.[89] In essence, he argues, they are being (ab)used as 'cannon fodder'. As noted earlier, within the tribal system, external threats were always the task of the tribal army (*lashkar*), not the *arbakai*.

Challenges in Arbakai-Government Cooperation

As noted earlier, the Afghan government has stepped in at times to 'co-opt' the *arbakai* through providing supervision and payment. The main question, however, is whether or not it is desirable to promote such integration, as it ultimately may change the autonomy of the *arbakai*. Drawing from the African experience, to function well, 'short of integrated policing policy, the non-state sector certainly needs some governmental attention'.[90] At present, however, the Afghan government lacks capacity to even monitor its own security forces,[91] let alone community-based policing structures. A better approach might be for the state to function as facilitator, as it did successfully during the presidential and parliamentary elections (with Chief of Police and Provincial Governor working with a multi-community *shura*). This would mean that *arbakai* retain their autonomy and community linkages, but still have some form of limited oversight – which is often readily desired by local communities.[92]

Another reason why the collaboration with *arbakai* worked during the election was that it was not just linked to the ANP, but to international security forces and UNAMA. While this is not useful as a long-term strategy, a community monitoring mechanism could potentially fulfil the monitoring task – possibly both for state and community-based policing. Such a body would have to be distinct enough from the *shuras* in charge of the *arbakai* in order no to be self-serving.

If over time the *arbakai* do merge within the state system, they would likely become part of the police and cease to be a community-based mechanism. This recently happened with the establishment of security for the Ainak copper mines in Khak-e-Jabar district, when the MoI approached local leaders to assist in building up the local ANP force. The elders from each of the four community (*wanda*) sections (two Tajik: Chakari and Khord Kabul, and two Pashtun: Karokhail and Malangi) agreed on a power-sharing arrangement, with each community providing exactly one hundred men to the ANP, increasing the total force to 400. The individuals would receive police training, uniforms, and salaries. So far, however, only about 200 men have been recruited, as an internal rivalry between the Chakari, Khord

Kabuli, and Malangi has arisen, showing the problems of coordination. Nevertheless, a similar policy is being discussed for Mohmand Agha and Azra districts of Logar in order to secure mines and recruit additional 800 men from local communities. For such collaboration to be effective, political will has to exist on both sides, and the state (MoI or IDLG) needs to work out an effective community engagement policy (to enable the management of rivalries if they arise). As such a state policy on community engagement is still lacking, it is up to the initiatives of individuals within the Afghan government (ministers, governors) to devise their own engagement strategies on an ad hoc basis.

The hiring of community members into the ANP (via community consultation, which provides community oversight in the selection of individuals, and as the Khak-e-Jabar example illustrates may also balance a local police force better), can also address the problem of state funding for a community-based policing structure. Local people in Paktia remain very poor, and raising funds for salaries and men to serve detracts directly from other economic activities. Thus, a volunteer police force, as it exists in some African countries, seems unlikely.[93] Yet, putting community leaders on government pay roll does not only strip them of their autonomy, but can also lead to corruption if there is no accountability on how they in turn pay the *arbakai* guards. A better alternative might be to find ways to support entire communities in return for their contributing to security. Then it becomes a mutual beneficial relationship rather than a one-way dependency. As the Afghan government at present has a hard time providing regular salaries to the ANP, it seems unlikely that anytime soon it will be able (or willing) to provide funds for a community police force that it does not fully control (funds during the election came from external donors). There are also conflicting interests within the MoI with strong links to strongmen and their militia.[94]

The Application of Arbakai *outside Loya Paktia*

It is important to re-emphasize that outside Loya Paktia the experience of communities with customary enforcement structures has been limited to the *lashkar* (tribal army) or tribal/ethnic militia. As such, it is important to recall that the *arbakai* has been indeed unique to the southeast of Afghanistan. A recent report of the British Agencies Afghanistan Group (BAAG) thus cautions an 'export idea': 'Proposals to extract the *arbakai* from their historical integrated relationship with the *shura* would essentially represent attempts to pervert tradition, and would sever the ties between *arbakai* groups and their traditional structures of community accountability.'[95] It is important to explain this further.

As emphasized earlier, one of the reasons that the *arbakai* works in Loya Paktia is its link to a homogeneous and cohesive tribal system, a universal pre-requisite for successful community policing anywhere.[96] In contrast to the tribal system in the southeast, the one that exists in the South is more fragmented due to the impact of the Afghan wars, the activities of post-Taliban governors, and recent insurgency tactics. *Mujahideen* parties and commanders (but also the Taliban promoting *sharia* governance over *pashtunwali*) had an extremely damaging effect on tribal cohesion and traditional leaderships, using their military power to eliminate tribal rivals and thus fuelling inter- and intra- tribal conflicts. Many commanders acted essentially as astute political 'entrepreneurs' using the fragmentation of tribes in order to enhance their own power.[97] Thus, *shuras* in these areas functioned less to serve communities than to serve strongmen; at times competing *shuras* were serving different power-holders. In such an environment an *arbakai*-like structure may backfire and be (ab)used more to create conflict rather than to resolve it. Baker observed a similar trend in Africa, where customary structures lost their authority during the war due to an inability to protect communities and challenges from rebel groups.[98]

The district of Zurmat in Paktia serves as a good example of what limits the *arbakai* even in the Southeast, and thus possibly even more so elsewhere. One of the most populated and diverse districts in the Southeast, Zurmat has always functioned as a strategic crossroads for fighters (for example, the *mujahideen* and now the insurgency) from southern Ghazni, Logar, Paktia, Paktika, and Khost. The district has a history of strong religious networks; more recently insurgents have tried to weaken customary structures as a way of gaining further control and undermining future efforts to use them to strengthen the Afghan government. Thus, *arbakai* have been weak in Zurmat.

In some districts of Khost (such as the Tani, Tereyzai, Bak, and Dwamanda/ Shamal), communities have resorted to employing something similar to privatized security companies, which still recruit from community members but are run by local entrepreneurs. They mainly provide security along reconstruction projects (for example, the road that goes via Sayed Karam to Jani Khail). Here essentially private entrepreneurs are picking up elements of the *arbakai* to provide security, yet the security force is not paid by communities but via project funds. In Paktika and Ghanzi the use of *arbakai* has been rather weak due to the greater insecurity, with election security posing an exception.

Conclusion

As in other (post)conflict countries, the array of sometimes indistinguishable security actors in Afghanistan today is bewildering for the uninitiated outsider. The aim of this article was to contribute to the current debate on the use of ANSA to assist the fledgling Afghan state in the area of security provision. Based on the discussion, three main problem areas can be identified.

First, despite the great diversity of ANSA in Afghanistan, discussions often uncritically lump distinct actors into the same category (such as customary structures and strongmen militia). Using the example of the *arbakai* in south-eastern Afghanistan, this article tried to enhance the understanding of community-based security structures by outlining who the *arbakai* are, how they differ from other ANSA, and in what areas they have functioned since 2001. Both strengths and limitations of the *arbakai* were discussed. The overall assumption that *arbakai* are still applicable in most of Loya Paktia in 2009 was also challenged by illustrating that a growing insurgency is threatening customary structures and community leaders willing to support it.

We argue that the security picture in Afghanistan has become much more complex since the fall of the Taliban, as it is not only the Afghan government that has ad hoc arrangements with ANSA, but also international military forces. If anything is to be learned from Afghan history, including the discussion of the *arbakai*, policy makers should carefully analyze the specific context ANSA operate in before designing engagement policies. One example discussed here was the limited transferability of the *arbakai* to areas where communities and customary structures are less cohesive. Research, however, can assess functioning community-based mechanisms in those areas of Afghanistan that have remained isolated from a strong state presence. The examples of the Hazara community based police in Gizab shows that communities with the right kind of initiative have the means to ensure the rule of law. Each mechanism, however, is unique. Instead of exporting pre-set structures it might be better to opt for a more flexible strategy adaptable to local realties and contexts.

A contextual understanding must take into account the scope and mandate of ANSA, in order to avoid pushing them beyond the limits of their capacities. This article showed that the *arbakai*, as with other community-based policing structures, are very hard pressed to engage in counter-insurgency activities and tend to be reluctant to become a fighting force. Linked to this is that government-ANSA cooperation can fundamentally change the nature of the ANSA or create distrust within communities.

Secondly, as Milliken and Krause suggest in their introduction to this special edition,[99] it is also important to work out formal and comprehensive mechanisms for engagement with ANSA in order to ensure clarity of mandates, division of labour, and commitment on both parts. One of the problems in Afghanistan has been a lack of a coherent policy in regards to ANSA. While historically the state has worked with customary structures and militia to consolidate the state, defeat internal uprisings and invasions, and to enforce law and order in remote areas, these arrangements have been ad hoc and informal. While this may have worked prior to the Afghan wars, the proliferation of ANSA since the *mujahideen* resistance against the communist coup in 1978 has made it much more difficult. The Afghan government needs to view the relationship between state and community-based policing in more of a wider sense than simply a reactionary 'more boots on the ground' approach. Instead of co-optation, the role of a facilitator of customary policing structures may be more feasible for the Afghan state at this stage. Communities would also have to be clearly informed as to the role and responsibility of any community-based police (*arbakai* or other) *vis-à-vis* the state security forces in order manage unrealistic expectations. In the case of the *arbakai*, for example, community leaders in Paktia were far more positive three years ago about merging with government structures due to the weakening legitimacy of the Afghan state. As Baker has demonstrated for post-conflict Africa, in the end, a hybrid model of policing may be more realistic for Afghanistan, as 'state power tends to [eventually] infiltrate non-state policing'.[100] The example of using communities to hire police in Khak-e-Jabar district seems to support this thesis.

Lastly, the Afghan government and international actors may want to weigh the pros and cons for engaging ANSA that have a history of challenging the state. It is important to differentiate those ANSA that are based on a 'personality cult' and those linked to customary structures that hold them accountable. Schneckener has already questioned whether 'it is possible to use these structures as temporary solutions and building blocks for reconstructing statehood, or whether this would simply increase the risk that they would be strengthened and legitimized so that the establishment of the state's monopoly of the use of force becomes even less likely'.[101]

As noted in the introduction, the collapse of the communist government can be attributed, at least in part, to a misdirected engagement with ANSA. This shows that quick fixes to security deficits, especially when involving ANSA, can easily backfire and lead to state failure. The long-term costs of arming militia in Afghanistan in order to fight the Taliban may simply be too high. It might be more advisable to work with existing community structures, such as the *arbakai* (or the example of the Hazara community-based police in Gizab) and begin to focus on providing governance and rule of law from the bottom up in Afghanistan.

ACKNOWLEDGEMENTS

This article builds on research conducted in 2004 and 2005 funded by the UK Department for International Development (DFID). We would like to acknowledge the input of Dr Conrad Schetter (ZEF) during the initial stages of research design. We benefited from discussions during workshop presentations involving military, UN, embassy and NGO participants that were held in Gardez (Paktia) and Kabul in 2005. Input from presentations and discussions during the conference 'Transnational and Non-State Armed Groups: Legal and Policy Responses', Graduate Institute of International Studies, Geneva, Switzerland, 24–25 April 2008, helped shape this article. We would especially like to thank Astri Suhrke, Bruce Baker, Tobias Hagman, Conrad Schetter, Nick Miszak, Jacob Rinck, Casey Johnson, and three anonymous interviewers for comments on earlier versions of this article.

NOTES

1. 'Agreement on Provisional Arrangements in Afghanistan Pending the Re-Establishment of Permanent Government Institutions', http://www.un.org/News/dh/latest/afghan/afghan-agree.htm (accessed 2 May 2009).
2. UNAMA, *Afghanistan: Annual Report on Protection of Civilians in Armed Conflict, 2008* (United Nations Assistance Mission to Afghanistan, Human Rights Unit, January 2009). http://www.reliefweb.int/rw/RWFiles2009.nsf/FilesByRWDocUnidFilename/JBRN-7PCD3P-full_report.pdf/$File/full_report.pdf, p.iii
3. Andrew Wilder, 'Cops or Robbers? The Struggle to Reform the Afghan National Police', Issue Papers Series, Afghanistan Research and Evaluation Unit (AREU), Kabul, July 2007; International Crisis Group, 'Reforming Afghanistan's Police', Asia Report No. 138, Brussels, 30 August 2007.
4. General James L. Jones (USMC, ret.) and Ambassador Thomas R. Pickering, 'Afghanistan Study Group Report: Revitalizing our Efforts, Rethinking our Strategies', Center for the Study of the Presidency, Washington, DC, 30 January 2008.
5. Afghan Civil Society Forum, 'Strengthening Civil Society in Afghanistan', Afghan Civil Society Forum, Kabul 2006; see also Susanne Schmeidl, 'Case Study Afghanistan – Who Guards the Guardians?' in *Private Security Companies and Local Populations. An Exploratory Study of Afghanistan and Angola*, Swisspeace Report, Berne, November 2007, pp. 14–45.
6. International Crisis Group, 'Reforming Afghanistan's Police' (note 3), p. 1; see also International Crisis Group, 'Policing in Afghanistan: Still Searching for a Strategy', Asia Briefing No. 85, Kabul/Brussels, 18 December 2008.
7. See for example Diane E. Davis, 'Non-State Armed Actors, New Imagined Communities, and Shifting Patterns of Sovereignty and Insecurity in the Modern World', this volume.

8. Ulrich Schneckener, 'Fragile Statehood, Armed Non-State Actors and Security Governance', in Alan Bryden and Marina Caparini (eds), *Private Actors and Security Governance* (Berlin: LIT Verlag, and Geneva Centre for the Democratic Control of Armed Forces (DCAF), 2006), pp. 23–40, p. 24.
9. Phil Williams, 'Violent Non-State Actors and National and International Security', International Relations and Security Network (ISN), Swiss Federal Institute of Technology, Zurich, 2008.
10. Schneckener, 'Fragile Statehood' (note 8), p. 35.
11. See Keith Krause and Jennifer Milliken, 'Introduction: The Challenge of Non-State Armed Groups' in this volume.
12. Bruce Baker, 'Who Do People Turn to for Policing in Sierra Leone?' *Journal of Contemporary African Studies*, Vol. 23, No. 3 (2005), pp. 371–90; see also Bruce Baker, 'Multi-choice Policing in Uganda', *Policing and Society*, Vol. 15, No. 1 (2005), pp. 19–41; and Davis, 'Non-State Armed Actors, New Imagined Communities' (this volume).
13. David H. Bayley and Clifford D. Shearing, 'The New Structure of Policing: Description, Conceptualization and Research Agenda', Department of Justice, Office of Justice Programs, National Institute of Justice, Washington, DC, July 2001, p. vii; see also I. Loader, 'Plural Policing and Democratic Governance', *Social and Legal Studies*, Vol. 9, No. 3 (2000), pp. 323–45.
14. Baker, 'Who Do People Turn To For Policing in Sierra Leone?' (note 12), p. 385.
15. See Davis, 'Non-State Armed Actors, New Imagined Communities' (this volume).
16. Schneckener, 'Fragile Statehood' (note 8).
17. See Milliken and Krause, 'Introduction: The Challenge of Transnational and Non-State Armed Groups' (this volume).
18. Williams, 'Violent Non-State Actors and National and International Security' (note 9).
19. Schneckener, 'Fragile Statehood' (note 8).
20. See British Agencies Afghanistan Group (BAAG), 'Community Defence Initiatives in Afghanistan – Implications to Consider', The Refugee Council, London, April 2008.
21. Sajjad Hussain, 'Formation of Lashkars a Means to Tackle Taliban', *Daily Outlook Afghanistan*, 1 December 2008; Michael Williams, 'The Militia Mistake: Expecting Tribal Militias to Help Solve Afghanistan's Problems is a Dangerous Error by America', www.guardian.co.uk, 29 December 2008, http://www.guardian.co.uk/commentisfree/2008/dec/29/afghanistan-middleeast (accessed 2 May 2009)
22. See Williams, 'Violent Non-State Actors and National and International Security' (note 9); Schneckener, 'Fragile Statehood' (note 8).
23. See BAAG, 'Community Defence Initiatives in Afghanistan' (note 20).
24. Davis, using her research on Mexico, also cautions on the use of militia for policing work, as she finds them leading to societal fragmentation, increasing distrust and violence, and a tendency to use guns to resolve conflicts. Diane E. Davis, 'Policing, Regime Change, and Democracy: Reflections from the Case of Mexico', Working Paper 22, Crisis States Research, Centre London School of Economics, London, November 2007, p. 19.
25. See BAAG, 'Community Defence Initiatives in Afghanistan' (note 20).
26. See Mike Brogden 'Commentary: Community Policing: A Panacea from the West', *African Affairs*, Vol. 103, No. 413 (2004), pp. 635–49; Robert C. Davis, Nicole J. Henderson, and Cybele Merrick, 'Community Policing: Variations on the Western Model in the Developing World', *Police Practice and Research*, Vol. 4, No. 4 (2003), pp. 285–300.
27. Pascal Bongard, 'Humanitarian Engagement with Non-State Armed Groups: Lessons Learned from Geneva Call's Experience on the Landmine Ban', Paper presented at the conference 'Transnational and Non-State Armed Groups: Legal and Policy Responses', Graduate Institute of International Studies, Geneva, Switzerland, 24–25 April 2008.
28. See here also William Reno's contribution on armed non-state actors in Africa, which demonstrates that the behaviour and actions of ANSA can contribute to state collapse, and that this is often linked to existing political strategies and local political economies that enabled this. See William Reno, 'Explaining Patterns of Violence in Collapsed States', in this volume.
29. This paper draws on various qualitative interviews and focus group discussion conducted by four researchers of The Liaison Office between 2004 and 2008 with representatives of the major tribes in Paktia with Arbakai forces in the past or present: Ahmadzai, Mangal, Zadran, and Zazee tribes, and their principal sub-tribes. The bulk of the research was conducted in late 2004. For each district in Paktia with Arbakai operations, focus group discussions with tribal elders and Arbakai commanders were conducted, supplemented by four semi-structured interviews with selected elders and Arbakai commanders. In addition to interviews with tribal elders and Arbakai commanders, government officials (District Police Chief, Provincial Police Chief, Ministry of Interior, Governor's Office,

President's Office) and UN officials (primarily UNAMA) were conducted. Initial findings were shared and discussed in early 2005 at a workshop in Gardez, Paktia that included tribal elders, Arbakai commanders, government officials as well as representatives from ISAF/NATO and the international community. Data was updated twice through interviews with selected tribal elders and Arbakai commanders and fighters during 2007 and 2008. This was done to gauge the changed situation of the Arbakai since the original research. The authors would like to thank Arsallan Mangal and Mohammad Nabi Tadbir for their assistance with these interviews.

30. Krause and Milliken, 'Introduction: The Challenge of Non-State Armed Groups' (this volume).
31. This is adapted from a framework put forth by Williams, 'Violent Non-State Actors and National and International Security', p. 8 (note 9).
32. See for example Antonio Giustozzi, 'Afghanistan: Transformation without End: An Analytical Narrative on State-Making', Crisis States Working Paper Series No. 2, Working Paper 40, Crisis States Research Centre, London School of Economics, November 2008, p. 1.
33. Krause and Milliken, 'Introduction: The Challenge of Non-State Armed Groups' (this volume).
34. Baker, 'Who Do People Turn to for Policing in Sierra Leone?' (note 12), p. 385.
35. See Milliken and Krause, 'Introduction: The Challenge of Transnational and Non-State Armed Groups' (this volume); Bongard, 'Humanitarian Engagement with Non-State Armed Groups' (note 27).
36. Community-based policing is meant to describe policing outside the regulatory framework of the state; Bruce Baker, 'Post-War Policing by Communities in Sierra Leone, Liberia, and Rwanda', Democracy and Security, Vol. 3, No. 2 (2007), pp. 215–36, p. 216.
37. It has been argued elsewhere that it is also linked to the Pashtu word for messenger, see Mohammed Osman Tariq, 'Tribal Security System (Arbakai) in Southeast Afghanistan', Occasional Papers, Crisis States Research Centre, LSE, London, December 2008, p. 3.
38. We would like to acknowledge that the arbakai label has also been wrongfully used for tribal para-state mechanisms in Shinwar and Mohmand areas of Nangarhar and rural areas outside Kabul. While these tribal structures had and have many similarities with the Arbakai, they were mostly set up upon the request of the state, such as to secure important trade routes. Thus, rather than speaking of a community-based mechanism, it is more a state-community collaboration, the government directing the purpose of the force and paying their salaries.
39. Conrad Schetter, Rainer Glassner, and Masood Karokhail, 'Beyond Warlordism. The Local Security Structure in Afghanistan', Internationale Politik und Gesellschaft, No. 2 (2007), pp. 136–52; www.fes.de/IPG/inhalt_d/pdf/10_Schetter_US.pdf (accessed 13 October 2009).
40. The division of geographical space among the tribes is determined on the basis of administrative sections (wand), where each tribe and its jurisdiction of responsibility are known. The wand constitutes the administrative framework for political action, such as shuras. The number of wands allocated gives an idea of the size, share in resources, and influence of a tribe. The term wand comes from the notion of Watan, which has an emotional quality close to the notion of 'home or the place one belongs to' (German = Heimat). It describes a small local region where one person knows the others face to face. Bernt Glatzer, 'War and Boundaries in Afghanistan: Significance and Relativity of Local and Social Boundaries', International Journal for the Study of Modern Islam, No. 3 (2001), pp. 379–99.
41. Wili Steul, Pashtunwali: Ein Ehrenkodex und seine rechtliche Relevanz (Wiesbaden: Franz Steiner Verlag, 1981).
42. Although the term 'Pashtunwali' is widely used in literature it is rarely used by rural Pashtuns themselves to describe their social system.
43. Steul, Pashtunwali (note 41).
44. See Erwin Grötzbach, Afghanistan: eine geographische Landeskunde (Darmstadt: Wissenschaftliche Buchgesellschaft, 1990).
45. Alfred Janata and Reihanoddin Hassas, 'Ghairatman – Der gute Pashtune: Exkurs über die Grundlagen des Pashtunwali', Afghanistan Journal, Vol. 2, No. 3 (1975), pp. 83–97.
46. Bernt Glatzer, 'The Pashtun Tribal System,' in G. Pfeffer and D.K. Behera (eds), Contemporary Society: Concept of Tribal Society (New Delhi: Concept Publisher, 1997), pp. 265–82.
47. One example is the practise of bad (exchange of women for crimes committed exemplifies how traditional justice is based on a communal rights system that stands contrary to Western and international laws emphasizing an individualistic rights interpretation. Under pashtunwali '[t]hose who have the ability to take vengeance but suffice to receiving Bad are named "good people" by the tribes and if they refuse Bad and resort to revenge-taking, they are called "unfavourable people"' [sic], as blood revenge may escalate conflict further. See Women and Children Legal Research

Foundation, 'Bad Painful Sedative', WCLRF Report, Kabul, 2004, p. 17. Unfortunately, these practices, decided and enforced by men (the tribal elders), 'deliberately victimize a girl for the crime her
father, brother, uncle or one of her relatives has committed', and quite possibly have longer-term consequences if the girl is treated poorly. Ibid., p. 18. This is quite often the case, and the psychological
long-term damage on the exchanged girl and her community is not usually considered by traditional
justice providers and communities, but is well demonstrated in the WCLRF report.
48. Barfield et al., *The Clash of Two Goods: State and Non-State Dispute Resolution in Afghanistan*
(Washington, DC: United States Institute for Peace, 2006).
49. Ibid. It is important to note that an integral part of a redistributive justice system tends to be a certain
set of values, principles, and lifestyle. It focuses on the needs of victim, the accountability of
offenders, while also giving offenders a way back into the community. By reinforcing community
values restorative justice empowers residents to improve their community. See Rachel Monaghan
'Community-based Justice in Northern Ireland and South Africa', *International Criminal Justice
Review*, Vol. 18, No. 1 (March 2008), pp. 83–105, pp. 89–90.
50. International Legal Foundation (ILF), 'The Customary Laws of Afghanistan. A Report by the International Legal Foundation', Kabul, September 2004, www.TheILF.org (accessed 21 April 2008),
p. 10.
51. The *jirga* has been also used in more recent years to govern relations between ethnic groups
within multi-ethnic districts, such as a Hazara-Pashtun *jirga* in Gizab district of Uruzgan. The
greater *jirga* (*loya kirga*) was also by Afghan rulers to consult with local leaders on key issues
(e.g., the constitutional *loya jirga* in 2003.
52. Steul, *Pashtunwali* (note 41), pp. 123–4.
53. Center for Policy and Human Development, 'Afghanistan Human Development Report 2007', Kabul
University, CPHD, 2007, p. 9. In the Southeast, however, religious figures generally do not take part
in the decision-making process, but can be important by giving their blessing to decisions made.
54. Originally the term *shura* was used for gathering of Islamic dignitaries ranging from *mullahs* to
ulema. During the Afghan wars the *mujahidin* introduced the term *shuras* for all kinds of gatherings
of official character (see Barnett, R. Rubin, *The Fragmentation of Afghanistan*, New Haven, NJ and
London: Yale University Press, 2002). *Shuras* can either function on a community level, or more
recently at district and provincial levels in an attempt to link up to state-drawn boundaries in order
to be flexible to collaborate with state authorities. The size of the *shura* depends on the population
size of a community (or area to be governed) with each community selecting their representatives.
See Glatzer, 'The Pashtun Tribal System' (note 46).
55. Community-based policing is meant to describe policing outside the regulatory framework of the
state. Bruce Baker, 'Post-War Policing by Communities in Sierra Leone, Liberia, and Rwanda'
(note 36), p. 216.
56. See also Williams, 'Violent Non-State Actors and National and International Security' (note 9), p. 8.
57. Mohammed Osman Tariq, 'Tribal Security System (Arbakai) in Southeast Afghanistan' (note 37),
p. 6.
58. Tom Coghlan 'Can Tribes Take on the Taliban?', *BBC News*, 26 December 2007, http://news.bbc.
co.uk/2/hi/south_asia/7155500.stm (accessed 21 April 2008).
59. Mohammed Osman Tariq, 'Tribal Security System (Arbakai) in Southeast Afghanistan' (note 37),
pp. 8–9.
60. Andreas Wimmer and Conrad Schetter, 'Staatsbildung zuerst: Empfehlungen zum Wiederaufbau und
zur Befriedung Afghanistans', ZEF Discussion Papers on Development Policy, Zentrum für Entwick-
lungsforschung, Bonn, 2002.
61. It is hard to obtain actual police figures, as in general only 'authorized numbers' not 'actual' ones are
known. 'Personnel records are weak, and there are incentives to inflate police numbers as salary payments in the past have been based on the number of authorized police positions rather than the actual
number of police'. Wilder, 'Cops or Robbers?' (note 3), p. 7.
62. Central Statistics Office, 'Settled Population by Civil Division (Urban and Rural) and Sex 2005–
2006', http://www.cso-af.net/cso/documents/estimated%20population%201384.xls (accessed 13
October 2008).
63. See, for example, Rachel Monaghan 'Community Based Justice in Northern Ireland and South
Africa', *International Criminal Justice Review*, Vol. 18, No. 1 (March 2008), pp. 83–105; Baker,
'Post-War Policing by Communities in Sierra Leone, Liberia, and Rwanda', (note 36); Bruce
Baker, 'Multi-Choice Policing in Uganda', *Policing and Society*, Vol. 15, No. 1 (2005), pp. 19–
41; Diane E. Davis, 'Policing, Regime Change, and Democracy' (note 24); Rachel Monaghan

'Community-based Justice in Northern Ireland and South Africa', *International Criminal Justice Review*, Vol. 18, No. 1 (March 2008), pp. 83–105.

64. Bruce Baker, 'The African Post-conflict Policing Agenda in Sierra Leone', *Conflict, Security & Development*, Vol. 6, No. 1 (April 2006), pp. 25–49, p. 26.

65. Wilder, 'Cops or Robbers? (note 3); International Crisis Group, 'Reforming Afghanistan's Police' (note 3).

66. Schmeidl, 'Case Study Afghanistan' (note 5).

67. Ibid., see also Susanne Schmeidl, 'The Good, the Bad and the Ugly – The Private Military and Security Sector in Afghanistan', in Alex Dowling and Eden Cole (eds), *Security Sector Governance in Afghanistan* (Geneva: Geneva Centre for the Democratic Control of Armed Forces (DCAF), 2009 (forthcoming)).

68. The word 'warlord' is intentionally not used. See Antonio Giustozzi, 'The Debate on Warlordism: The Importance of Military Legitimacy', Working Paper 13, Crisis States Research Centre, London School of Economics, London, October 2005.

69. Mafia-like and criminal networks are certainly not new to Afghanistan, albeit they have seen a proliferation in the post-2001 era. They are linked the illegal export of goods, the drugs and weapons trade, and other areas such as land-grabbing. See Irvine, Stephanie, 'Powerful Grab Afghanistan Land', *BBC News Eurasia*, 6 September 2007, http://news.bbc.co.uk/2/hi/south_asia/6981035.stm (accessed 26 September 2008); also Barnett R. Rubin, Humayun Hamidzada, and Abby Stoddard, 'Afghanistan 2005 and Beyond: Prospects for Improved Stability Reference Document', Netherlands Institute for International Relations, Clingendael, Conflict Research Unit, April 2005.

70. For an overview of PSCs in Afghanistan see Schmeidl, 'Case Study Afghanistan' (note 5).

71. For a good discussion see Antonio Giustozzi, *Koran, Kalashnikov, and Laptop: The Neo-Taliban Insurgency in Afghanistan* (New York: Columbia University Press, 2007).

72. Ongoing research of The Liaison Office in Uruzgan province (since 2006).

73. Kristian Berg Harpviken, 'Transcending Traditionalism: The Emergence of Non-State Military Formations in Afghanistan', *Journal of Peace Research*, Vol. 34, No. 3 (1997); Antonio Giustozzi and Noor Ullah, '"Tribes" and Warlords of Southern Afghanistan, 1980–2005', Working Paper 7, Crisis States Research Centre, London School of Economics, London, September 2006.

74. See Schmeidl, 'Case Study Afghanistan' (note 5); Wilder, 'Cops or Robbers? (note 3).

75. Astri Suhrke, 'A Contradictory Mission? NATO from Stabilization to Combat in Afghanistan', *International Peacekeeping*, Vol. 15, No. 2 (2008), pp. 214–36.

76. Wilder, 'Cops or Robbers? (note 3); International Crisis Group, 'Reforming Afghanistan's Police' (note 3).

77. See Giustozzi, 'Afghanistan: Transformation without End' (note 32), and Harpviken, 'Transcending Traditionalism (note 73).

78. See Giustozzi, 'Afghanistan: Transformation without End' (note 32), and Harpviken, 'Transcending Traditionalism (note 73).

79. See Schmeidl, 'Case Study Afghanistan' (note 5); Wilder, 'Cops or Robbers? (note 3).

80. Giustozzi, 'The Debate on Warlordism' (note 68).

81. Ibid.

82. Baker asserts for the Sierra Leone case that there is a 'danger that alternative policing structures fail in the near future because of its evident limitation'. Baker, 'Who Do People Turn To For Policing in Sierra Leone?' (note 12), p. 381.

83. Barfield *et al.*, 'The Clash of Two Goods' (note 48); Centre for Policy and Human Development, 'Afghanistan Human Development Report 2007' (note 53).

84. Ibid.; Women and Children Legal Research Foundation, 'Bad Painful Sedative' (note 47). This is not uniquely so in Afghanistan, but also the case for most African communal laws. See Baker 'Who Do People Turn To For Policing in Sierra Leone?' (note 12).

85. BAAG, 'Community Defence Initiatives in Afghanistan (note 20), p. 5.

86. Christine Noelle-Karimi, 'Village Institutions in the Perceptions of National and International Actors in Afghanistan', Amu Dary Series, Paper No. 1, Center for Development Research, University of Bonn, 2006, pp. 8–9.

87. See Liz Alden Wily, 'Looking for Peace on the Pastures: Rural Land Relations in Afghanistan', Synthesis Paper, Afghanistan Research and Evaluation Unit (AREU), Kabul, December 2004.

88. International Crisis Group, 'Policing in Afghanistan: Still Searching for a Strategy', Asia Briefing No. 85, Kabul/Brussels, 18 December 2008.

89. Wilder, 'Cops or Robbers? (note 3); International Crisis Group, 'Reforming Afghanistan's Police' (note 3), p. 46.

90. Baker, 'Who Do People Turn to for Policing in Sierra Leone? (note 12), p. 386.
91. Wilder, 'Cops or Robbers? (note 3); International Crisis Group, 'Reforming Afghanistan's Police' (note 3). Again, this is not unique to Afghanistan, but also a clear dilemma for African government, see for example Baker, 'Who Do People Turn to for Policing in Sierra Leone? (note 12).
92. Susanne Schmeidl, 'Successful Cooperation or Dangerous Liaison? Integrating Traditional and Modern Justice Mechanisms in Southeastern Afghanistan', Paper presented at the 50th Annual Convention of the International Studies Association, New York, 15–18 February 2009.
93. Baker, 'Post-War Policing by Communities in Sierra Leone, Liberia, and Rwanda', (note 36); Baker, 'Who Do People Turn to for Policing in Sierra Leone? (note 12); Bruce Baker, 'Reconstructing a Policing System Out of the Ashes: Rwanda's Solution', *Policing and Society*, Vol. 17. No. 4 (December 2007), pp. 344–66.
94. Ibid.
95. BAAG, 'Community Defence Initiatives in Afghanistan' (note 20), p. 5.
96. Robert C. Davis *et al.*, 'Community Policing: Variations on the Western Model in the Developing World' (note 26), pp. 286–7.
97. See also Giustozzi and Ullah, '"Tribes" and Warlords of Southern Afghanistan' (note 73).
98. Baker, 'Who Do People Turn to for Policing in Sierra Leone? (note 12).
99. See Milliken and Krause, 'Introduction: The Challenge of Transnational and Non-State Armed Groups' (this volume).
100. Baker, 'Post-War Policing by Communities in Sierra Leone, Liberia, and Rwanda' (note 36), p. 216.
101. Schneckener, 'Fragile Statehood' (note 8), p. 36.

Staging Society: Sources of Loyalty in the Angolan UNITA

TERESA KOLOMA BECK

In 1992–1993 the city of Huambo in the Central Highlands of Angola was held by the insurgent armed group UNITA. At that time, civil war had been consuming the country for more than 15 years. Angola's Central Highlands had always been a UNITA stronghold, since the Ovimbundu, the ethno-linguistic group traditionally inhabiting this region, had formed its historic core constituency. Hence, initially, popular opinion in Huambo was not per se hostile to UNITA's seizure of the city. The ruling Movimento Popular de Libertação de Angola (MPLA) government answered with a strategy of siege: unable to enter the city, they started to lock it from outside, hoping that increasing supply shortages would turn public opinion against the UNITA occupiers. Finally, in order to demoralize the population further, air raids were launched against the city.

It is said that among the pilots charged with this order were men who themselves came from the region. They are said to have refused to destroy the city where they knew their families to be living. Instead, they dropped the bombs on unoccupied grounds. If they had followed orders, people from Huambo say the city would have been even more badly damaged.[1]

A common image of armed groups in civil wars, cultivated first and foremost by public media, is that of a violent intruder into an otherwise peaceful social milieu. Yet, armed groups do not come out of the blue. They emerge in particular contexts at particular moments in time. As organizations, they are embedded in a particular social environment, and they do not and cannot exist independently from the latter.

This problem is particularly pronounced in armed groups' efforts to create a stable and loyal following. The story told about the bomber pilots from Huambo illustrates how ignoring pre-existing social ties or acting against them may jeopardize armed group efficiency.

During my field research in the region, I was not able to verify if things had actually happened the way I was told, or if the story was rather a rumour that had emerged to make sense of otherwise inscrutable observations.[2] Yet, be that as it may,[3] the narrative broaches an important issue: it portrays members of an armed force who – in a decisive situation – were torn between competing loyalties; and it shows how their inner conflict led to a decision countering the intentions of the armed group's leadership. To prevent such situations and to secure success armed groups systematically engage pre-existing social structures in order to use them for their own benefit. They also become inventive in order to overcome the limitations imposed by those structures. And, in doing so, they become agents of social change.

In this article, I will examine the importance of the social environment for the stability of armed groups as organizations. In a case study of the Angolan UNITA, I will show how this armed group engaged and transformed existing social structures to recruit members and create a stable and loyal following. The basic background of these considerations is data collected during seven months of field research, from September 2005 to April 2006, principally in the region of the Huambo and the Central Highlands, complemented by literature review.[4]

First, I will briefly consider the state of research on the issue. The second section introduces the socio-historical background of the case, including a sketch of UNITA's history and evolution. The third section focuses on the question of how UNITA secured and conditioned membership and support, illustrating how this armed group dealt with the conditions found in its social as well as its natural environment.

My basic argument is that UNITA's most loyal following was created in a far-reaching project of social engineering. At its base was a practice of forced recruitment of young boys and girls. Those teenagers were raised in a society run by UNITA's rules, and they continued to live there as adults. When the war ended in 2002, this was the only life they knew. Their loyalty thus outlived the armed group itself. And it is a powder-keg to social peace in post-war Angola.

Armed Groups and Society: State of Research

Despite the growing body of academic literature on armed groups, there is still little known about the interdependencies between armed groups and their broader social context, between their actions on the one hand and the transformation of society on the other. The reason for this is (at least) twofold. First, to analyze how armed groups relate to the social environment in which they move micro-level data is needed. For obvious reasons, the latter is not easy to obtain in contexts of war and violence. Against this background, it comes as no surprise that among the pioneers in this field are a number of anthropologists, who methodologically seem to be especially prepared for conducting research in such sensitive settings.[5]

Yet, the technical problem of data collection is but one part of an explanation. Another important aspect is the theoretical framework. During the last decades, rational choice has become the dominant concept in political science writing. Research on armed groups is no exception in this regard. With its focus on self-interest and choice, and the associated problems of information and coordination, the introduction of this concept significantly enlarged the horizon of research on the issue. This turn is particularly obvious in the analysis of factors stimulating individual participation in armed groups, where the focus of research shifted from collective grievances[6] to more individual motivations. Most frequently, however, a materialistic interpretation of the concept of self-interest prevailed: the prospect of individual gains, in terms of current or future income (opportunities), was concluded to be decisive in determining participation. Accordingly, the resource endowment of armed groups moved into the focus of attention.

The importance of material benefits in the recruitment process cannot be denied. Yet, limiting the analysis to this aspect means reducing the complexity of the relationship between armed groups and the broader social context.

From the perspective of an armed group, a stable and compliant following cannot be created simply by convincing individuals to join. Instead, securing membership of and compliance with armed group rule is an ongoing task. In this context, the engagement of pre-existing social structures is a decisive factor.

This is illustrated, for example, in Stathis Kalyvas' studies on violence in civil wars. He shows how in local arenas political conflicts come to overlap with pre-existing intra-personal quarrels,[7] and how armed groups' relationships to local populations become crucial to their use of violence.[8] As many armed groups mimic state behaviour, important insights on the issue can also be drawn from earlier studies on the relationship between armed action and state formation, such as Charles Tilly's work on state formation in Europe,[9] or Joel S. Migdal's study on *State in Society*.[10] Analyses like these suggest that in the perspective of an armed group society is at the same time an invaluable resource and a serious limitation. In this sense, society poses a problem to armed groups: not one that cannot solved, but one that needs to be managed.

In the following, I am going to reconstruct how these problems were manifested in the context of the civil war in Angola, and how UNITA, the armed group challenging state power for almost 30 years, tried to address them.

The Background

Civil War in Angola

Angola looks back upon one of the longest lasting wars in the modern history of the African continent: it started in the late 1950s and early 1960s with the Liberation Movement. Three groups – MPLA (Movimento Popular de Libertação de Angola – Popular Movement for the Liberation of Angola), FNLA (Frente Nacional de Libertação de Angola – National Front for the Liberation of Angola) and UNITA (União Nacional para a Independência Total de Angola – National Union for the Total Independence of Angola) – started to fight for independence from Portugal. Each one of the movements was rooted in a different social and ethno-linguistic milieu, and each one supported by different foreign agents. Yet, finally, Angolan independence was not won on the battlefield: in 1975 increased protest against the Salazar regime within Portugal led to his overthrow. In the course of the political reforms following this event the country also renounced its overseas territories. Angola's authority was to be put into the hands of a joint interim government comprising the three major independence movements. However, this plan was thwarted when one of the movements, the MPLA, occupied the country's capital and declared a People's Republic.[11] Thus began, in the autumn of 1975, a struggle for state authority which lasted nearly 30 years. After the FNLA was defeated militarily in 1976, there remained only two protagonists in this civil war. One on side was the ruling MPLA, initially under Agostinho Neto and since 1983 under Eduardo dos Santos. It was supported by the so-called Eastern bloc, principally by Cuba and the Soviet Union. On the other side was, as the challenger, the Western-oriented UNITA under Jonas Savimbi. The first peace agreement, the Bicesse Accords, was signed in 1991. It foresaw a DDR program and elections to be held in September 1992. When the polls declared the MPLA government the winner, UNITA took up arms again and war re-erupted, now more violently than before. After another failed peace agreement, the Lusaka Accords in 1994, the Angolan civil war ended in early 2002, after Jonas Savimbi had been killed by government armed forces and UNITA conceded military defeat. The signature of the Luena Memorandum of Understanding, on 4 April 2002, marked the official end of the civil war. It was a ceasefire agreement that confirmed the Lusaka Accords, thus paving the way for the transformation of UNITA into a political party and its integration into a formal power-sharing arrangement.[12]

Creation and Evolution of UNITA

Among the three major independence movements UNITA was the last to be founded. Yet, saying this means more than stating a mere chronology. While MPLA and FNLA[13] were created in the mid 1950s with rejection of the colonial state at the core of their organizational program, UNITA was created almost ten years later in 1966. The decisive context conditioning the emergence of this third independence movement was not so much colonial society as the failures and problems of the already existing movements. A first point of critique referred to the composition of these movements: while the majority of FNLA leaders and followers came from the Bakongo-speaking rural regions in northern Angola, MPLA, at its core, was composed of urban intellectuals, principally *mestiços* and so-called assimilated black Africans, from the region of the capital Luanda. The second point of critique was that neither of the movements was based in Angola itself but operated out of safe havens in neighbouring countries, namely Congo-Kinshasa and Congo-Brazzaville. Hence, in a double sense, the two dominant independence movements were detached from the Angolan population: first because they lacked inclusiveness and representativeness, and second, because they were spatially cut off from the people in whose interest they pretended to fight.

It was against the background of this critique that UNITA was founded in 1966, setting out to overcome the faults denounced in the FNLA and MPLA organizations. This was no easy task, since contrary to the image presented in many recent publications as well as in the publications of the movement itself at the time of its foundation, there were various groups challenging FNLA and MPLA authority, all competing for followers, recognition, and funds.[14] Yet, in the case of UNITA, several factors combined to lead to its emergence as a credible 'third force'.

The enterprising personality behind UNITA's creation, Jonas Savimbi, had been himself a high-ranking FNLA official and a member of the revolutionary exile government,[15] created by this movement. In a spectacular move, on the second summit of the Organization of African Unity (OAU) in 1964, Savimbi resigned from all his posts, denouncing FNLA's inefficiency and its lack of representativeness, and started out to create his own movement. Based on the social and symbolic capital accumulated as a minister in the FNLA-created exile government, he succeeded, in a relatively short period of time, to mobilize followers, funds, and international attention. To found the first organizational core, three partially overlapping networks of pre-existing social ties became important:[16] first, a group of other dissident members of the exile government, which shared Savimbi's frustration with FNLA politics; and second, a circle of politically active students abroad, also critical of the FNLA, which was headed by a long-standing confidant of Savimbi. The third source for the recruitment of UNITA's first members was a circle of nationalist leaders from central and southern Angola.

Savimbi himself belonged to the Ovimbundu, the biggest of the ethno-linguistic groups in the country, concentrated in the central highlands. Several factors had set the central and southern regions apart from those in the north of the country. There was first the general ethno-linguistic divide in Angola. The Bakongo and Mbundu of the north belonged to the group of northern Bantus and had traditionally cultivated strong ties with the regions of central Africa. The people of south and central Angola were linguistically as well as in the orientation of their in socio-economic activities closer to the peoples in the south of the continent. Missionary history had further nourished that divide: while in the north Portuguese Catholic missionaries had been dominant, the central and southern hinterland had been left to Protestant missionaries from North America and Europe. True to the Protestant project, the latter had introduced their philosophy of self-organizing communities and had created a black African elite who, different from the one in the capital, was in no ways detached from its cultural roots, who had preserved, for example, the local languages as a lingua franca.[17] Finally, the colonial state had exploited this already existing gap between north and south by employing Ovimbundu and other southerners as contract workers on the coffee plantations and, more importantly, in the military forces fighting the insurgency in the north. Within Angola, the Ovimbundu in particular had thus earned a reputation as willing collaborators of the colonizers.

In the further evolution of UNITA's organization, four different stages can be distinguished: the first phase comprises the formation of UNITA as an anti-colonial movement and the ten years of its independence struggle. It ends with the military defeat of the movement and its retreat to the South Angolan bush in 1976.

At the beginning of stage two, UNITA was, in the words of one high-ranking member, 'in a state of complete disorganization. We had to run away from the cities', he continues, 'at the beginning without any distinct destination. We were walking for the purpose of walking.'[18] Yet, against all odds and expectations, the armed group succeeded in reorganizing. Semantically, the 'struggle against colonial rule' was transformed into a 'struggle against the Russo-Cuban expansion' in Angola. A Congress held in 1977 launched a process of organizational differentiation and operational professionalization. This second phase, which ends with the signature of the Bicesse Accords in 1991, is the time of UNITA's biggest successes. Headquarters where created in Jamba, deep in the south-east of the country, and until the mid 1980s, they were expanded into a veritable city, with schools and hospitals, running water and electricity, and, most importantly, an airstrip. Starting from this region, the armed group began to expand its territorial control. By the end of 1985, UNITA had 30,000 guerrillas[19] and basically taken control of the Provinces of Cuando Cubango and Moxico. Its areas of operation stretched out into the Provinces of Bié, Malange and the Lundas, with single operations staged as far west as in the coastal town of Sumbe.[20] By the late 1980s, the Angolan government started to recognize that, to settle the conflict, direct negotiations with the insurgents were inevitable.

The third and last stage in the evolution of UNITA as an armed group is launched by the failure of the Bicesse Accords and the renewed outbreak of civil war. It is marked by growing internal dissent, the withering of international support, and finally, an increasing fragmentation of the movement. This stage ends with the death of UNITA's leader Jonas Savimbi and the signing of the Luena Memorandum, which initiates the transformation of the insurgent armed group into a political party.

Throughout those years, the Ovimbundu were considered to be UNITA's core constituency. Therefore, the armed group had been sometimes be mistaken for a 'tribal movement'.[21] Yet, as we are going to see in the following, the cohesion of UNITA as an organization cannot simply be explained by ethnic ties. Rather, it was created in a systematic effort by UNITA's leadership to secure membership as well as compliance with the rules of the organization.

Engineering Normality: UNITA's Social Project

Gangs of men, dancing to the tune of violence – such is our common conception of armed groups, especially in African conflicts. Yet, the violent images transmitted evening after evening by news stations around the globe represent but a fraction of armed groups' reality. Those acts of violence are embedded in a network of rules regulating the exercise of physical force. The efficiency armed groups attain in controlling the use of violence, in guarding against its unintended consequences, and in conditioning combatants' behaviour in this sense is crucial to their success.[22] Contingent upon the socio-political and cultural context, systems of rule and punishment emerge as armed groups attempt to face this challenge. The Angolan UNITA is an interesting case in this regard.

Right after independence, the country's military and political situation led to a spatial polarization of the two main opponents. As described in the preceding section, the self-appointed party in power, MPLA, consolidated its power bases in the cities, while the remaining members of the defeated UNITA fled to the scarcely populated regions in the far south-east of the country. In Angola, those regions not yet appropriated by humans, at best passed through by travellers are referred to as *mata*. 'There was nothing but trees and wild animals,' as an interviewee, who had witnessed UNITA's expulsion from the cities, explained.[23] The hostility of the natural environment quickly translated into a hostile popular discourse, denouncing the armed group's bush existence.[24] Fusing colonial rhetoric and traditional beliefs, life in the cities and villages was praised as tough but civilized, while UNITA combatants and their families were branded as living 'in the bush like wild animals'.[25] Hence, living with UNITA came to mean foreswearing humanity.[26]

The reorganization of the armed group from 1976 onwards seems to have been guided by an effort to prevent it from becoming the feral bush guerrilla as which it was already represented. As in any armed group, regulating combatants' behaviour became a central objective of UNITA's organizational structure. Yet, the armed group approached this problem in a very particular way. Instead of conditioning combatants' behaviour simply by a network of rules and regulations, UNITA leadership set out to design and control their entire life world. In a far-reaching project of social engineering 'normal', in the sense of civilian, life was staged in UNITA's military bases so as to counter the threatening wilderness of the surrounding *mata*.

In the following let us explore this social project more closely, considering how members were recruited and how life in the bases was organized.

'I Have Always Been a Soldier':[27] Recruiting Members

UNITA's strategies for raising combatants altered with the armed group's various history. During the independence struggle, the mobilization of pre-existing social ties was the central recruitment mechanism. As pointed out above, the people of the central and southern regions had been utterly underrepresented in the FNLA and MPLA struggle. Nevertheless, in these regions, too, a couple of small, mostly tribal-based organizations had emerged with the advancement of Angolan interests at the core of their program. Playing on his Ovimbundu identity, Savimbi succeeded in rallying these leaders to his cause, and they in turn mobilized their own small constituencies to form the UNITA core organization. The nexus of people educated at the Protestant mission schools were decisive in this process.

Yet, when UNITA transformed itself into an insurgent armed group in an intrastate war, this recruitment pattern changed. As the organization grew, and especially, as the armed forces expanded in size and scope of their operations, ethno-linguistic ties and similar patterns of socialization were no longer enough to supply it with reliable combatants. Hence, in the second phase of UNITA's history, from the late 1970s onwards, a second mechanism for engaging and binding members, especially for the organization's rank and file, prevailed: the involuntary recruitment of adolescents, more commonly known as 'kidnapping'. Boys and young men as well as girls and young women were taken from their families in villages or at roadblocks. They were brought to Jamba or to other military bases, where they were raised among other kidnapped children. Usually, they received primary education, and were then prepared for military life. Eventually, the boys were integrated into the armed forces, while most of the girls came to provide assistance services, acting as porters, nurses, cooks or teachers.

Considering UNITA's recruitment practices at this stage, it is important to note that in this case the actions commonly referred to as 'kidnapping' vary heavily regarding the degree of physical force involved. The cases where adolescents were violently abducted at roadblocks, in villages or during fieldwork are well documented.[28] Yet, with the expansion of territorial control in the 1980s, the armed group began to mimic state behaviour. UNITA leadership sought to channel recruitment into an orderly process of military enlistment. Raising combatants became an organized process between UNITA representatives and the *soba*, the traditional head of the village: UNITA officials arrived at appointed times during the year, and the local leaders would already have chosen a group of boys and girls to leave with them. In a group interview, village people pointed out that this demand was a heavy burden to the community and its leaders. But, according to them, the *soba* had no choice. He would be killed if he refused to comply. The village would be raided and the requested number of adolescents taken by force.[29] Regardless of their initial preferences concerning UNITA's political project, those village people came to cooperate with the armed group, as acquiescence to its demands appeared as the only way to ensure local peace. Yet, despite this cooperation, UNITA never abstained entirely from irregular violent raptures, presumably to satisfy short-term recruitment demands.

The forced recruitment of adolescents became UNITA's most important strategy for raising long-term combatants and created UNITA's most stable and most durable following. Being young and still malleable, these youths were socialized into the armed group in a process I will explain in more detail further below.

Nevertheless, pre-existing social ties, such as ethno-linguistic origins and kin, did not become completely insignificant. They came to play a role in a third type of UNITA combatant who gained in importance during the late 1980s and 1990s: the part-time soldier who joined more or less voluntarily to participate in regional campaigns. Those men relied heavily on their extended families for securing their basic supply in food, clothing, medicine, and money. Also in those cases, local people came to support UNITA, independently of their political preferences. One interviewee vividly described this situation:

> Especially in the villages it happened, for example, that at night it knocked on the door of father. And his son, who was fighting on the other side, stood there, asking for money. Money for medicine, money for food. 'Father, we are dying out there!' he would say. What would this man do in such a situation? Would he act as one from the other side? Or as a father?' (Interview Luanda 18 October 2005).

From the late 1990s onwards, the time of crisis, however, it became apparent that those forcibly recruited at an early age formed the backbone of UNITA's organization. During this period, the armed group's leadership collapsed. In the end, it was reduced to a close circle of people from Savimbi's Bailundo clan. The rest had either deserted to join the MPLA government or were marginalized or simply 'eliminated'.[30] Yet, this process of disintegration at the top did not directly affect the many rank and file, who were socialized into the organization. It was through the increasing number of military defeats, especially after the destruction of Jamba in 2000, that a process of decomposition set in. Disoriented and left by their leadership, UNITA troops collapsed into small units of survival. Their loyalty, however, in many cases remained unbroken until present day. Considering this raises the question of how UNITA succeeded in creating this loyalty.

'Weapon, Hoe and Pen': Forming the UNITA Combatant

Mobilizing membership by forced recruitment was of course but a first step. The constant influx of members could secure the survival of the organization, but not its efficiency as a military, political and administrative force. To succeed, a socio-structural framework conditioning the behaviour of the members according to the goals of the organization was needed. The guiding idea in creating this framework seems to have been to guard against the negative impact of the absence of social rules in the surrounding environment on the combatants' behaviour, and especially to guard against the derailing of violence.

Thus, UNITA leadership set out to regulate combatants' behaviour. Yet, most interestingly, this project of behavioural regulation was not limited to the immediate situations of battle and confrontation, but aimed instead at all domains of the combatant's life. The UNITA combatant became embedded in a milieu in which 'society' was staged, under supervision and according to the rules of the UNITA leadership.

Most rigorously, this project was realized in the military bases. In sharp contrast to the common image of armed groups, UNITA soldiers there were embedded in a civilian life of family, education and agricultural work. *Arma, inchada e lapis*, weapon, hoe and pen, were said to be the tools of the UNITA combatant. It meant that, besides participating in military campaigns, he had to attend school and to work on the fields for defined periods of time.

Even more important was the leadership's insistence on embedding its combatants within families. Each one was urged, or, if necessary, coerced, to marry and to have children (this, by the way, was the central reason why UNITA 'kidnapped' boys and girls alike). The latter were an integral part of the population of the military bases. These social structures were framed by a draconian jurisdiction, within the framework of which, for example, adultery or the abuse of women could be severely punished.

It was thus by mimicking 'normal' social life, yet under the full observance and control of the organization, that UNITA's leadership tried to reliably and durably condition the behaviour of its members and to secure thus organizational efficiency. Nowhere were those efforts more pronounced than in Jamba. UNITA's self-declared capital not only harboured the armed group's military headquarters, but was also the epicentre of its social project. It was a city with concrete roads and houses, with running water and electricity. Its medical services were well equipped and the personnel well trained. One of my interviewees proudly told me that the dentures he was wearing were made in Jamba.[31] The school system included not only primary and secondary schools, but also institutes of higher education for the armed group's high-ranking cadres. Clergymen of all major Angolan denominations provided church services and pastoral care. Hence, Jamba became the symbol of the well-ordered civilian life within UNITA. With living standards well above those in the rest of Angola, in Jamba the illusion of a civilian normality was almost perfect. The order of social life there inspired social organization in all the UNITA bases.

The administrative strategies UNITA leadership developed to condition combatant's behaviour produced a particular warrior habitus that can be observed until present day among the armed group veterans. It is dominated not so much by classical martial values such as strength and skilfulness, but by self-discipline and education. Its prototype is the high-ranking veteran, so polished in his demeanour and so elegant in his speech that his past 30 years as a military man are almost inconceivable.[32]

A survey conducted among demobilized UNITA combatants[33] in the Central Highlands, 18 months after the Luena memorandum, further illustrates the scope of the social project of this armed group: the average demobilized combatant had entered the armed group at the age of 17, had spent 17 years with UNITA, and was now around 36 years old. Some entered at a much younger age (from three years onwards), to spent their lives with the armed group. More than 90 per cent were married, most of them by common law; 81 per cent were accompanied by their spouses as they returned to the resettlement areas, 76 per cent brought children with them.[34]

A Legacy for Post-War Angola

UNITA was defeated as a military force in 2002. As a political party it was formally integrated into the Angolan government, but remained with marginal political influence. In the short run, this situation is not going to change, as in the first elections since the end of the civil war, in September 2008, UNITA had to accept the victory of the party in power. Yet, the social project of the armed group left a critical legacy to post-war Angola.

During the years of civil war, UNITA created a state within a state.[35] Of the women and men who spent their life with UNITA, many remain like aliens in today's Angolan society. Talking to ex-UNITA people, for example in Bailundo, where a large number of demobilized combatants are concentrated, is like meeting people from a different world. When they speak admiringly and full of hope about 'our president', it takes a moment of confusion to understand that the president they are talking about is dead. They appear stuck between a society that has ceased to exist and a life in a state by which they feel rejected. They feel excluded by many policies and laws. One recurrent point of dispute, for example, is the partial recognition of educational and professional degrees acquired while living with UNITA.[36] The persistent discontent of this group of people and their social as well as economic marginalization are the most important risk to social peace in post-war Angola, and should be recognized as a major challenge to policy-making.

Conclusion

In the survey cited above, 96 per cent of the 603 UNITA ex-combatants interviewed were native Umbundu speakers.[37] They thus belonged to the ethno-linguistic group said to have been the backbone of the armed group. This article, however, has shown that shared language and origins are not a sufficient explanation for the strong loyalty which can be found to the present day among many of UNITA's rank and file. The social environment of armed groups in intra-state wars is an important, yet still underestimated factor for understanding their organization and operations. The case explored here illustrates that those structures can be a valuable source, for example when engaging family or ethno-linguistic ties for attracting members or rallying support, as it had been the case with UNITA's part-time combatants and, more generally, in the early years of the armed group's existence. Yet, this article also shows how the conditions in the social environment can become obstacles to the armed group's successful operation and how strategies emerge to circumvent the latter. Most evidently, in this process armed groups come to engage with local populations. In a history of interaction, interdependencies prevail. Not only do armed groups adapt to their social environment; the social environment also changes and adapts to the presence of armed groups, as UNITA's interaction with village people in the recruitment process shows. In this sense, armed groups become important agents of social change.

During the years of civil war, UNITA created a state within a state; a society within society. Yet, in the end, the party in power prevailed. To policymakers in the post-war context, this situation poses a major challenge. To facilitate a rapprochement of the UNITA people to the majority society and the institutions of the state will take time and effort. The latter will have to be as intensive as the social project of UNITA itself had been.

NOTES

1. Interview by the author, Huambo, 19 January 2006. According to the interviewee, radio communication between pilots was sometimes received by household radios. In this way, the refusal of pilots to obey their orders had become known.
2. In a seminal study, Robert Knapp defined rumour as 'a proposition for belief of topical reference disseminated without official verification'. Robert H. Knapp, 'A Psychology of Rumor', *Public Opinion Quarterly*, Vol. 8, No. 1 (1944), p. 22. As such, rumours represent a particular form of information. Knapp also points out that war conditions foster the emergence of rumours, because official information on important events (e.g. the preparation of attacks) is scarce while at the same time the 'emotional life of the public' is intensified (p. 23).
3. If merely rumour, the function of the story would be to spread division. In Knapp's classification it would be a 'wedge-driving or aggression rumour' designed to divide groups or undermine loyalties. See Knapp, 'A Psychology of Rumor' (note 2), p. 24.
4. The research was part of a PhD project about the transformation of societies in civil wars, realized in the context of the research group 'Micropolitics of Armed Groups' at Humboldt University Berlin, Germany. During the seven months of field research in Angola data was collected chiefly through interviews, complemented by the study of archival material accessible in Huambo.
5. The works of Carolyn Nordstrom are the most prominent examples in this regard (see especially Carolyn Nordstrom, *A Different Kind of War Story* (Philidelphia: University of Pennsylvania Press, 1997); Carolyn Nordstrom, *Shadows of War. Violence, Power, and International Profiteering in the Twenty-First Century* (Berkley: University of California Press, 2007). In the eye of the political scientist, the anthropologist's advantage in gathering information is often outweighed by a certain conceptual weakness. Yet, works such Stephen Lubkemann's study on Mozambique show that anthropological research might very well indicate strong conceptual propositions. See Stephen C. Lubkemann, *Culture in Chaos: An Anthropology of the Social Condition in War* (Chicago, IL: University of Chicago Press, 2008).
   or Ivana Maček's works on Sarajevo that shows that this is not necessarily the case. See Ivana Maček, 'Predicament of war: Sarajevo experiences and ethics of war', in Bettina E. Schmidt and Ingo W. Schröder (eds), *Anthropology of Violence and Conflict* (London, New York: Routledge, 2001); Ivana Maček, 2007. 'Imitation of Life. Negotiating Normality in Sarajevo under siege', In: Xavier Bougarel, Elissa Helms, and Ger Duijzings (eds.), *The new Bosnian mosaic. Identities, memories and moral claims in a post-war society* (Aldershot: Ashgate, 2007).
6. Ted Robert Gurr, *Why Men Rebel* (Princeton, NJ: Princeton University Press, 1970).
7. Stathis Kalyvas, 'The Ontology of Political Violence' Action and Identity in Civil Wars', *Perspectives on Politics*, Vol. 1, No. 3 (2003), pp. 475–94.
8. Stathis Kalyvas, *The Logic of Violence in Civil Wars* (Cambridge: Cambridge University Press, 2000).
9. Charles Tilly, *The Formation of National States in Western Europe* (Princeton, NJ: Princeton University Press, 1975).
10. Joel S. Migdal, *State In Society. Studying How States and Societies Transform and Constitute Each Other* (Cambridge: Cambridge University Press, 2001).

11. For detailed overview on the period of anti-colonial struggle until the end of the post-colonial transition John Marcum's two-volume oeuvre *The Angolan Revolution* remains unmatched. John A. Marcum, *The Angolan Revolution, Vol. I: The Anatomy of an explosion 1950–1962* (London: MIT Press, 1969); John A. Marcum, *The Angolan Revolution, Vol. II: Exile Politics and Guerrilla Warfare 1962–1976* (London: MIT Press, 1978), pp. 318–20. A recent contribution focussing on comba-tant-civilian relations during this period is Inge Brinkman's study of Southern Angola: *A War for People. Civilians, Mobility, and Legitimacy in South-east Angola during the MPLA's War for Independence* (Köln: Rüdiger Köppe, 2005).
12. Academic writing on the Angolan civil war mirrors the state of world politics as well as conceptual developments in the field of conflict studies sciences. During the Cold War, the conflict was described either as terms of collective deprivation. See for example: W. Martin James, *A Political History of the Civil War In Angola 1974–1990* (New Brunswick, NJ: The East-South Relations Series, Transaction Publishers, 1992). It has also been denounced as a proxy war launched and maintained by imperialistic powers; see for example George Wright, *The Destruction of a Nation. United State's Policy Towards Angola since 1945* (London and Chicago, IL: Pluto Press, 1997).
    From the late 1990s onwards, attention moved to the economic dimension of the conflict. See for example: Tony Hodges, *Angola. From Afro-Stalinism to Petro-Diamond Capitalism* (Bloomington: Indiana University Press, 2001); Assis Malaquias, *Rebels and Robbers. Violence in Post-colonial Angola* (Uppsala: Nordiska Afrikainstitutet, 2007). For a detailed (yet not impartial) reconstruction of the military events until 1991 see Edward George, *The Cuban Intervention in Angola, 1965–1991. From Che Guevara to Cuito Cuanavale* (London and New York: Frank Cass, 2005). For the denunciation of the conflict as a proxy war launched and maintained by imperialistic powers, see: for example Wright, *The Destruction of a Nation* (note 13). From the late 1990s onwards, attention moved to the economic dimension of the conflict. See for example Hodges, *Angola. From Afro-Stalinism to Petro-Diamond Capitalism* and Malaquias, *Rebels and Robbers* (above). For a detailed (yet not impartial) reconstruction of the military events until 1991, see George, *The Cuban Intervention in Angola* (above).
13. The date, 1956, refers to the foundation of the FNLA's principal predecessor, the UPNA (União das Populações do Norte de Angola – Union of the Northern People of Angola), renamed UPA (União das Populações de Angola – Union of the People of Angola) in 1958.
14. From the outset, the broader Angolan liberation movement had been fragmented into panoply of organizations. FNLA and MPLA were but the tip of an iceberg. In what he calls 'a partial list of Angolan nationalist movements', John Marcum names 86 organizations for the period 1962–1976 alone. See Marcum, *The Angolan Revolution*, Vol. II (note 12), pp. 318–20.
15. GRAE – Govêrno revolucionário de Angola no exílio.
16. Marcum, *The Angolan Revolution* (note 12), pp. 161–7.
17. Linda M. Heywood, *Contested Power in Angola, 1840s to the Present* (Rochester, NY: University of Rochester Press, 2000), pp. 154–5.
18. Interview by the author, Huambo, 30 December 2005.
19. George, *The Cuban Intervention in Angola* (note 13), p. 193.
20. Ibid.
21. The Minorities At Risk Project, for example, listed UNITA as a 'communal contender'. See Ted Robert Gurr, and James R. Scarritt, 'Minorities Rights at Risk: A Global Survey', *Human Rights Quarterly*, Vol. 11, No. 3 (1989). For a more differentiated discussion of the issue see Linda M. Heywood, 'UNITA and Ethnic Nationalism in Angola', *The Journal of Modern African Studies*, Vol. 27, No. 1 (1989).
22. Klaus Schlichte, *In the Shadow of Violence. The Micropolitics of Armed Groups* (Frankfurt/M: Campus, 2009).
23. Interview by the author, Huambo, 30 December 2005.
24. Inge Brinkman, 'War and Identity in Angola. Two Case Studies', *Lusotopie* (2003), pp. 195–222.
25. Interview by the author, Huambo, 30 January 2006.
26. For more on the relationship between 'physical' space and social order see: Pierre Bourdieu, 'Physischer, sozialer und angeeigneter physischer Raum', in Martin Wenz (ed.), *Stadt-Räume* (Frankfurt/Main: Campus, 1991). For a modified version in English, see Pierre Bourdieu, 'Site effects', in Pierre Bourdieu (ed.), *The Weight of the World. Social Suffering in Contemporary Society* (Oxford and Stanford, CA: Polity Press and Oxford University Press, 1999).
27. Interview by the author, Bailundo 24 March 2006. The interviewee had joined UNITA in 1979 and was demobilized in 2002.

28. See for example Médecins sans frontières (MSF) (ed.), *Voices from the Silence. Testimonies from Angola* (Toronto: MSF, 2004).
29. Interview by the author, village km25, 1 December 2005.
30. Fred Bridgland, 'Savimbi et l'exercice du pouvoir. Un témoignage', *Politique Africaine*, No. 57 (1995), pp. 94–102.
31. Interview by author, Huambo, 30 December 2005.
32. Teresa Koloma Beck and Klaus Schlichte, 'Nature and Civilization in the Habitus of the Warrior', *Working Papers Micropolitics 1*. Working Paper series of the research group *The Micropolitics of Armed Groups*, Humboldt University Berlin, 2007.
33. Note that the vast majority of those considered as 'combatants' who could thus register for demobilization (95 per cent in the cited survey) were men, in spite of the fact that most of UNITA's women have been combatants in the broader sense, providing rear support as porters, cooks, etc. See: João Gomes Porto, Imogen Parsons, and Chris Alden. *From Soldiers to Citizens. The Social, Economic and Political Reintegration of UNITA Ex-Combatants*. ISS Monograph Series No. 130, Institute for Security Studies, Tshwane, 2007, pp. 40–1.
34. Ibid., chapter 2.
35. See also Jutta Bakonyi and Kirsti Stuvøy, 'Violence & Social Order beyond the State: Somalia & Angola', *Review of African Political Economy*, Vol. 32, No. 104/105 (2005).
36. Interviews by the author, Bailundo, 24 March 2006.
37. Porto et al., *From Soldiers to Citizens* (note 34), p. 41.

Explaining Patterns of Violence in Collapsed States

WILLIAM RENO

Imagine the shock of an African time-traveller coming from an anti-colonial struggle to a recent war. Our visitor might wonder why insurgents now toss aside strategies and resources that could help them overthrow governments and take power. The conversation might come around to why these insurgents seem to be so disinterested in offering political programs to mobilize local populations to fight with them against governments, that most people view their rulers as corrupt and oppressive. Why do they not try to build effective insurgent administrations – 'liberated zones' – and instead forego access to local information, willing recruits, and social institutions that could be applied to subvert enemy control and strengthen their own positions? Why not articulate ideological goals that attract aid from foreigners?

Analyses of predatory violence that stress individual fighters' pursuits of short-term opportunities for enrichment explain why insurgents seem so uninterested in taking time to propagandize, recruit, and organize local populations to fight. This behaviour produces real consequences. Fighting in Sierra Leone in 1999 over diamond mines displaced about 30 per cent of the country's population.[1] Loot and the quest for power drove fighting in neighbouring Liberia, where five years earlier about 30 per cent of the population had fled the country.[2] International efforts to resolve this kind of conflict often aim to sever this link between resources, conflict, and these short-term goals.

Alongside this mayhem, our time-traveller might see something familiar in recent landscapes of conflict. Congo's diamond-mining area in the south-central region has enjoyed relative order and peace when compared to violence in the resource-rich east. As early as 1993, young men in some of Sierra Leone's diamond-mining communities organized to protect local people from the predations of the Revolutionary United Front (RUF) and marauding army units, even though young men from similar circumstances in communities not far away joined in the scramble for loot. Violence in Nigeria's Niger Delta is uneven, with some communities able to control armed young men while others become their targets. Meanwhile, predation appears in conflicts where it would seem that there are few opportunities for enrichment, as in periods of Somalia's turmoil and in fighting in Chad and Central African Republic.

Despite this variation in behaviour, Weinstein is largely correct that 'rebel groups that emerge amidst abundant natural resources or with the external support of an outside patron tend to commit high levels of indiscriminate violence'. Quick opportunities do attract certain kinds of people and shape how they organize and how they fight.[3] But even though the cases in which observed behaviour does not bear out these assumptions may be relatively few, I argue that they are disproportionately important. These critical cases rarely turn up in analyses that link local resources to propensities for predation. This is partly because these conflicts are more limited, or because islands of order are subsumed under the labels that are applied to wider conflicts. The absence of predation, or even more interesting from a methodological point of view, its control once it begins, should interest policymakers and scholars. This behaviour may indicate the construction of new institutions that contribute to post-conflict stability such that people with guns obey people without guns. Historically this obedience to community leadership or to political cadres has been integral to the mobilization of insurgents with political programs and liberated zones, and ultimately, the creation of new versions of state authority.

I consider this variation in degrees and uses of violence and provide a framework to explain relations between conflict and resources. The argument below is that extremes of predation are consequences of particular pre-conflict political strategies and the local political economies that they created in the patronage-based political systems that account for the bulk of Africa's recent conflicts. These political strategies produced militarized forms of clandestine commerce and other rent-seeking activities that enjoyed support from key state officials. Though these officials and their associates enjoyed access to the prerogatives of sovereign statehood, their authority was not based upon conventional notions of legitimacy or imposed through bureaucratic administration. Instead, they manipulated markets, especially in natural resources and cross-border trade, to control other people's access to economic opportunities to enhance their power. This strategy focused on monopolizing formal and informal economic channels to limit the autonomy of other social groups outside the influence of this political network.

This analysis is based upon two key observations. First, state collapse is directly connected to the fragmentation or decentralization of the kind of patronage politics described above. The analysis of violence in this essay is focused on this particular context, which encompasses a significant portion of the cases of large-scale violence in sub-Saharan Africa in the last two decades, most of which show a direct evolution in the uses of violence to control markets as a way of asserting power over communities and to limit threats to that power. Second, my explanation of varied outcomes rests on an empirical analysis of local elements of this political economy that shape the relationships between political authority, resources, and coercion. These relationships in turn influence the interests of key actors. Thus the organization of pre-conflict patronage networks in these places loom large in this analysis. The analysis links wartime variations in the behaviour of armed groups and degrees of community control of them in the earlier differences in the degrees to which local political bosses were integrated into or had to defend themselves against prewar political networks that were centred in the capital city.

These observations generate two propositions: First, those who were most marginal to prewar networks had to deal with other local authorities, including customary leaders such as elders and whoever else could guarantee commercial transactions and other deals outside of the hostile reach of state administration and its grasping political networks. These local relationships put more constraints on how these strongmen could mobilize fighters and use violence once conflicts broke out. Second, regions that were more closely connected to prewar capital-based patronage networks were more likely to host predatory armed groups. Local commanders there operated with less constraint from local authorities, since they could rely on the favour of their patrons in the capital to get resources. Even though this argument rests upon findings that do not fit most analyses of the behaviour of armed groups, it accepts core propositions concerning the rational nature of insurgents and other actors. Nonetheless, it arrives at new conclusions through adding to the analysis the details of the political economies of state collapse.

Rational Predators and the Importance of Group Organization

Explaining the behaviour of individual insurgents in terms of responses to available opportunities is useful. Longer-term motives do not feature in most recent scholarship that explains why people fight or how they fight. While it was once thought that decades of stagnant or falling per capita incomes in many countries, inequality, and widespread frustration with official corruption that generates significant gaps between expectations and opportunities would cause political violence,[4] frustration in and of itself does not seem to explain why people fight. Otherwise, Africa would have a lot more wars. An alternative is the 'looting model of rebellion' in which 'opportunities are more important in explaining conflict than are motives',[5] a proposition that informs Weinstein's work noted above. Collier and Hoeffler's analysis of 78 civil conflicts between 1960 and 1999 confirms that the availability of natural resources provides such opportunities. Others point to a wider range of opportunities directed at individuals, such as increased access to small arms and easier access to lucrative global criminal networks, which enable insurgents to grab resources without taking into account the interests of local communities.[6] These resources make the insurgent organizations attractive to self-interested recruits who personally benefit from conflict.

Non-academic observers of some of Africa's recent conflicts also identify opportunist impulses.[7] John Hirsch, the US ambassador to Sierra Leone at the height of its 1991–2002 war, wrote of the leader of the RUF: 'Documents taken from Sankoh's residence revealed his flagrant disregard of the Lomé Agreement's ban on illegal mining... he was continuing to systematically exploit the country's diamonds for his personal benefit.'[8] Eyewitnesses reported that they saw fighters who were prone to excessive violence and who used disorder to improve their personal lot. 'Death and humiliation puts the genuine adults and achievers into their shells', wrote a refugee from the Liberian conflict. 'The vacuum is them filled in by the young ones who become daredevils, not caring about death or any related end. For them, chance (and not age, valuable time and energy) creates material wealth.'[9]

Most versions of the 'looting model' do not reject out of hand that insurgents might care about some element of community interests. Collier and Hoeffler point out: 'Opportunity can account for the existence of either for-profit, or not-for-profit, rebel organizations.'[10] That is, insurgents need resources to field fighters, whether they pursue the economic interests of members or seek some broad political goal. But then, Weinstein explains, opportunists show up among initial recruits attracted by the promise of loot and force leaders to permit indiscipline as the only way to maintain even minimal organizational control.[11] This entrenches a path dependent course as fighters' behaviour alienates local people and drives away what he calls investors, or political activists. These opportunities engage calculating and ideologically flexible personalities such as the head of the National Patriotic Front of Liberia (NPFL), Charles Taylor, who was willing to take risks and use violence to gain his position. The murders early in the conflict of popular civilian political leaders and charismatic commanders, allegedly on Taylor's orders, point to the threats that ideologues with political programs encounter when materially motivated rivals appear. Taylor was good at getting resources to buy guns and attract followers while rivals tried to mobilize people on the basis of political programs. Ideologues might have offered better long-term prospects for individual and group success, but ultimately Taylor's short-term gains crowded out their efforts to organize people around a political program.

Every insurgency has to find means of support and individuals seeking personal gain have always exploited opportunities in these enterprises, and thus looting and other personally aggrandizing activities have appeared in wars throughout history.[12] But, though opportunity clearly is an important element shaping insurgents' behaviour, motivation may be a less productive analytical avenue, at least for reaching beyond proximate causes. A hint of this may be found in the surprise that this researcher encounters when explaining to insurgents, including rather violent ones, that some scholars in America think that political grievances are relatively unimportant in causing conflicts. Political scientists who study public opinion in more settled circumstances also cast doubt on the primacy of calculations of personal gain. They, along with pollsters, expect that attitudes change in ways that are meaningful for the conduct of politics, and that this varies over time and context. For these scholars, framing of issues matter a great deal in how individuals respond to opportunities.

Scholars of insurgencies once placed greater stock in socio-political context as a sort of framing that shaped how motivations and group behaviour were connected. Building on Maoist ideas, Eric Wolf explained how cohesive, disciplined insurgencies developed out of what he called 'fields of leverage'. These were the places where people experienced the intrusion of the state and 'capitalist imperialism' (local rebels' label for 'globalization'), yet were removed enough from it that ideologues could organize their anger and instil in them a commitment to overthrowing the established order.[13] These political spaces, relatively abundant in Sub-Saharan Africa at the end of colonial rule, have become harder to find where patron-client networks and politician-led rackets and their co-opting tendencies have taken over from state institutions as a primary basis for exercising authority. These places also host many of Africa's recent conflicts.

James Scott focused on the importance of these 'fields of leverage'. He explained that people join insurgencies for all kinds of reasons. They want revenge against a neighbour who stole their girlfriend, protection for their family, income, status, or they may seek excitement. It is the role of 'commissars' to aggregate these diverse motives and convince a critical mass of these people to fight for a political program or idea. Thus diverse insurgencies can recruit from pools of people who are similar in terms of individuals' susceptibilities to material or ideological appeals. Commissars turn them into committed followers through exploiting circumstances and instil codes of conduct and enforce rules.[14] This supports Kalyvas's observation that violence is endogenous to civil wars, and that 'political actors use violence to achieve multiple, overlapping and sometimes mutually contradictory goals'.[15]

Scott's commissar-ideologues require 'fields of leverage' to emerge. In the mid 20th century Africa, insurgent leaders and their commissars typically came from universities. Universities provided the bulk of leaders in anti-colonial rebellions and in insurgencies that gained power in Uganda, Rwanda, Ethiopia, and Eritrea. Universities suffered under government repression and externally engineered economic austerity programs in the 1980s considerably hindered their capacities to play these old political roles. While one does not need professors to lead a rebellion, it helps to have a political space where ideologues can make plans and recruit followers and figure out how to control the opportunists before the shooting starts. In contrast, opportunism plays a central role in the organization of violence where strongmen build their authority on controlling people's access to economic opportunities, including even illicit commerce. The bosses of these networks and their associates who use violence to regulate other people's access to markets find themselves in the best positions to acquire weapons and attract followers. This is why proximity of communities and local notables to centres of prewar patronage is associated with the scarcity of program-driven insurgencies in wartime, as noted in the propositions in the last section.

Social structures are central to this explanation. Resources in Wolf's and Scott's 'fields of leverage' sustained ideological insurgencies in other times and places, including in Africa. But now the political networks of collapsing states – collapsing from the perspective of formal institutions or a moral duty to serve a public good – undermine prewar leaders with real popular appeal. The Movement for Justice in Africa, a pan-Africanist group active in Liberia in the 1970s and 1980s, and Congo's democratic opposition led by Étienne Tshisekedi were highly successful at mobilizing people. But these and other groups were unable to disrupt or redirect the material resources upon which the personalist dictatorships they opposed were built, so they ultimately played minor roles in the conflicts of the 1990s in those countries.

Anton Blok showed in his studies of mafia politics in Sicily how particular kinds of relationships between patronage, resources, and the uses of violence can monopolize political space. Local Sicilian landowners and politicians used their links to the mafia to consolidate their power. Both of these groups employed young men from the communities that they exploited. This was a clever strategy, for 'rather than actual champions of the poor and weak, bandits quite often terrorized those from whose very ranks they managed to rise, and thus helped to suppress them'.[16] They used violence in the service of predation to exploit opportunities for personal gain. For Blok, the available resources are incidental as the appearance of violent organizations, such as mafias, create their own rent-seeking possibilities. Protection rackets, permission to outsiders to dump toxic wastes, and hiding fugitives are like diamond mines for the resource-poor. It is more important how these social relationships develop and how they shape uses of violence than what particular resources are under or above the ground. Different social relationships channel resources differently, a banal but necessary observation.

Blok did not find that outright opportunism drove Sicily's violent politics. Instead, people joined organizations became they wanted to become clients of strongmen with good connections to corrupt state officials and mafiosi. This was a reasonable path of upward mobility for young men in rural areas where state officials were in league with criminals. Even those who hated this situation and who complained about corruption realized that they had to hone their skills of violence if they were to be useful to potential patrons. Patrons in turn used their status and connections to the state – true of mafiosi as much as for state officials – to give clients selective access to opportunities in the regional and global economy and to protect them and their families from other predators. Local notables and not bandits or their families were the real beneficiaries of plunder. Predation in Sicily had political causes. It followed from conscious efforts on the part of those in power to limit people's political options in an age of rising mass engagement in politics and to tie young men to hierarchies of state and non-state authority.[17]

An advantage of looking at violence in insurgencies in this fashion is that one can explain group behaviour without having to assume that a person's opportunist propensities are fixed or that these personal motives inevitably drive organizational behaviour. This insight is useful for explaining variation in the behaviour of insurgents who have similar resource opportunities. This variation is manifest in a sharp rise in the appearance of certain kinds of predatory insurgencies in Sub-Saharan Africa in the 1990s. Diamonds have been mined by hand in Sierra Leone, Congo, and Angola for a long time, but fighting in these places before the 1990s appeared to outsiders to be driven by popular anti-colonial sentiments, anger at arbitrary exploitation by local authorities, and so forth. The collapse of formal bureaucratic institutions is important in unchaining opportunism, but that does not account for the variable levels of discipline and order or the degree of articulation of political programs in the micro-politics of subsequent conflicts.

The relative dearth of predatory insurgencies elsewhere sheds light on the central role of pre-conflict patronage networks, especially those that take over from formal bureaucratic state agencies as primary vehicles for exercising authority, in shaping conflicts. Lebanon and Palestinian Gaza can be seen as 'failed states' from an institutional perspective. Both experienced colonial rule. Clans figure in violence, as in Somalia and Sudan. Illicit commerce in many cases is linked to the influence of politicians. There are also a lot of armed young men who are responsible for internecine violence. These should be great places for opportunists. Yet most people there do not fight like most contemporary African insurgents. HAMAS won a free election in Gaza in which it mobilized a lot of willing supporters. Hezbollah fighters showed enough discipline and cooperation to beat Israel's army in 2006 and have become a virtual state-within-a-state in Lebanon, a 'liberated zone' if one prefers 1970s lingo.

Can insurgents give up predatory opportunities? Afghanistan's Taliban cut opium production in areas they controlled to just four per cent of a year earlier by the fateful

11 September 2001, foregoing an income of $100 million, even while they fought the Northern Alliance.[18] Perhaps Taliban tried to restrict supplies to raise the price of drugs. Even if this was so, Taliban showed that its members were not slaves to immediate gains. Foregoing this income in the face of military pressure indicated that the group could control short-term opportunistic impulses among followers. It could shape the behaviour of agents who came out of a fractured, predatory pre-Taliban conflict and who might have wanted to continue serving their individual interests in this lucrative resource-driven economy. This discipline, a reversal of an opportunity-fuelled path dependent predation, was an impressive feat, especially given the subsequent return of some local warlords to these opportunities once Taliban was chased out of cities and towns after 2001. What distinguished Taliban from *most* contemporary African insurgencies?

Taliban utilized its legitimacy and its ties to indigenous social structures to establish a broader social basis for its power. Taliban's pronouncements emphasized public goods of a sort – a religious society that does not engage in sins like drug trafficking, for example. It also is likely that Taliban leaders really did fear that local strongmen might divert proceeds from the drug trade to assert their local authority against Taliban. Even if Taliban members really were opportunists, Taliban's decisions and means looked very different from Sierra Leone's predatory RUF or Liberia's NPFL, even though all operated in factionalized societies with extremely weak state institutions in which clan and regional political networks were important. Taliban was both self-interested and capable of providing public goods in terms of generating benefits that were greater than the individual interests of its members.[19] The organization also had to deal with local strongmen who commanded authority in their own right. Attention to their interests and priorities were important elements of Taliban's strategy of control, even as the group pursued its goals in the illicit drug economy.

This variation in insurgent behaviours beyond Africa and across seemingly similar circumstances shows how context matters, particularly the how local networks of authority control the use of resources and those who benefit from them. If leaders shape and direct the interests of fighters while other groups with similar cultural and material backgrounds engage in wanton predation, this contrast suggests the presence of an underlying factor that a focus on individual motives obscures. This underlying factor is the pre-conflict social context, to which I turn next.

Coercion, Violence and the Political Economy of Collapsing States

Most regimes in Africa adhere to the pronouncement in Article III, Paragraph 3 of the charter of the Organization of African States (now African Union) that all 'Respect for the sovereignty and territorial integrity of each State' as mapped by colonial rulers out of a fear that challenging existing borders would expose all to counterclaims.[20] International recognition of even the weakest states created what Robert Jackson called 'quasi-states' with 'governments [that] are often deficient in the political will, institutional authority, and organized power to protect human rights or provide socio-economic welfare'.[21] Jackson showed that exemption from external threats had direct bearing on the role of coercion and violence in these political communities and gave many post-colonial rulers licence to undermine the rule of law.

Threats were mainly internal as many rulers feared that rivals might hijack effective state agencies as bases to attract followings. These rulers were reluctant to build strong institutions to which they would have to delegate authority.[22] This threat was real. More than two-thirds of African countries have experienced violent transitions of government, a trend that has recent political reforms have not halted.[23] Since 1990, elections helped spark violence in Kenya, Congo-Brazzaville, Nigeria, Tanzania, Guinea-Bissau, and Côte d'Ivoire. Between 2000 and 2006, internal wars produced at least 1,000 deaths in 14 of Africa's 52 countries.[24] Coups and contested transitions affected Mauritania, Guinea, and Madagascar over just 12 months in 2008–2009. Rulers facing such threats are inclined to preempt even potential competitors.

Thus sprawling patronage networks replaced failing state bureaucracies and services that were taken as indicators of state collapse in the 1990s. With time, patronage politics moved deep into commercial, religious, generational and other realms that once harboured Wolf's 'field of leverage'. This kind of political patronage may have been conceived as a means of integrating diverse groups into regime politics. But this private use of state office had a destructive impact on economies and non-state social organizations. What Joseph calls a prebend became the focus of power in the private realm too, and undermines other forms of authority.[25] It is networked with overseas economies, political cliques in neighbouring countries, and clandestine commercial networks. These networks can be difficult to control and generate violent battles for spoils once the political centre's power wanes.

Rulers at first focused on manipulating economic regulations and distributing state assets to political allies, including those who could mobilize violence – youth gangs and paramilitary forces – on behalf of the regime. Immediate political priorities came to trump interests in economic efficiency, and formal economies dwindled and state revenues shrank. Politicians then extended their economic activities to clandestine markets. State office gave rulers the capacity to declare activities illegal and then sell exemption from prosecution to political favourites to accumulate wealth while still using the law to punish opponents. Poor economic conditions contributed to the short-term stability of this system, since regime critics and even the politically passive had to consider integrating into these political networks to secure exemption from insecurity and want, much like Blok's Sicilian peasants in search of upward mobility. A striking feature of states like Congo, Sierra Leone, Liberia, and Nigeria from the 1970s was the extent to which market control replaced state administration as means of dominating people and to which misery and obvious corruption did not translate into broad-based social movements or rebellion.

Common measures of corruption shed light on the political role of patronage. The table below compares country standings on Transparency International's corruption perceptions index, the World Bank's measure of per capita growth, and the UN Development Programme's measure of citizens' well being. While neither Senegal nor Tanzania is a collapsed state, both show that corruption is associated with anaemic growth and poor well-being. The surprise is that corruption in China and in Vietnam is compatible with economic growth and citizens' well-being, unlike in Africa.[26]

Why is corruption compatible with economic growth in East Asia? That is like asking why individual opportunism in parts of Sierra Leone and the Niger Delta is compatible with community-based insurgencies in a few instances. David Kang explains this East Asian compatibility in terms of 'crony capitalists' and rulers mutually benefit from strong state institutions and rising state capacity to lay claim to societal resources. They use their informal relationships to distribute economic opportunities on the basis of personal loyalties. This is not the most economically efficient arrangement, but it preserves the bonds of mutual interests in policies that promote economic efficiency within the bounds of favouritism.[27] East Asian crony capitalists resemble Olson's 'stationary bandits' in which victims gain some leverage over predatory rulers.[28] In these instances, greedy rulers recognize that promoting the long-term prosperity of their 'victims' increases available resources. But if coups are a real threat and tend to be more violent than a typical Thai affair, as has been the case in Africa, partners are dangerous and political allies should not be too popular or dependent on their local communities.

In most weak and collapsing states, patron-client relationships are highly unequal. This is reflected in the political economies of some states such as Congo (Zaire), Liberia, Sierra Leone and Somalia where rulers took steps that predictably resulted in dramatic damage to their societies' economic prospects. This diminished their own access to resources in gross terms, though not relative to real or potential rivals. From the perspective of patrons with insufficient institutional or social tools for controlling people, this keeps beneficiaries insecure and dependent on the largesse of the ruler. Impoverishment reinforces the exclusivity of this relationship, giving the ruler the capacity to sell selective exemption from the negative consequences that the ruler's own choices created and undermines 'fields of leverage' based upon societal groups' own control over resources.

Regimes that exercise authority through this organization of patronage fail in large part to consistently provide public goods such as order to wider society. Abjuring the task of providing order, whether through repression or willing compliance, undermines prospects that rulers will provide other public goods. In any event, asserting an exclusive right to exercise violence in order to provide public goods is an essential element of governance.[29] Its contrast is found in racketeers who create disorder so as to charge individuals for exemption from harm and thus are unwilling

TABLE 1
COMPARING CORRUPTION AND PERFORMANCE

	TI: Corruption Index	World Bank: Per capita economic growth	UNDP: Human Development Index
Senegal	71 (not too bad)	2.1%	156
Tanzania	94	3.9%	159 (horrible!)
China	72	9.2%	81 (getting by)
Vietnam	123 (just awful)	6.3%	105

to provide order to all. Effective racketeers have incentives to be especially violent and destructive. This prevents other groups from recruiting victims as their own clients and limits the chances that people will accidentally receive security for free. In extreme cases, one must chose the 'right' protector to survive, and cannot simply withdraw.[30] Following this logic, one may identify some 'quasi-state' regimes that might actually be more like racketeers than like governments, if one defines the latter in Hobbes' and Olsen's senses as providers of public goods.

Like racketeers, rulers who preside over collapsed states make citizens poorer and less secure as they control as much economic opportunity as possible, including clandestine varieties, and then sell exemption from harm to individuals who have something to offer the regime. Experts in violence often find niches in these regimes. They can trade these skills for access to commercial networks to join what are essentially violent private commercial syndicates, like Blok's mafia–*patron* networks. From this perspective, whether one fights in a context where providers of public goods or racketeers hold sway shapes how violence is organized and used in relation to non-combatants.

In extreme cases, the fusion of violence, political power, and commerce can overwhelm alternative forms of politics, For example, UN investigators estimated that commercial transactions under Liberian President Charles Taylor's personal control, mostly diamond and logging deals that financed his personal networks of armed gangs and supported his associates, were about five times larger than Liberia's official budget in 2001 and 25 times greater than Liberia's domestic revenues that year.[31] Likewise, Zimbabwe's economically disastrous policies benefit a political clique. With access to a national bank and official documents and passports that foreign officials accept as legitimate, the president's personal allies dominate the economy. Economic contraction reinforces the position of these presidential associates and enhances the president's control over them. They are so tightly bound to his political network that his death may prove fatal to them too. What is important is not that political turmoil and conflict generates predation. The novelty of predation in contemporary cases like this lies in its social context, especially the shared interests in organizations that forego the benefits that even their unilateral provision of public goods can provide, and I argue next that this is directly relevant to the variation in the behaviour of insurgents.

Violence, Opportunism and Public Goods

Contemporary norms of sovereignty tell us little about whether insurgents or states provide more public goods. The self-styled Republic of Somaliland has built a relatively stable political order that taxes and regulates commerce, yet no other government accords it the status of a sovereign state. Its leadership reined in local warlords and militias by the mid 1990s and provides citizens with a measure of personal security beyond that in many recognized states. UN investigators reported that 'Somaliland security forces are paid and equipped principally with tax revenues raised by the administration' and were able to maintain order throughout most of Somaliland's territory, while the armed forces of the globally recognized government based in

Somalia's old capital were 'disorganized and undisciplined, and to a large extent function as semi-autonomous militias'.[32]

Insurgents also can protect communities in spite of international failure to recognize this. The decision of the UN-mandated Special Court in Sierra Leone to indict the head of an ethnic militia, the Civil Defense Forces (CDF), for human rights abuses drew local criticism. Protestors argued, 'Chief Hinga Norman stayed to confront the rebels and renegade soldiers... without his contribution and tenacity, the rebels would not have come to the peace table and would have still been in the city, killing and maiming at will.'[33] Though responsible for considerable violations of human rights, the CDF battled elements of the government's army that had joined Revolutionary United Front (RUF) fighters in their 'Operation No Living Thing' attack on the capital in 1999. In the space of a week the RUF coalition killed about 250 policemen and targeted law offices and other state and private institutions of public order.[34] As the indictment was made public, the militia's second-in-command offered to assist efforts to stem incursions of Liberian fighters, reflecting the opinions of many that the CDF was better able to protect the country than was the government army.[35]

Data from Sierra Leone indicate that differences in the behaviour of insurgents were systematic. RUF was responsible for 60 per cent of over 40,000 violations of human rights where perpetrators were known that postwar researchers were able to collect. The national army and its renegade factions were responsible for 18.1 per cent of these violations, and CDF fighters committed six per cent of these violations.[36] More telling is the ratio of violations committed against children. CDF fighters committed one violation against a child (age 17 or younger) for every 11.83 violations against adults. The RUF's ratio was 3.89 adult victims for every child victim,[37] indicating that RUF fighters either operated beyond the discipline of their commanders or that the insurgency intentionally focused violence against people who might reasonably be considered non-combatants. This is not to say that CDF fighters were innocent of human rights abuses. Instead, these data draw attention to different uses of violence.

Different uses of violence among armed groups reflect the influences of the social institutions shaping the opportunities available to armed actors. These institutions can include clan and ethnic associations, bureaucratic remnants of collapsing states, clandestine business arrangements, and diaspora networks. Their relationships are central to determining who controls coercion and how it is exercised. Building on the propositions above, the empirical evidence provides a framework to explain variations in the uses of resources and violence, including by insurgents that arise as political order breaks down. They contextualize the exercise of coercion, distinguishing between violence in the pursuit of personal interests and that which is tied in some way to deals with local communities. This approach does not automatically identify resources, including clandestine and illicit rackets, as causes of predation. Instead it shows how resources fit into or change social relationships between insurgents and communities.

Political actors may use clandestine economic networks, such as in diamonds that are usually associated with predation and chaos can be used in ways that can include providing order. If these actors exercise enough control over these resources, they can starve violent political entrepreneurs of resources that they need to mobilize alternative sets of followers. Control of this sort is more sustainable if entrenched local political networks, such as 'traditional' or religious authorities, youth initiation societies and the like, dominate clandestine commercial operations. Moreover, actors are more likely to use these resources to provide public goods if they have been marginal to pre-conflict political networks based in the capital. This is because local strongmen and other would-be warlords who were not intimates of old capital-based cliques have to rely upon local authorities as alternatives to presidential protection.

These variations in how resources are used in violent conflicts suggest that it may be a bad idea *in some instances* to block certain clandestine trades. Sanctioning certain armed actors might reduce short-term violence, but risk strengthening predatory groups or individuals if targets of sanctions were providing communities with order. International actors often ignore informal local authorities and officials of seemingly low status who do not speak a European language or lack social practices that outsiders associate with authority. Yet they may exercise social control over significant resources and prove crucial to restoring order. In southwest Nigeria, for example, certain elderly ladies play critical roles in the organization and control of urban vigilante groups.[38]

Details of the social backgrounds of armed groups illustrate the variable nature of violence. In Somalia, for example, President Siad Barre (1969–1991) built a political network from the late 1970s through distributing parts of the formal and clandestine economy to strongmen who he thought he could trust and through manipulating bonds of shared kinship and clan to exercise power. Suspicious of his own state's institutions after losing a war against Ethiopia in 1978 and surviving a coup attempt in 1979, he financed this alliance through skimming foreign aid and exploiting creditor-mandated land tenure reforms to distribute land to his political allies. The president used a political calculus in handing out these resources, offering some political allies opportunities to exploit places outside their home areas. Their tendency to bring along private militias made up of otherwise unemployed youth insulated them from the social consequences of their predations since they owed their power to the president's favour and were insulated from local customary sanctions for anti-social behaviour. Their autonomy from the obligation to heed local community interests gave them opportunities to construct violent and exploitative quasi-commercial operations, at least with regard to people outside of their immediate networks. Had these presidential clients been more selective in their opportunism, they might have strengthened their positions through recruiting local followers through mobilizing popular grievances. But the president was careful to punish any among his associates who showed signs of becoming popular outside of their own circumscribed social or kinship group.

Those on the margins of the old president's political networks faced difficulties in pursuing this predatory strategy. Some were on the wrong side of old political battles or drew presidential suspicion because of their kinship ties. As among backers of the old Somali Youth League that the army had overthrown in 1969 when the dictator came to power, their political marginalization forced them to organize their own clandestine economic activities outside 'official' illicit activities. Unable to secure presidential protection, some local strongmen, especially those who remained in the area that later became the Republic of Somaliland, turned to turn to kinship networks for protection and local elders to guarantee and adjudicate business agreements. The decision of the Ethiopian government to kick their militias out of Ethiopia in 1988 from which others had opposed the president's regime reinforced this dependency of armed groups after members of this group lost their foreign patron. In the opinions of some leaders of the Somali National Movement (SNM), the Ethiopian decision strengthened the hands of clan elders and limited the opportunities for enterprising commanders to loot their own communities to recruit and arm followers to join the gathering battle for power in Mogadishu. In fact, these authorities forced some who had become more predatory to change their behaviour.[39]

By the time serious fighting started in the north in 1988, enterprising figures who under other circumstances might have become predatory found it difficult to finance their militias through looting local communities without suffering negative consequences. They still had to deal with local clan elders to raise funds, through them gaining access to overseas remittances to finance their militias. Gerard Prunier describes the consequences of this arrangement when he visited the region in 1989. He noted that armed young men looted aid convoys from outside the region. But he also noted the 'difficulty of shooting young apprentice shiftas because their clan and family backgrounds have to be taken into account, and the same holds for any person who might kill',[40] which meant that those who misbehaved had to deal with consequential clan elders. These clan authorities and their authority over the exchange of resources were part of the glue that bound those who wielded violence to those who enjoyed deep-rooted legitimacy in local communities.

Tests of these propositions appeared later in the north. Intra-community violence in 1992 and 1994 threatened to escalate into predatory factional fighting, based on old feuds and the ambitions of a former Barre appointee in the prewar police force. This commander occupied the airport, a source of supplies and revenues, and recruited young men by giving them car keys that he told them could be redeemed for automobiles on 'Victory Day'. But he was driven off to the capital (where he owned real estate) after recruits were 'encouraged' to switch sides, partly through appeals to their family members who were reminded of the considerable harm that would come to their standing in the community and finances if their relatives persisted in this use of violence.[41]

It is significant, in light of the power of local customary authorities, that Somaliland officials decided to restrict UN political involvement in their territory and ban local participation in peace talks, lest this disrupt their social control over resources, and thus control over violence. The Ethiopian government, on the other hand, has discovered that promoting peace talks is the best way of ensuring that no centralized state that could pose a threat to it – it fought a war in 1977–1978 against a Somali army invasion and Somali government sponsored rebels – could ever arise. The fractious dynamic of outside mediation appears further south in Mogadishu, too. Militias proliferated again in 2001–2002 as negotiations provided a new external arena and the prospect of wealth and power associated with an externally guaranteed sovereign state without regard for popular legitimacy or socially accepted methods. UN investigators reported 'some leading businessmen have outflanked militia leaders from their own clans and have started buying the backing of individual militia fighters'.[42] This they attributed to 'part of the competition between Somali groups in advance of the anticipated conference of concerned parties in Nairobi under the auspices of IGAD [Intergovernmental Authority on Development] peace negotiations'.[43]

Similar relationships between violence, resources, and authority appeared in Sierra Leone. Military setbacks forced the RUF into peace negotiations that produced the 1999 Lomé Agreement, which brought Foday Sankoh, the insurgent's primary organizer of diamonds-for-arms transactions into a coalition government – as head of an agency administering Sierra Leone's diamond resources! He used his new prerogatives of office to sell diamonds abroad without having to rely upon intermediaries who demanded hefty risk premiums when dealing with him as a rebel leader. A year later the RUF took several hundred UN peacekeepers hostage, a crisis that ended when British forces intervened and coordinated with the CDF militia to rescue the hostages and fight the RUF and renegade elements of the government army.[44]

Some among the CDF militias used illicit diamond mining to serve their interests in ways that combined personal opportunity and violence with at least a modest provision of security to communities. Like many Somaliland leaders, the militias' organizers came from among the local elite that had been relatively marginalized in prewar politics. They too relied on local customary practices, specifically the mobilization of young men's initiation societies, to fend off attacks from capital-based political networks. Some local elites also used young men in illicit commercial activities, as did corrupt politicians in the capital. But because they attracted the suspicion of the old president, they needed these youth to protect their operations against poaching from 'official' clandestine operators. Thus the wartime armed group developed in a context that already integrated locally legitimate practices for controlling youth into armed gangs that protected the community from predatory outsiders. When war came to these areas, young men from the same social category from which RUF drew recruits over time were increasingly likely to join the CDF to protect their communities. This wartime behaviour built on the obligations of local strongmen and miners to guarantee each other's security, a fundamental element of the social relationship that underlies the creation of political order, no matter whether the international community regarded their mining activities as greedy or otherwise.

Young fighters' relations to local authority appear to have been more important than resources in shaping how they organized and used violence. Where local authorities had grown distant from networks of patronage tied to state power and had developed defensive mechanisms, these social institutions and practices helped to recruit and socialize young men, even ones from outside of the specific communities into a particular mode of fighting. Resources were important to fight – at the very least. But one could even make the argument that even the 'resource rich' in that conflict were actually resource poor. According to a postwar commission documenting human rights violations in Sierra Leone's war, 'RUF pioneered the policy of

forced recruitment in the conflict. The RUF bore a marked proclivity towards abduc-
tion, abuse and training of civilians', and that 'youths and children were recruited by
explicit force that included coercing them at gunpoint'. The commission 'holds the
RUF responsible for the majority of violations involving forced recruitment of children', 76.2 per cent by its count.[45] The RUF's reliance on kidnapping children, particularly the 10–14 age group, to carry supplies and fight suggests that this
insurgency lacked material means to attract sufficiently motivated recruits or even
enough opportunists.

Sierra Leone also shows how clandestine economies can be integral components of
strategies to control violence and create order as a public good in a context where an
incumbent government is organized more like a predatory private business syndicate.
It also shows the difficulties of international engagement of these groups within the
existing framework of states. Once a private military service company and then
Nigerian and British expeditionary forces moved CDF units outside their home areas
to fight RUF rebels, these units split into factions, looted, and became more general
abusers of human rights. This was due in part to their removal from mechanisms of
social control that bound them to the communities they protected. Further afield,
armed young men found they could use their weapons for personal gain without suffering the social consequences of misbehaviour they would have faced earlier. But inside
their home areas, CDF organizers proved able to recruit RUF fighters to switch sides.
This was explained in fighters' interviews to the Sierra Leone Truth Commission as an
alternate means of seeking status and personal 'empowerment'.[46]

This difference in the social relations underpinning uses of violence mattered a lot
for foreign intervention forces which were looking for proxies capable of maintaining
order that would gain them the acceptance of local populations. Nigerian and British
expeditionary forces assisted CDF units to fight the RUF in 2001,[47] well after the promulgation of UN Resolution 1325 of 14 August 2000, which called for the formation
of an independent Special Court to prosecute serious violations of international
human rights law. In 1998 after RUF and renegade elements of the army had captured
the capital, officials in London, the British ambassador to Sierra Leone, and the West
African expeditionary force cooperated with the CDF to import weapons in contra-
vention of a UN embargo and expel rebels from the city.[48] The urgent need to
bring order to the country overrode concerns about uniform adherence to human
rights norms or concerns about fighters' motivations. Thus the CDF was deemed a
more reliable proxy than the national army, or certainly the RUF, in what became
a state-building effort. This was because the CDF used violence in a more state-
like manner and less like a criminal syndicate. This recognition of the impact of
social relationships on uses of violence has become a staple of intervention forces
in Afghanistan, Iraq, and elsewhere which seek out indigenous allies who can
claim local legitimacy and maintain order.[49] However, once Sierra Leone's war
ended, the UN-sponsored Special Court issued indictments for Chief Sam Hinga
Norman, the former CDF National Coordinator and Minister of Internal Affairs,
and two of his associates.

Russia's Ingush Autonomous Republic's former President Ruslan Aushev also
used clandestine economic channels and informal social institutions to control

predation, thus avoiding the spread of Chechnya's war. This kept his country out of
the usual conflict datasets and thus beyond the consideration of most scholars who
study conflicts. Doing his best to preserve order, Aushev confronted fighters from
neighbouring Chechnya who recruited local young men to kidnap people to
finance their struggle and to challenge local authorities. Many Ingush people regarded
these fighters as bandits, and tried to carry out vendettas against the families of local
recruits who participated in this racket. But outside financial support and armed protection for kidnappers undermined this sanction, as did families' concerns for the
welfare of the kidnapped in a part of Russia without effective police. Aushev expelled
Arab guests who had come from Chechnya and asked for the consent of village elders
to close new mosques that the outsiders had built. He asked families of kidnapping
victims to forgive local fighters, and help find them jobs in the many rackets that
found their way to Aushev's land-locked republic, which he decreed was a tax free
'offshore economic zone'.[50]

Since Ingushetia's economy has been in desperate straits, many people rely on
connections to Caucasian mafias and legal financial networks in Russia. Aushev
was thought to be well connected and generous, using his influence to employ as
many local young men as possible. He also legalized vendetta and organized the
local police – recruiting more young men – to assist aggrieved families to punish
misbehaviour. This arrangement appears to have helped keep predation at bay,
with help from young men who easily could have been off committing opportunist
mayhem.[51] Most households in this region have substantial private arsenals, offering
ample opportunities to prey on others, but the region's order contrasts with neighbouring Chechnya.[52] Ingushestia's leader used methods that seem dubious from
the perspective of global norms. Mobilizing patriarchal customs against the threat
of militancy is bound to upset some people and is a hard practice to generalize.
Nonetheless, these strategies established order on the basis of shared bonds of
social reciprocity that restrained opportunist individual desires.

Dealing with the Complex Uses of Violence

The point of this argument is that social context matters a lot, perhaps more than individual motives in shaping the uses to which violence is put. The notorious Charles
Taylor is a case in point. He stands accused of war crimes and crimes against humanity before a tribunal in The Hague. In other contexts, his aggressive and socially
destructive impulses could have been turned to his advantage as a risk-taking obnox-
ious CEO of the sort that American investors and the producers of *American Psycho*
love. In fact, he was a businessman in the US in the 1980s before he returned to
Liberia. Social context – Liberia's collapsed state, America's rule of law – shaped
his various interactions with other people and state power.

This wider focus moves beyond the rigid determinism of resources and individual
interests. As the evidence above shows, some resources are used to constrain and redirect violence against non-combatants, while in other instances the resource-poor behave
very harshly toward non-combatants. Occasionally, these insurgents as organizations
and individual members change their behaviour toward non-combatants. They

usually do this when their relation to authority, either the state or local people who provide governance, changes.

This is not to say that individuals' interests are irrelevant. Instead, the point here is that they present an incomplete picture of the behaviour and organization of insurgents. A more complete explanation entails looking more closely at the relation of insurgents to non-combatants and to the politics of patronage, or the 'state' as it has become in the most extreme examples of state collapse. The reader may object and point out that relatively few states, even in Africa, are truly collapsing states. That is true. It is also true that a significant portion of states that host internal wars in Africa and a few other places exhibit political authorities in which personalist networks and patron-client relationships outside of the formal structure of state institutions are decisive instruments of power.

Critics might deploy the 'Dick Cheney defence'. That is, one argues that even the US is riddled with insider politics, and point to Cheney as an exemplar of one whose interests combined his official position and his previous occupation as the head of one of the main recipients of US government contracts in the war in Iraq, of which he was such an ardent supporter, and as a manipulator of laws and law enforcement to increase his clique's power. But it is hard to imagine American politicians splitting off from the political establishment like Taylor did from Liberia's and using their insider connections to build private paramilitaries, and using these to get rich. Nor does patronage politics in the US occupy political space to such an extent as it did in Liberia or Congo. Moreover, it needs to be pointed out again that most African states are not collapsed states. Most experts do not expect war in Tanzania, despite its proximity to so many conflicts, nor worry about Botswana's or Senegal's political situations. Attention focuses instead on countries where politicians are most proficient at combining patronage politics and violence, such as Kenya, Sudan, and Chad, places where patronage-based political systems have integrated otherwise very local and parochial conflicts into their exercises of authority.

Explaining these variations in insurgent behaviour requires an analytical framework that can deal with the complexity of politics. It has to account for why opportunism matters sometimes and sometimes not, and sometimes in different ways. Otherwise, the uses of political science research are limited. As a field director for President Obama's successful presidential campaign said, 'I try to throw out all the political-science majors when I do hiring' in favor of people who understand the processes in which the variables that political scientists study can be contingent and changed in ways that promote a candidate's prospects.[53] Real life also shows the importance of taking seriously the context and uses of violence, particularly if one wants to account for some very significant outliers, such as those insurgencies that end up acting more like state-builders and less like predators.

ACKNOWLEDGEMENT

An earlier version of this paper was presented at 'Mikropolitik bewaffneter Gruppen', Institut für Sozialwissenschaften, Humboldt University, Berlin, March 2007.

NOTES

1. United Nations High Commissioner for Refugees, *Refugees and Others of Concern to UNHCR: 1999 Statistical Overview* (Geneva: Registration and Statistical Unit, UNHCR, 2000), p. 29.
2. Office of the United Nations High Commissioner for Refugees, *Populations of Concern to UNHCR: A Statistical Overview, 1994* (Geneva: UNHCR, 1995), Table 7.
3. Jeremy Weinstein, *Inside Rebellion: The Politics of Insurgent Violence* (New York: Cambridge University Press, 2007), p. 7
4. For example, Ted Gurr, *Why Men Rebel* (Princeton, NJ: Princeton University Press, 1970).
5. Paul Collier and Anke Hoeffler, *Greed and Grievance in Civil War* (Washington, DC: World Bank, 2001), p. 2.
6. *Journal of Conflict Resolution*, Vol. 46, No. 1 (2002). Special Issue: *Understanding Civil Wars*, edited by Paul Collier and Nicholas Sambanis.
7. United Nations, *Report of the United Nations Conference on the Illicit Trade in Small Arms and Light Weapons in All Its Aspects* (New York: UN, 2001) and other experts' reports on commerce in arms and natural resources in conflicts in Sierra Leone, Liberia, Congo, Angola, and Somalia.
8. John Hirsch, *Sierra Leone: Diamonds and the Struggle for Democracy* (Boulder, CO: Lynne Rienner, 2001), p. 89.
9. K. Moses Nagbe, *Bulk Challenge: The Story of 4,000 Liberians in Search of Refuge* (Cape Coast, Ghana: Champion Publishers, 1996), p. 53.
10. Collier and Hoeffler, *Greed and Grievance* (note 5), p. 17.
11. Weinstein, *Inside Rebellion* (note 3), p. 9.
12. Stathis Kalyvas, '"New" and "Old" Civil Wars: A Valid Distinction?' *World Politics*, Vol. 54, No. 1 (2001), pp. 99–118.
13. Eric Wolf, *Peasant Wars of the Twentieth Century* (Norman, OK: University of Oklahoma Press, 1999).
14. James Scott, 'Revolution in the Revolution: Peasants and Commissars', *Theory and Society*, Vol. 7, No. 11 (1979), pp. 97–134.
15. Stathis Kalyvas, *The Logic of Violence in Civil Wars* (New York: Cambridge University Press, 2006), p. 23.
16. Anton Blok, 'The Peasant and the Brigand: Social Banditry Reconsidered', *Comparative Studies in Society and History*, Vol. 14, No. 4 (1972), p. 496.
17. Anton Blok, *The Mafia of a Sicilian Village, 1860-1960: A Study of Violent Peasant Entrepreneurs* (Oxford: Blackwell, 1974), esp. pp. 99–102.
18. United Nations Drug Control Program, *Afghanistan Annual Opium Poppy Survey 2001* (Islamabad: UNDCP), pp. iii, 11.
19. Some policymakers and NGOs conflate odious governance with predation in ways that obscure the possibility that such groups provide public goods to definable communities, regardless of their policies on kite-flying and education for girls.
20. Organization of African Unity, 'Charter of the OAU', in Ian Brownlie (ed.), *Basic Documents on African Affairs* (Oxford: Clarendon Press, 1971), p. 3.
21. Robert Jackson, *Quasi-States: Sovereignty, International Relations and the Third World* (New York: Cambridge University Press, 1990), p. 21. See also Charles Tilly, *Coercion, Capital and European States, AD 990-1992* (Oxford: Blackwell Publishers, 1992), pp. 192–227.
22. Joel Migdal, *Strong Societies and Weak States* (Princeton, NJ: Princeton University Press, 1988), pp. 139–41.
23. Patrick McGowan, 'African Military Coups d'état, 1956–2001: Frequency, Trends and Distribution', *Journal of Modern African Studies*, Vol. 41, No. 3 (2004), pp. 339–70.
24. Uppsala Conflict Data Program & International Peace Research Institute, Oslo, 'UCDP/PRIO Armed Conflict Dataset Codebook, 4-2007' and 'Main Conflict Table' (Uppsala & Oslo: UCDP& PRIO, 2007).
25. Prebend: an official position that gives the holder assurances of access to personal economic benefits and opportunities beyond salary. See Richard Joseph, *Democracy and Prebendal Politics in Nigeria* (Ibadan: Spectrum Books, 1991), pp. 55–7.
26. Transparency International, http://www.transparency.org/policy_research/surveys_indices/cpi/ 2007; per capita growth, World Bank, *World Development Report 2008*, http://siteresources. worldbank.org/INTWDR2008/Resources/2795087-1192112387976/WDR08_24_SWDI.pdf and United Nations Development Program, *Human Development Report 2007*, http://hdr.undp.org/en/ statistics/ (all accessed 18 January 2008).

27. David Kang, *Crony Capitalism: Corruption and Development in South Korea and the Philippines* (New York: Cambridge University Press, 2002).
28. Mancur Olson, 'Dictatorship, Democracy and Development', *American Political Science Review*, Vol. 87, No. 3 (1993), pp. 567–76.
29. Thomas Hobbes, *Leviathan* (New York: Oxford University Press, 1996), pp. 82–95.
30. Diego Gambetta, *The Sicilian Mafia* (Cambridge, MA: Harvard University Press, 1993).
31. Compare International Monetary Fund, *Liberia: Staff Report for the 2001 Article IV Consultation and Overdue Financial Obligations to the Fund* (Washington, DC: IMF, 11 February 2002), paras. 35, 56; United Nations, *Report of the Panel of Experts Appointed Pursuant to Security Council Resolution 1395 (2002), Paragraph 4, in Relation to Liberia* (New York: UN, April 2002), pp. 23–34.
32. United Nations Security Council, *Report of the Monitoring Group on Somalia pursuant to Security Council Resolution 1811 (2008)*, 10 Dec. 2008, paras. 44 &17.
33. Augustine Beecher, 'A Tale of Two Betrayals', *Standard Times* (Freetown), 27 May 2003, p. 3.
34. Commonwealth Human Rights Initiative, *In Pursuit of Justice: A Report on the Judiciary in Sierra Leone* (Freetown: CHRI, 2002), p.2 8.
35. International Crisis Group, *Sierra Leone: The State of Security and Governance* (Freetown: ICG, 5 September 2003), p. 13.
36. Truth & Reconciliation Commission, *Witness to Truth: Report of the Sierra Leone Truth & Reconciliation Commission* (Accra, Ghana: Graphic Packaging, 2004), p. 38.
37. Richard Conibere, Jana Asher, Kristen Cibelli, Jana Dudukovich, Rafe Kaplan, and Patrick Ball, *Statistical Appendix to the Report of Truth and Reconciliation Commission, Report of Sierra Leone* (Palo Alto, CA: Human Rights Data Analysis Group, The Benetech Initiative, 2004), p. 19.
38. These *Iyalodes* regulate urban markets. Observations associated with the author's research in Ibadan, Nigeria and conversations with one over a chicken dinner that she bought for the author.
39. Interviews with former SNM commanders, Hargeisa and Borama [Somaliland], June–July 2006.
40. Gerard Prunier, 'A Candid View of the Somali National Front', *Horn of Africa* (1991), p. 109.
41. Interview with John Drysdale, Somaliland resident and former advisor to the UN, Hargeisa, 23 June 2006.
42. United Nations Security Council, *Report of the Team of Experts Appointed Pursuant to Security Council Resolution 1407 (2002), Paragraph 1, Concerning Somalia* (New York: UN, 3 July 2002), para. 32.
43. Ibid., para. 28.
44. United Nations, *Tenth Report of the Secretary-General on the United Nations Mission in Sierra Leone* (New York, UN, 25 June 2001), para. 16.
45. Truth & Reconciliation Commission, *Report*, Vol. 2: *Findings* (note 36), p. 43.
46. Ibid., p. 36.
47. Author's observation, Daru Headquarters, Kailahun District, Sierra Leone, May–June 2001.
48. United Kingdom, House of Commons, *Select Committee on Foreign Affairs Second Report: Sierra Leone* (London: HMSO, 21 Aug 1999).
49. This is articulated in Department of the Army, *US Army Field Manual No. 3–24* (Chicago, IL: University of Chicago Press, 2007).
50. Patrick Tyler, 'In Caucasus, Peaceful Separatists', *New York Times*, 2 February 2002, p. A12.
51. Matthew Evangelista, 'Ingushetia as a Microcosm of Putin's Reforms', PONARS Policy Memo 346, Program on New Approaches to Russian Security, 2004.
52. This and the preceding paragraph reflect the author's investigations and ideas in Georgi Derluguian, 'From Afghanistan to Ingushetia', unpublished manuscript. The author conducted research in the Caucasus in collaboration with Derluguian and enjoyed the hospitality and protection of some of these networks.
53. Quoted in Ryan Lizza, 'Battle Plans: How Obama Won', *New Yorker*, 17 November 2008, p. 51.

The Changing Ownership of War: States, Insurgencies and Technology

AARON KARP

Twenty years after Fourth Generation Warfare theorists first proclaimed the transformation of armed conflict, we continue to struggle with the consequences. As the state loses not only its monopoly over legitimate warfare, but also control over military initiative and dominance of military technology, how will the ends and means of armed violence be redefined? If non-state actors are the new owners of war, how must our understanding of the *artefacts of violence* adapt as well?

This essay examines the effects of changes in the legitimacy of violence, stressing their physical manifestations. Weapons technologies, it is argued here, have ceased to be an independent variable of violence and become consequences of strategic and doctrinal choice. With states losing their ability to use technology to dominate warfare, technological virtuosity no longer is defined by the state; instead it belongs to the initiators of violence. It follows that the most important violent technologies no longer are state-generated. They are the inventions and adaptations of terrorists and insurgents.

No irony of contemporary international security is more confounding than the sight of the most advanced Western military technology stymied by social inhibitions and the banal implements of insurgent enemies. It has become common wisdom to attribute the weaknesses of Western-style armed forces to their inability to rapidly adapt to the needs of counterinsurgency warfare.[1] Fully adapt to insurgent challenges, goes this line, and success can be regained. While there undoubtedly is much to this logic, it also conceals more basic changes in the nature of armed conflict. The greater problem, rather, is the declining relevance of the entire Western Way of War.[2]

It is argued here that the declining capability of Western militaries and the concomitant rise of non-state forces are parts of the same process. What we are witnessing is a consequence of broader changes in world order. As the meaning of warfare is redefined, leadership in the use of violence shifts. The nature of warfare and military technology is being transformed, as states give up the ability to use their most destructive military technology, and non-state actors gain greater freedom to use their own. The Western Way of War, with its reliance on advanced technology, no longer leads change in the use of force. Instead it faces a crisis of relevance, challenged by non-state actors who increasingly seem to control initiative over the use of violence, its intensity and duration.

The essential contrast between the state and the insurgent is explored here through examples from the Middle East and Afghanistan, where the limitations of the statist military technique and the advantages of insurgency are readily seen. While most documentation from these wars examines the progress of industrial armed forces, the same material can be read as a rolling illustration of non-state adaptation.

What does the record of Gaza, Afghanistan, and Iraq, then, show about the adaptability of insurgencies to use violence in pursuit of their goals?

This essay examines the transformation of warfare as part of a larger political process, associated with the declining myth of the state. As the state loses its Weberian grip on legitimate violence, its citizens and institutions reveal ever-greater discomfort with the official use of political violence, regardless of the exact purpose. Although its physical capabilities may remain virtually unimpaired, the state is compelled to be ever more defensive in its use of force, restricted literally to territorial self-defence (itself a declining need) or struggling to define its problems as issues of self-defence in a quest for legitimacy. But such claims tend to fail, with results that are mixed, at best, as illustrated by international reaction in August 2008 to Russia's unconvincing claims of self-defence against Georgia. As even the world's only superpower discovered to its dismay in 2003, without the aegis of self-defence or collective security, states are gravely weakened.

Instead it often is rival claimants, non-state actors, who find it easier to assume the Weberian cloak of legitimate force.[3] While the question of who starts wars tends to be impossibly controversial (it was always the other guy), the ability of insurgents and terrorists to dominate the technology of warfare is easier to resolve. Ignoring traditional measures like cost and engineering virtuosity, the only important measure of technology used here is its ability to achieve specific political goals. Non-state actors increasingly control military initiative; they chose the kinds of technology that dominate contemporary conflicts. While state armed forces struggle to make their equipment relevant, non-state actors make the determining decisions about how killing will occur and when. Their control of technological initiative gives them increasing ownership over contemporary warfare, the ability to use violence to achieve their goals.

The changing balance between legitimate force and non-state violence is examined here not as an impartial problem of world order, but through the lens of counterinsurgency. The relationship between counterinsurgency and other approaches to dealing with non-state violence (such as conflict resolution, mediation and good offices, peacekeeping or disarmament, demobilization and reconstruction) is naturally tense. This reflects fundamental differences in the motives of their advocates and the means they permit themselves. Counterinsurgency, after all, involves systematic force in pursuit of the clearest possible victory for one side, almost always the state. Although it acknowledges the fundamental importance of political accommodation for success, it also relies on lethal violence to repel attacks and advocates offensive operations when advantageous. Its greatest advantage for our purposes here is as a mature system of thought, with a systematic understanding of the relationship between different international actors expressed through political violence. Other approaches may better explain the motives and causes that drive men to rebel, but counterinsurgency offers a distinct explanation for why insurgencies are gaining greater initiative.

The State Loses Ownership of War

It was not supposed to be this way. The script popularized immediately after the Cold War left no one in doubt of the winner. The remarkable success of Desert Storm fostered the belief that state power was continuing to develop along the same path it had followed for the past two centuries, only much faster. The Revolution in Military Affairs (RMA) foreshadowed in Iraq would inevitably give states (especially America) unprecedented freedom of action.[4] In retrospect, the RMA literature took far too much for granted, including the immutability of the state, its strategic salience of the state and the traditions of industrial warfare. The equipment was there, to be sure. But somehow dramatically new capabilities did not confer comparable choice.

The RMA outlook received a major shock from the 1999 Kosovo war, which showed that capability came with constraints. Not only were the motives for the use of force seemingly revolutionary – divorced from national interest – but also the political limits on its use. Post-modern, humanitarian sensibilities made it hard for states to resist requests to go to war, even though they had no immediate national interest in its outcome.[5] Compelled to use force, but unwilling to see widespread destruction, the state was anything but the superman envisioned by the RMA. Successful force was defined by minimal death and destruction to all sides, what Edward Luttwak called post-heroic warfare.[6]

The most incisive critiques of the 79-day bombing campaign portrayed it as a turning point, as states no longer fought to the full extent of their capabilities, but felt compelled to tailor the use of force to the task.[7] This may be an historical exaggeration – limited war is nothing new – but the critiques were on to something. Previously states restrained themselves out of military necessity, because multiple obligations made it hard to reduce deployments elsewhere, or limited operations were tactical desirable, or strategically less provocative. In Kosovo, however, limitations were politically essential to the conduct of war. Without restraint, political acceptance of the war would disintegrate. Force was not limited by military consequences so much as domestic political concerns. Allied commander Wesley Clark described his greatest task not as fighting Serbia, but placating NATO country political leaders and defence ministry lawyers.[8] Advanced technology was essential to the conduct of such conflicts; network-centric communications and the precision-guided JDAM all but replaced unguided bombs. But its greatest role was as an expression of self-control, used not to maximize destruction but to minimize damage.[9]

Not all observers accepted the limitations. In the American Department of Defense, influential officials led by Arthur Cebrowski, Andrew Marshall, and William Owens advocated that these technological innovations created unprecedented disparities, permitting the United States to rapidly deploy small forces to resolve political disputes.[10] As described by Owens, a System of Systems would enable commanders to direct deadly force exactly where it would be most effective. The enemy would not be destroyed, but unable to respond, with no choice besides flight or capitulation. This image of Network-Centric Warfare was not predicated on any particular new technology. Rather, it exploited innovations in information technology, sensors, and guidance systems. These, it was argued, not ships, tanks, planes and rifles, were the most instrumental military tools of the future.[11]

The image of small detachments attacking centres of gravity to destroy rival governments was intoxicating to the Neo-Cons who inherited the Pentagon after George W. Bush's Electoral College victory. Released after 11 September, their enthusiasm also reaffirmed the limits noted by their contemporaries during Kosovo. Politics and justifications had become more important than technology. Iraq was overthrown for higher causes – whether counterterrorism, world order, humanitarianism or democracy – but not to make America more powerful.

Transformation to Network-Centric Warfare was another way of acknowledging the redefinition of war, as a privilege rather than a right of the state. It was implicitly about making war acceptable to domestic and international audiences, the essential requirement for acquiescence to its use.

Trying to Salvage Industrial Warfare

In the 1990s, advocates of the Revolution in Military Affairs were more likely to be accused or triumphalism than modesty. In retrospect, though, their assertiveness can be interpreted as an effort to preserve the utility of a declining instrument in the face of more powerful trends. Against the growing constraints on the state, the RMA was more a plea than triumph. Subsequent iterations – Network Centric Warfare, Transformation and System of Systems – always seemed more statements of optimism than cruel calculations about killing and winning. The more sophisticated each effort to reassert the utility of force, the more questionable.

The last-ditch effort to salvage the RMA was Effects Based Operations (EBO). Lead by the US Air Force, EBO stressed carefully calibrated use of force, combined with a full range of economic and political initiatives, to overcome an adversary's will to resist.[12] Instead of outright destruction of adversaries, it was more efficient and much more acceptable to find ways to circumvent their advantages. Here was a step beyond the RMA and Transformation, both of which still emphasized physical destruction of an enemy's ability to act. EBO emphasized not outright destruction but a full spectrum of military, economic, and political measures that made resistance meaningless. To be sure, violence remained a vital arrow in the tactical quiver, but only one among many alternatives. This approach self-consciously tried to turn the limitations of the post-modern environment into a source of strength. The most legitimate weapons were those without secondary effects, reinterpreting constraints on the use of force as a justification for the very weapons that military aviation has begun to master. Other armed services would mostly implement political and economic developmental assistance, providing the positive incentive to balance the punishing threats of air power.

Promising economy of force and giving a prominent role to civil affairs, EBO made a virtue of necessity. Its inherent adaptability gave widespread appeal, or perhaps made it all things to all sides. EBO was just as consistent with the White House's War on Terror as with Europe's Responsibility to Protect (R2P). It was especially appealing to audiences searching for ways to justify intervention without major use of force. Accepted by NATO as the Comprehensive Approach at its 2006 Riga Summit, it offered a rationale for the engage-as-you-want tactics of Afghanistan, transforming national caveats into a source of strength.[13] Avoiding combat operations no longer was shirking responsibility; it became desirable specialization. Since EBO potentially applies every transformational tool an intervening country is willing to offer, everything fits. Operational cherry-picking ceased to be an alliance problem. Everyone was pulling their weight.

Except that everyone really knew better. EBO has been condemned for indulging wishful thinking when hard strategic choices are what are needed most.[14] Superficially, the logic of EBO is clear; successful intervention requires getting a lot of different things right. In practice, efforts to plan this strategically border on utter impossibility.

In hindsight it is easy to appreciate that in Afghanistan NATO was fooling itself, especially now that the price for strategic inattention has risen. As stability in Afghanistan deteriorated beginning in spring 2006, pressure for strategic reassessment mounted. Once foreign casualties in Afghanistan began to surpass those in Iraq – American combat deaths in Afghanistan became dominant in May and June 2008 – this became imperative (Figure 1).[15]

It is no accident that EBO was officially abandoned at the same moment that the seriousness of the Afghan situation became clear. In August 2008, General James N. Mattis, the American Joint Forces Commander – responsible for joint military doctrine for all four US armed services – published an unclassified letter declaring,

> I am convinced that the various interpretations of EBO have caused confusion throughout the joint force and amongst our multinational partners...EBO has been misapplied and overextended to the point that it actually hinders rather than helps.[16]

In a related document, he concludes, 'The underlying principles associated with EDO, ONA (Operational Net Assessment), and SoSA (System of Systems Analysis) are fundamentally flawed and must be removed from our lexicon, training, and operations.' To his credit, Mattis does not offer an alternative. Contemporary war, he seems to be saying, defies doctrine and technology, because we are not in control.

FIGURE 1
AMERICAN MONTHLY COMBAT FATALITIES, MARCH 2003–APRIL 2009

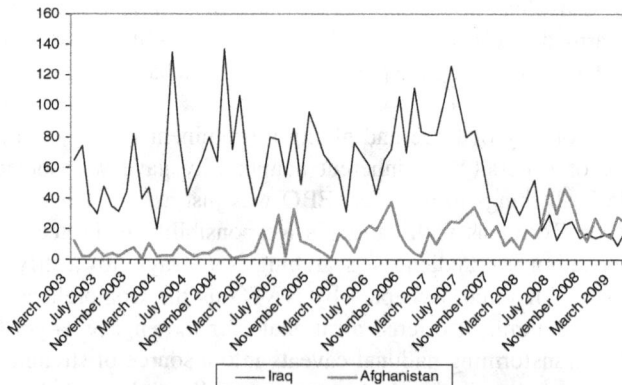

Source: adapted from data in http://icasualties.org/oef/

The amazing success of technology-intensive force in Kosovo increasingly is understood as a singular event, a precedent for nothing. Efforts to rely on technical dominance in the early stages of war in Afghanistan and Iraq did not pay off. As the Iraq Surge showed four years later, people and the ideas they carry matter much more.

The State Loses Control Over Technology

Faith in perfect weapons is nothing new. But the holy Ramayana and legendary Excalibur were mythic, not models for emulation.[17] This attitude changed during the industrial revolution, as the process of invention was mastered to serve the state. Sixty years ago, no less an observer than J.F.C. Fuller could write with complete certainty that

> weapons, if only the right ones can be discovered, form 99 per cent of victory...
> Strategy, command, leadership, courage, discipline, supply, organization and all the moral and physical paraphernalia of war are nothing to a high superiority of weapons.[18]

Such themes were commonplace through the 20th century – the key ingredient in Reagan's 1983 Star Wars speech, for example – but they sound ridiculous today.

We now appreciate that Fuller was not describing war in general. His perspective was confined to a particular – and peculiar – manifestation; the Western Way of War, and Industrial Warfare in particular. In an era when all other aspects of economic and social life were dominated by industrial manufacturing, Fuller's logic seemed self-evident. After the extraordinary spectacles of two world wars, there was no reason to believe that warfare was different from any other element of industrial society; nothing mattered so much as being first with the most.

Industrial perspectives never totally dominated global strategy. Few states had the resources to invest in perfect weapons. Especially for middle and smaller countries, the emphasis on advanced technology tested their ability to compete, pushing them to the periphery of the Cold War. Lacking the civilian economies required to sustain industrial war, they essentially quit. The best organized found effectiveness by stressing geographic roles or niche capabilities approaches still emphasized by many. With few direct threats to their state security, this strategy gave a satisfying role for the armed forces and was economically sustainable, avoiding the need for difficult military-industrial investment. Many other countries maintained armed forces exclusively for territorial defence or constabulary duties, relying mostly on vintage equipment.

Events since 1991 have revealed the limits of Fuller's faith, transforming his iron rule into a romantic anachronistic. Its truth always was limited to the narrow boundaries of the Westphalian international system, where evenly armed states fought virtually identical counterparts. Other memories like declarations of war, unconditional surrender, and the Geneva Conventions reflected the same historical roots. Even during the 19th and 20th centuries, the shortcomings of industrial military logic were repeated demonstrated, but usually along the geopolitical periphery where greater powers only challenged each other indirectly. In the Philippines, the

Middle East, the Caribbean, China, and Southeast Asia, it was guerrilla forces with little or nothing more than basic infantry equipment who repeatedly pushed state forces to the brink of defeat, sometimes further.[19] The limits of industrial warfare were apparent at the time and widely respected. For most industrial militaries, the implications were obvious: avoid guerrilla war at all costs.

Among the most graphic evidence of the decline of industrial warfare is the irrelevance of its previously dominant artefacts. State-of-the-art systems like American F-22 and Russian SU-35 fighters no longer assure victory. Instead we ask, are they even relevant? They have no obvious military mission; there are comparable weapons, but no comparable foes for them to challenge. Their programmatic success testifies exclusively to institutional importance. Over time tactical roles will be found for them – their existence has to be justified – but such uses will not resemble their designed functions in the least.

The clearest expression of this rule is the ultimate artefact of industrial warfare, the nuclear weapon, more than ever an instrument of deterrence or a prestige symbol, without any war-fighting role.[20] Many major powers appear to be done buying nuclear weapons (like Britain, probably America and Israel, and maybe France), or only buy new ones slowly (like China, India, Pakistan, and Russia). Conventional weapons procurement also has become untenably arduous. While turning out weapon systems designed in the 1970s and 1980s remains easy enough, developing new ones seems to be virtually impossible. The old Western model of continuous technical improvement no longer provides guidance. The most striking evidence is the inability of the American armed services to buy new weapons. This is not because of engineering or industrial weakness. Rather, the services cannot agree on basic requirements. In lieu of an industrial enemy, the only guidance comes from technology itself. The result is an endless spiral of improvements and cost, leading to weapons that are unaffordable and of questionable tactical relevance.[21]

The declining salience of technology brings into doubt the entire superstructure it supported, the Western Way of War, or as it matured in the 19th century, Industrial Warfare. Liberating itself from the rules of hand-to-hand chivalry that had defined military legitimacy since classical Greece, the Western Way of War re-emerged simultaneously with the introduction and mastery of gunpowder in the 14th and 15th centuries.[22] Far more recognizable to contemporary eyes was its emphasis on reducing risk to combatants through long-range fire. The connection between war and technology, previously very idiosyncratic now became a firm weld, so much that in the 20th century technology and war became virtual synonyms. Like Fuller, everyone could assume the side with the best weapons won. Post-modern warfare severs this seemingly unassailable bond.

Not that post-industrial technology is irrelevant, far from it. But its role is increasingly marginal. The JDAM probably is the most important major weapon of Afghanistan and Iraq, making it impossible for insurgents to concentrate their forces, impossible for them to win militarily, and allowing coalition forces to engage enemies without exposing their personnel to the most extreme risks.[23] Low-tech armoured vehicles like the monstrous MRAP (a reworked South African design from the early 1980s) and personal items like body armour and QuikClot are essential in the contemporary combat, if only because they suppress fatalities to politically tolerable levels. But none of these are decisive in the sense of shortening wars.

Unable to control the battlefield through overwhelming violence or technological advances, Western warriors are systematically disadvantaged. Because they are *reacting* to insurgent challenges, states are all but unable to regain military initiative. As the swift reassertion of state power over national financial markets in October 2008 showed, states seem better at reclaiming economic initiative, playing to their strengths as development agents, focusing on societies instead of enemies. But there is no evidence of a coming substitute for technology's role assuring Western military power. Observers with historical axes to grind may find satisfaction in the sight of Western armies floundering against regional adversaries. But there is no evidence either of any winners from the resulting disorder.

Redefining War

The migration of military-technical initiative to insurgents and terrorists, the only actors readily able to use weapons to advance political goals and transform expectations, is part of larger change in perceptions of justifiable violence. The shifting legitimacy of violence, entangling states to the advantage of non-state actors, is the core theme of Fourth Generation Warfare (4GW). This school goes even further, maintaining that insurgency has become the predominant form of warfare. Since the birth of the modern state system in 1648, war was almost exclusive an instrument of state power. This was the case with First Generation linear tactics, widely employed until the mid 19th century. State dominance was even more profound under Second Generation tactics, attrition through mass fires so characteristic of the American Civil War and World War One. It became complete with Third Generation manoeuvre and envelopment associated with Blitzkrieg, a high-tech stunt that only states could even attempt.[24] From this perspective, Network-Centric Warfare was an advance. It revitalized Third Generation concepts, but with less effect for want of comparable state adversaries.

Other actors could try to use force, and often did, but so long as they tried to fight like a state, they were doomed. In an era of globalisation and the erosion of hierarchy, what the state loses, other actors are only too ready to pick up. While orthodox Maoist guerrilla warfare starts with opportunistic raiding and progresses to conventional tactics, Fourth Generation warriors do not try to defeat their opponents. The goal, rather, is to inflict enough pain and humiliation to convince the adversary to give up. In Bill Lind's prophetic words, the new goal is

> collapsing the enemy internally rather than physically destroying him. Targets will include such things as the population's support for the war and the enemy's culture. ... fourth generation warfare seems likely to be widely dispersed and largely undefined; the distinction between war and peace will be blurred to the vanishing point. It will be nonlinear, possibly to the point of having no definable battlefields or fronts. The distinction between 'civilian' and 'military' may disappear.[25]

Fourth Generation insurgent and terrorist tactics are almost the opposite of Third Generation industrial or network-centric warfare. Instead of decisive attacks on well-guarded centres of gravity, it seeks symbolic targets of opportunity. It eschews massive confrontations, and relies on continuous raiding to create unendurable pain and sorrow. Rather than restrict the news media, it exploits the press to exaggerate emotional impact and question the successes of the other side. Everything is calculated to prolong a struggle that state forces are politically compelled to wrap up as quickly as possible. Under such a regime, the impact of a few isolated gunmen can be enormous.

Much of the difference can be summarized in terms of the political role of death. In Third Generation, industrial or network-centric warfare, the infantryman represents weakness, because he *risks death* and death undermines already weak commitment. By dying, however, a Fourth Generation insurgent demonstrates the moral superiority of his cause. Fourth Generation tactics restore the essential salience of the rifleman or suicide bomber, transforming them into a source of strength, because they are *prepared to die*. While states usually feel compelled to minimize human suffering, insurgents often have much greater freedom with the lives of their combatants, their people, and their adversaries.

As the tactical opposite of network-centric warfare, Fourth Generation conflict intentionally emphasizes the very weapons governments want to use least. At one extreme this might mean WMD terrorism, which would surpass idiocy if done by a state, but might seem the epitome of reason to a non-state actor.[26] At the other extreme it leads to a vigorous embrace of small arms and light weapons, suicide bombs and improvised explosive devices (IEDs), specifically because their use elicits bloodshed that states must avoid.

Redefining Weapons

Perhaps the most pertinent finding of the 4GW school is that the insurgent emphasis on simple technology is not a phase; it is an essential characteristic of contemporary warfare. Mao assumed that low-tech reliance on whatever weapons was a phase (the second stage of guerrilla warfare), necessary as guerrillas accumulated the strength to fight state armies as military equals. In the final stage of Maoist theory, guerrillas triumph by matching the industrial capabilities of their state enemies, defeating them in formal battles. This was the path to victory used by Mao himself and by Giáp in Vietnam.

But the transition to industrial war is not essential. Hammes credits the Sandinistas with the insight that they could overthrow the Nicaraguan government in the 1970s without making the leap to major weaponry or pitched battles. In essence and fact, they went directly from the jungles to the capitol. The PLO's attempt to create a conventional industrial army in the 1970s and early 1980s was a strategic disaster, provoking the Israeli invasion of 1982 and permanently fracturing the Palestinian movement. The first intifada of 1987–1991, by comparison, fought almost exclusively with stones, was a remarkable success, leading directly to the 1993 Oslo Accords. Ever since, insurgents have understood that by cultivating international pressure through the media, they do not have to defeat their enemy's army.[27] Consequently, they have no need of major conventional weapons. Simple weapons are not a steppingstone to bigger things, but sufficient in-and-of themselves.

In the math of post-modern violence, no relationship matters as much as the synergism of men and guns. Since the rise of systematic research on sub-state conflict in the early 1990s, armed conflict has been structured around this trope, so much so that many of us (myself included) assumed that small arms and armed conflict were synonyms. No one thought the gun-conflict connection was exclusive, but it seemed sufficient to explain most post-modern organized violence. Other weapons often appeared on contemporary battlefields, including major weapons systems like MANPADS and armoured vehicles, but they seemed more decorative than decisive.

As many observers have rightly noted, non-state actors tend to rely on old-fashioned infantry weapons. The Kalashnikov is the weapon that changed armed conflict more than any other, the universally understood symbol of insurrection and mayhem. The seemingly limitless reservoirs of aging Kalashnikovs, so easy to use and maintain, seem sufficient to plague the planet for a very long time. This technical fact of life seems sufficient to insure that insurgencies will continue to be a major global problem.[28]

Beyond Small Arms

But there are limits to Kalashnikov logic. To be sure, sheer numbers insure they will litter the background of virtually any violent conflict. But they may not dominate the foreground of contestation. Experience in the Middle East and Afghanistan shows that Fourth Generation warriors have lost none of the insurgent's traditional willingness to innovate. As the offensive force of the future, insurgents control the pace of innovation. When Kalashnikov rifles no longer bring the results they need, they will find something else.[29]

This has been seen through successive waves of insurgent adaptation in Iraq. The reaction to the American-led invasion was led by the Saddam Fedeyeen, Sunni irregulars armed with AKs. This rifle-armed guerrilla infantry largely collapsed after the fall of Baghdad. Subsequent insurgents, their ranks swelled by then-Director of the US Office for Reconstruction and Humanitarian Assistance in Iraq, L. Paul Bremer's decision to fire the entire Iraqi military and Ba'ath Party, continued to try infantry warfare, including formal battles in Falluja in April and November 2004.

Although the timing is rough, rifle-armed insurgents already were yielding tactical leadership to suicide bombers, who emerged as a near equal instrument of warfare in 2004. Even at its height, suicide bombing did not replace rifle fire. But since its first major success in 1983, when suicide bombers destroyed American and French installations in Beirut, killing hundreds and compelling both countries to pull out of Lebanon, it continues to expand to more and countries. Widely used against civilians, leaders and military personnel in Israel, Sri Lanka, and elsewhere, suicide bombing was firmly established before 11 September. But after the American-led invasions of Afghanistan and Iraq, suicide bombing metastasized. Of 1,850 suicide attacks (successes and failures) recorded since 1983, more than 260 occurred in Afghanistan, 920 in Iraq.[30]

Suicide bombing escalated the conflict, but it could be ameliorated through counter-measures, above all the simple expedient of dividing people behind massive blast walls. As a result, suicide bombing declined in Israel and Iraq, although continues to be a major threat, especially in the vast areas of Iraq beyond reach of blast walls.[31]

Some observers believe suicide bombing is too effective to be suppressed for long.[32] In the meanwhile, counterinsurgency success creates enormous pressure for further insurgent innovation. Unable to challenge Israeli or American dominance through small arms or suicide bombing, insurgents in Palestine and Iraq gradually found alternatives. Against Israel, the unguided rocket became the principle weapons. Iraqi insurgents shifted to emphasize IED attacks. While all tactics remain in widespread use, the IED has become the most deadly weapon in the insurgent arsenal, as shown by Figure 2, now causing over half of all American military fatalities in Iraq, and roughly as many in Afghanistan.[33]

Most intriguing to specialists in small arms is the declining role of 'other hostile causes'. These are they very small arms we previously thought to be dominant. The reasons why fewer American soldiers are dying of gunshot are complex. Universal use of body armour and revolutionary medical treatments (especially QuikClot and cryogenics) have an enormous effect, as do armour-plated Humvees and Mine Resitant Ambush Protected (MRAP) vehicles. But the switch to insurgent reliance on bombing was largely a matter of tactical choice and adaptation. Afghan and Iraqi insurgents were learning faster than Western armed forces. How insurgents learn remains poorly understood; Hammes suggests that the process is largely informal and intuitive, based a culture of continuous experimentation and reactions to media reporting.[34] In more formal terms, insurgent organizations reward innovation more than industrial armed forces.[35]

Easy availability of artillery ammunition facilitated the switch to IEDs, but mostly by creating opportunities. Contrary to much commentary from the time, Iraq's ammunition stockpiles were not exceptionally large, but they were exception-ally distributed.[36] By late 2005 or early 2006, though, the caches had been mostly

FIGURE 2
PROPORTIONATE CAUSES OF AMERICAN MILITARY FATALITIES IN IRAQ

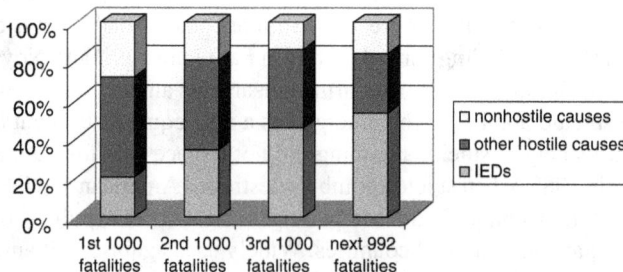

Source: adapted from 'Most Now Killed By Bombs', *New York Times*, 25 March 2008, p. A21.

Notes: 'Other hostile causes' include SALW attack, rockets and mortars, aircraft destruction, suicide bombing, stabbing and kidnap-murder. 'Nonhostile causes' include friendly fire and combat-related accidents.

cleaned away. Evidence of the insurgent dedication to their revised strategic concept can be seen in their further adaptation, improvising explosives for bombs. Shia bombers clearly had a partial source of supply in Iran. Sunnis had to be more creative. In lieu of artillery shells, they began to rely on homemade mixtures of nitrate fertilizer and diesel fuel.[37]

In Lebanon and Gaza, warfare has witnessed a similar process. The second or al-Asqa intifada that began in September 2000 was much more violent than the first uprising of 1987–1991. Killing Israelis was an unambiguous goal from the start. Having acquired tens of thousands of automatic rifles through the Oslo Peace Process to arm various Palestinian security agencies and political factions, Palestinians started a deadly sniping campaign. This was suppressed through a series of Israeli raids against militants, who turned out to be surprisingly vulnerable to Israeli Defense Force (IDF) interdiction. Although the exact timing needs careful research, it appears that suicide bombing became more common as sniping diminished. Israel's security wall, which started to go up in the summer of 2002, was extremely successful against both.[38]

As sniping and suicide bombing lost their impact, Shia and Palestinians found their own weapon of choice in unguided rockets. For Hezbollah, with reliable access to weapons from Iran and Syria, unguided artillery rockets became the weapon of choice. Their arsenal was estimated by Israeli sources at over 10,000 before the July 2006 War. Since then, Israeli sources estimate the total at over 20,000. These range from large numbers to short-range, 1940s vintage Katyushas (BM-21s) to much larger Iranian-made weapons able to reach Tel Aviv and Jerusalem.

When Israeli leaders ordered the invasion of 12 July 2006 to deal with Hezbollah provocations, suppressing the rocket threat was an explicit goal. Yet after 33 days of combat operations, the IDF – led by the Israel Air Force – was unable to suppress the rocket fire, which caused 53 fatalities, wounded hundreds, and shut down most activity in northern Israel.[39]

The rocket threat from Gaza has a very different character, determined largely by the territory's isolation. After the outbreak of the Al Asqa intifada in 2000, Hamas tried to import artillery rockets from Hezbollah and directly from Iran, but its efforts were vulnerable to the Israeli interception. One year into the confrontation, in September 2001, Hamas and affiliated factions began launching locally made al-Qassam rockets at Israeli settlements in Gaza. The rocket attacks increased every year since, more than 3,000 so far, more than 200 a month in the first half of 2008.[40]

Since Israel evacuated its civilians from Gaza in 2005, about half of these rockets have been directed at nearby Sderot, a town of 23,000. Larger rockets, capable of hitting Ashkelon, 10 km away, have been attempted, bringing 190,000 Israelis within range. Although complete numbers are not readily available, there appears to be an inverse relationship between the decline of successful suicide bombing in 2003–2005 and the rise of rocket attacks.

In every sense, the rockets are Hamas' greatest technical success. Although other forms of attack continue – including suicide bombings, sniping, mortars, raids on border posts and tunnelling – rockets attract far and away the greatest media attention. Other forms of attack undoubtedly are more deadly; al-Qassams have killed 14 and wounded at least 500 to date.[41] But the rockets are uniquely provocative, the direct cause of Israeli preemptive raids against workshops, launch parties and cadres, often killing or wounding bystanders. The genius of al-Qassams is making Palestinians simultaneously strong and victims. Either way, rocket tactics are made to appear justified.

The rockets are hardly impressive. Except for an explosive warhead of 2–5 kg, they are little different from large hobby rockets popular among North American enthusiasts. Typical al-Qassams rely on a propellant mixture of diesel fuel and nitrate fertilizer or sugar oxidizer, cast inside a sheet metal tube roughly 80 cm long.[42] The warhead probably is the hardest part to make. As primarily political weapons, they only have to work well enough to encourage Palestinian unity and keep pressure on Israel for political concessions.

Efforts to find technical or tactical responses have been weak. In the July 2006 war, the Israeli Air Force was highly effective destroying the very largest (and least mobile) Hezbollah rocket launchers, but had virtually no impact on smaller rockets.[43] There is no evidence that preemptive attacks in Gaza have done more than hinder the rain of al-Qassams. Israel has several major projects currently underway to develop defences against al-Qassams. Interception is technically straightforward, but reducing the costs sufficiently to permit defence against a large proportion has proven impossible so far.[44] Because of the extremely short distances involved, moreover, interception would tend to shift the battlespace from one inhabited area to another. Israeli experts increasingly seem to think there is no technical solution.[45] Instead, the Israeli government has encouraged a cult around Sderot, trying to reclaim the status of victimhood.

So great was the technical success of al-Qassams, our greatest challenge is to explain the truce between Hamas and Israel, announced on 19 June 2008. The truce, brokered by Egypt, did not end the cycle of attacks and retaliation, but it led to sudden and unexpectedly improvement. In first weeks there were routine violations, apparently as the enemies tested each other's intentions. Even now, several months later, the diplomacy behind the truce – especially on the Hamas side – and the internal politics of its enforcement remain obscure. One explanation poplar among Israeli observers is the Hamas leadership needed a pause to moderate the continuous radicalization and loss of its authority brought on by the fighting.[46] But the impact is much clearer. The truce substantiated Israeli allegations that Hamas, despite previous insistence otherwise, could control the attacks; they may have begun spontaneously, but their growth required official acceptance if not formal encouragement. Hamas reportedly arrested some would-be rocket teams. The rocket attacks never ended completely, but subsided greatly in frequency and destructiveness.[47]

The rockets may be largely symbolic weapons, creating much more psychic insecurity – a serious challenge for the Israeli government – than physical casualties. Baiting Israel to overreact may have been a deliberate goal of the decision, apparently by Hamas leaders in Syria, not to continue the ceasefire after it ended on 19 December 2008. The return to uninhibited mortar and rocket attacks precipitated the Gaza war of 29 December 2008–21 January 2009. This time the Israeli Defense Forces showed deliberate restraint, much more than they did in 2006.[48] But the extreme difference in fatalities, with over 1,300 Gazan dead compared to 13 Israeli deaths, only served the reinforce Hamas legitimacy throughout the Muslim world and much of Europe. Months later, with its political base more secure than ever, Hamas was restraining rocket attacks; reportedly trying to reestablish a ceasefire.[49]

Welcome to Unpredictability

The primary goal of war-planning throughout the long modern era was to impose predictability within chaos. A brilliant captain was someone with a gift for seeing order through the Clausewitzian fog. Success meant overcoming the exceptional forces of human inventiveness, the near certainty that his adversary was trying to change everything to make his job impossible. Yet within the framework of previous generations of war, this goal was routinely achieved. War worked, not all the time, but often enough to justify the risk.

With the rise of 4GW, however, this basic calculation of statecraft may be permanently obsolete. The near absence of war between democracies has been widely observed.[50] The decline of war between states of all stripes is only a little less striking.[51] War increasingly appears to belong to non-state adversaries (NSAs). To be sure, states are involved in these conflicts most of the time, but it is their non-state adversaries who often have greatest influence over when and how fighting occurs.

For states, the shift in ownership brings unprecedented unpredictability. Frank Hoffman described this as hybrid warfare, in which restrained but powerful states struggle to establish control over weaker but more agile insurgencies.[52] Just as the place and tempo of operations is much harder to predict, so are the vital technologies and their effects. Useful insights can be drawn from the experience of smaller state forces in recent wars. British armed forces in Iraq were much smaller and suffered much less in absolute terms than the Americans. With their smaller profile, they are much more typical of the state forces likely to find themselves engaged in future peace enforcement or stability operations. Smaller size made them much more vulnerable to relative fluctuations in casualties. British combat fatalities display none of the consistency of their American counterparts, varying between months with no one killed to other months with over a dozen dead. The dramatic highs and lows reflect particular tactical choices, unpredictable accidents and disasters.[53]

This roller coaster creates its own special burdens for intervening states. How to justify the worst moments before an unconvinced public? Other American allies gradually abandoned Iraq, leaving the British the largest other foreign presence, a situation that gradually become politically untenable. British commanders coped with the weakness of their position by gradually withdrawing their personnel and avoiding fire-fights, to the point of great embarrassment, before leaving altogether. Britain left not because their mission in Iraq was complete, but because it no longer could be sustained.[54]

Whether the weakening commitment of states and their own control over the tempo and severity of fighting helps NSAs is not clear. As counterinsurgency experts never tire of pointing out, insurgents win about as often as they lose.[55] The ability to pick dominant weapons is a new advantage though, one that suggests to me that insurgents are gaining more from current transformations than they lose. They may not be more likely to win, but they probably are less likely to lose. Armed conflicts, in other words, seem likely to become stalemated, continuing without much hope of resolution.

The constant change of 4GW has immediate consequences for orthodox international responses to non-state actors. The switch from reliance on SALW to suicide bombing, IEDs or rockets, suggests limits to what can be achieved through NSA disarmament, for example. Collecting small arms and ammunition, the basic theme of Disarmament, Development and Reintegration (DDR) disarmament, is unlikely to impact war-making potential permanently. While NSA disarmament may serve many very important roles, its effect on the ability to resume combat is easily exaggerated. Insurgents can and will find other ways.

Nor are there technical solutions to the weapons of insurgent and terrorists. There are no panaceas for weapons like Kalashnikovs, IEDs, rockets, MANPADS and more distant prospects like terrorist WMDs. Their risks can be managed, but not countered outright. Even responses like armour or short-range missile defences only help reduce – never eliminate – their risks. And if outstanding technical fixes can be found, the basic rules of 4GW leave no doubt that alternative threats will rapidly emerge. If solutions are to be found, by exclusion they must be political or social.

Ironically, more may be achieved through revival of traditional arms control and disarmament. Statist methods of arms control – developed in recent years through the Proliferation Security Initiative and United Nations Security Council Resolution 1540 to restrain the illicit trade in WMD technology – remain highly relevant, creating barriers to access. The same is true of old concepts like export control, especially restrictions on brokering and transfers to NSAs. Disarmament also can play a crucial role by eliminating items non-state actors might want, whether they are guns, MANPADS or fissile materials. Such measures will not eliminate the dangers of new forms of armed conflict, but they will make existing risks more manageable.

Behemoths Without Conviction

States are far from powerless. Non-state actors have enormous advantages in the new environment, enabling them to resort to force with greater ease and often with greater political effect. But the enormous resources that only states can mobilize make them tough competitors. If they can invoke the trope of self-defence, a state can sustain military operations or decades, potentially long enough to outlast insurgents. Although there is disagreement on the exact numbers, states win or at least prevent rebels from winning about half the time.

Nor are their traditional capabilities irrelevant. State-against-state warfare is in sharp decline, but it is not unknown. Wars of the last ten years include furiously bloody contests between Eritrea and Ethiopia in 1999–2001, and the much shorter war between Georgia and Russia in 7–12 August 2008. Although heavily outnumbered by conflicts involving insurgencies, such examples are sufficient to conclude that familiar ways of conflict are not quite obsolete. Russian observers saw the war with Georgia as a reaffirmation of the continuing relevance of the Red Army's conventional capabilities.[56] The capabilities of even a seemingly weak state should not be underestimated. The accomplishments of the Colombian and Sri Lankan armed forces in 2008–2009 against their insurgent foes can be criticized on ethical grounds, but still stand out for their competence.

Other observers, following the path blazed by Colin Powell in the early 1990s, stress that state militaries are poorly suited for counterinsurgency and stability missions, but still must be prepared for traditional problems of defence and deterrence against other states.[57] They fear a tight embrace of counterinsurgency will detract dangerously from the ability to maintain a stable balance of power between states and deter destabilizing actions, making remaining statist threats much tougher to address. Thus American Defense Secretary Robert Gates has pressed his agency not to switch outright from industrial warfare to counterinsurgency, but to strike the right balance.[58]

Missing from such calls for adjustment is a clear sense of strategic priorities. There is a tendency for observers and increasingly for leaders, confronted with a seemingly endless emergence of new dangers, to call for expanding the instruments of policy-making. But lacking Weberian ownership of war, they are hard-pressed to say which instruments matter most or when. Strategic planning is out of fashion; reactive options are in. One result is ever longer menus, like NATO's Comprehensive Approach.

There is consensus among Western security planners that military tools are not a sufficient response to contemporary challenges; conflict can only be resolved with a quiver holding many more political and economic arrows than before. The most widely used international expression for this interest in interagency collaboration is Whole-of-Government. The term itself has been used in many contexts with maddening slipperiness. Although it always involves overcoming traditional barriers and demarcations between government agencies, it means very different things in America and elsewhere. The United States comes to the theme at an almost opposite angle from Canada and Europe, for example. For the United States, Whole-of-Government justifies elevation of civilian agencies, above all State Department and the US Agency for International Development. For Canada and Europe the problem usually means the exact opposite; giving defence ministries a systemic role in matters previously controlled by foreign policy, emergency relief, and development agencies. In every case, though, the Whole-of-Government approach means elevating interagency processes.

Despite rigidly excluding civilian decision-makers for most of the George W. Bush presidency, the United States now is having an easier time with systemic interagency cooperation. After the election of President Obama, the American process is guaranteed to rapidly advance, especially since important advocates – like Defense Secretary Robert Gates, National Security Advisor James Jones, and Undersecretary of Defense Michèle Flournoy – have high positions in the government.[59] In essence, the US Department of Defense is being asked to share responsibilities it has no desire to monopolize. Institutional momentum favours inter-agency cooperation.

For other countries the process will be slower and more arduous. Their job is to convince dominant civilian agencies to share power with defence ministries and the armed forces. Actors who often are antagonistic to the military, in other words, are being asked to act against their natural inclinations, something they are likely to do only begrudgingly. The results there are, accordingly, less predictable.

Conclusion: Romantic Longing

The transformation of warfare helps explain one of more curious enigmas of the contemporary world: if armed conflict is becoming less common, why are we more sensitive to it? The processes described here show that rising anxiety is not normal human pining for perfection. It expresses a loss of statist control over the not just the tools of warfare, but the means and causes.

There is no reason to doubt that the Newtonian reaction from Western warfare to insurgency will be long lasting. Asymmetric warfare, in other words, is not a secondary form of armed conflict, but the inevitable and increasingly dominant manifestation of its core meaning. If insurgency and terrorism were tolerated so far by most states and international organizations, this was because they also were distant menaces or controllable ones. Except for strokes of deadly genius (or stupidity) like 11 September, they touched the people of most states only if those states deliberately went looking for them. Over time, though, this crucial separation is becoming less sustainable. Against the twin tides of economic globalization and rising immigration, the ability to insulate unpleasant parts of the world is going away. Fourth Generation warriors do not have to be globally organized, in other words, to pose global threats. At the worst, there is the threat of nuclear-armed terrorists – the ultimate symbol of global unpredictability – the possibility that aroused Dick Cheney's one percent logic (if there is a one percent chance of terrorists acquiring nuclear weapons, we must act as if it were a certainty).[60] Even if the specific dangers are less awesome, they are unprecedented and unlikely to decline for many years to come.

The challenge is adapting institutions and attitudes created for a world of sovereign states to deal with the slipperiness of flexible security challenges. That it is tough is no surprise. What is more striking is the ability of those institutions to adjust when given the chance. It took the American armed forces four year of warfare in Iraq to become satisfactorily effective there, embracing counterinsurgency doctrine, learning to make political deals, and how to integrate economic development and political recognition into and overall package. While the results have not been as amazing as some would like to believe, the declining fatality statistics alone show they were not completely wrong either. Not all military institutions can make the leap. The relative failure of the British Royal Army in Basra is a cautionary example.[61]

Convincing military organizations to change is hard enough. Far tougher is the task of persuading whole societies. If this has been avoided so far, it is largely because the risks of intervention have been structured to minimize the demands on civilian society. Insulated by military professionalization and reliance on relatively discrete aid missions, dangers were as remote as the places themselves. When the scale of involvement and danger of the cases rises, though, this insulation stops working. As the extreme experiences of the Japanese Self-Defense Forces in Iraq and German soldiers in Afghanistan show, many societies lag far behind their militaries in their willingness to face Fourth Generation security challenges.

The conflicting desires to do good and to be left alone frame the antinomies of foreign intervention today. Few societies are equipped to deal with such conflicting motives, especially in environments promising uncertain results. As the relative successes discussed here show, the international community and even individual states are far from being helpless. But we remain very far from the goal of being able to address the problems of Fourth Generation Warfare with predictable success.

ACKNOWLEDGMENTS

This essay is the result of an invitation from Keith Krause, who encouraged me – as he often has before – to forage in fields where I otherwise would have hesitated to go. The essay owes further strength to comments from David Capie, Antonio Giustozzi, TX Hammes, my wife Regina Karp, David Keithly, Stéphanie Pézard, Pablo Policzer, Chet Richards, and Mimmi Söderberg.

NOTES

1. John Nagl, *Learning to Eat Soup with a Knife: Counterinsurgency Lessons from Malaya and Vietnam*, revised ed. (Chicago, IL: University of Chicago Press, 2005).
2. Geoffrey Parker, 'The Future of Western Warfare', in Parker (ed.), *The Cambridge History of Warfare* (Cambridge: Cambridge University Press, 2006), pp. 413–32.
3. Departing from Max Weber's seminal lecture from January 1919, 'Politics as a Vocation', where he argued that 'a state is a human community that (successfully) claims the *monopoly of the legitimate use of physical force* within a given territory.' Charles Tilly's development of this concept, most completely in *Coercion, Capital, and European States, AD 990-1990* (Cambridge, MA: Basil Blackwell, 1992), places the connection between war and the state at the heart of the entire international system.
4. Eliot A. Cohen, 'Revolution in Warfare', *Foreign Affairs*, Vol. 75, No. 2 (March–April 1996), pp. 37–54; and Andrew F. Krepinevich, 'Cavalry to Computer', *The National Interest*, No. 37 (Fall 1994), pp. 30–42. The RMA always had its doubters. To his credit, Cohen eventually joined their ranks.
5. Mark R. Brawley and Pierre Martin (eds), *Alliance Politics, Kosovo and NATO's War: Allied Force or Forced Allies?* (New York: Palgrave, 2001).
6. Edward N. Luttwak, 'Toward Post-Heroic Warfare', *Foreign Affairs*, Vol. 74, No. 3 (May/June 1995), pp. 109–22.
7. Colin McInnes, *Spectator Sport War: The West and Contemporary Conflict* (Boulder, CO: Lynne Rienner, 2002); and Stephen D. Wrage (ed.), *Immaculate Warfare: Participants Reflect on the Air Campaigns over Kosovo and Afghanistan* (Westport, CT: Praeger, 2003).
8. Wesley K. Clark, *Waging Modern War: Bosnia, Kosovo and the Future of Combat* (New York: Public Affairs Press, 2002).
9. Andrew J. Bacevich and Eliot A. Cohen (eds), *War Over Kosovo: Politics and Strategy in a Global Age* (New York: Columbia University Press, 2002). On the JDAM (Joint Direct Attack Munition) a useful overview is Peter Grier, 'The JDAM Revolution', *Air Force Magazine*, September 2006, pp. 610–63.
10. Arthur K. Cebrowski and John J. Garstka, 'Network-Centric Warfare: Its Origin and Future', *Proceedings*, January 1998. William A. Owens, 'Creating a US Military Revolution', in Theo Farrell and Terry Terriff (eds), *The Sources of Military Change: Culture, Politics and Technology* (Boulder, CO: Lynn Rienner, 2002).
11. William A. Owens, *Lifting the Fog of War* (New York: Farrar, Straus, Giroux, 2000).
12. A vigorous defense of EBO from the Air Force point of view is Robert S. Dudney, 'It's the Effect, Stupid', *Air Force Magazine*, November 2006, p. 2.

13. Brooke Smith-Windsor, *Hasten Slowly: Nato's Effects Based Comprehensive Approach to Operations*, Research Paper No. 38 (Rome: Nato Defence College, July 2008).
14. The classic criticism is Milan N. Vego, 'Effects-Based Operations: A Critique', *Joint Force Quarterly*, No. 41 (Spring 2006), pp. 51–7.
15. 'May Combat Deaths in Afghanistan Outpace Iraq', *Associated Press*, 13 July 2008. Anthony H. Cordesman reminds us that all such comparisons are imperfect and argues that comprehensive figures including combat wounds are equally revealing, but the general trend seems clear enough. Cordesman, *US Casualties: The Trends in Iraq and Afghanistan* (Washington, DC: Center for Strategic and International Studies, 6 August 2008).
16. J.N. Mattis, 'Memorandum for US Joint Forces Command' (Norfolk, VA: US Joint Forces Command, 14 August 2008), p. 4.
17. J.N. Mattis, 'USJFCOM Commander's Guidance for Effects-Based Operations' (Norfolk, Virginia: US Joint Forces Command, 14 August 2008), p. 4. The Western Way of War, as originally inherited from Greece, had no place for magical weapons, as Hansen and Keegan make clear. It was Geoffrey of Monmouth's development of the Arthurian Legend in the 13th century and his invention of Excalibur that instilled the idea, which became a fetish only in the 20th century. Geoffrey Ashe, *The Discovery of King Arthur* (London: Guild Publishing 1985), pp. 185–7.
18. J.F.C. Fuller, *Armament and History: A Study of the Influence of Armament on History from the Dawn of Classical Warfare to the Second World War* (London: Eyre and Spottiswoode, 1946), p. 31.
19. Nagl, *Learning to Eat Soup with a Knife* (note 1).
20. Scott D. Sagan, 'Why Do States Build Nuclear Weapons? Three Models in Search of a Bomb', *International Security*, Vol. 21, No. 3 (Winter 1996/97), pp. 54–86; Nina Tannenwald, 'Stigmatizing the Bomb: Origins of the Nuclear Taboo', *International Security*, Vol. 29, No. 4 (Spring 2005), pp. 5–49.
21. Hans Ulrich Kaeser, *Abandon Ships: The Costly Illusion of Unaffordable Transformation* (Washington, DC: Center for Strategic and International Studies, *draft*, 19 August 2008); and Anthony H. Cordesman and Hans Ulrich Kaeser, *America's Self-Destroying Airpower: Becoming Your Own Peer Threat* (Washington, DC: Center for Strategic and International Studies, *draft*, 1 October 2008).
22. There are many fine reviews of this transformation. My personal favorite is John Keegan's *History of Warfare* (New York: Alfred Knopf, 1994), esp. ch. 5.
23. In Tora Bora fire-fights of winter 2001–02, the Taliban quickly learned that if they massed, they died. They quickly learned to melt away and wait for more auspicious opportunities. Stephen Biddle, *Afghanistan and the Future of Warfare* (Carlisle, PA: Strategic Studies Institute, US Army War College, November 2002).
24. This scheme is the creation of William S. Lind in Lind et al., 'The Changing Face of War: Into the Fourth Generation', *Marine Corps Gazette*, October 1989, pp. 22–6.
25. Ibid., p. 23.
26. Jessica Stern, *Terror in the Name of God: Why Religious Militants Kill* (New York: HarperCollins, 2003).
27. This insight into the evolving nature of global insurgency was articulated first by T.X. Hammes in *The Sling and the Stone: On War in the 21st Century* (Osceola, WI: Zenith Press, 2004).
28. Larry Kahaner, *AK-47: The Weapon that Changed the Face of War* (New York: Wiley, 2007).
29. 4GW makes fools of everyone who fails to anticipate constant innovation. I wish my own early work on the small arms revolution at least mentioned IEDs. Fortunately my omissions were not as grotesquely influential as those of Cebrowski and Marshall. Aaron Karp, 'Arming Ethnic Conflict', *Arms Control Today*, Vol. 23, No. 7 (September 1993).
30. Robin Wright, 'Since 2001, A Dramatic Increase in Suicide Bombings', *Washington Post*, 18 April 2008, p. A18.
31. Isabel Kershner, 'Israel's Tactics Thwart Attacks, With Trade-Off', *New York Times*, 3 May 2008, p. A1.
32. Ronen Bergman, 'Living to Bomb Another Day', *New York Times*, 10 September 2008, p. A27.
33. Kris Osborn, 'Bomb Attacks Worsen in Afghanistan', *Defense News*, 4 May 2009, p. 36.
34. T.X. Hammes, 'Information Operations in 4GW', in Aaron Karp, Regina Karp, and Terry Terriff (eds), *Global Insurgency and the Future of Armed Conflict* (London: Routledge, 2007), ch. 20.
35. James Q. Wilson, 'Innovation in Organization: Notes Towards a Theory', in James D. Thompson and Victor Harold Vroom (eds), *Approaches to Organizational Design* (Pittsburgh, PA: University of Pittsburgh Press, 1971) pp. 195–218.
36. *Small Arms Survey 2008* (Cambridge: Cambridge University Press, 2008), ch. 3.
37. John Bokel, 'IEDs in Asymmetric Warfare', *Military Technology*, Vol. 31, No. 10 (October 2007), p. 37.

38. Hillel Frisch, '(The) Fence or Offense? Testing the Effectiveness of "The Fence" in Judea and Samaria', *Democracy and Security*, Vol. 3, No. 1 (2007).
39. Uzi Rubin, *The Rocket Campaign Against Israel During the 2006 Lebanon War* (Ramat-Gan: BESA Center, June 2007).
40. *Rockets from Gaza: Facts and Figures* (London: Britain Israel Communications & Research Centre, 21 February 2008); and Margaret Weiss, *Weapon of Terror: Development and Impact of the Qassam Rocket*, PolicyWatch No. 1352 (Washington, DC: Washington Institute for Near East Policy, 11 March 2008).
41. Ibid.
42. Ibid.
43. 'Interview: Maj. Gen. Elyezer Shkedy', *Defense News*, 19 May 2008, p. 62.
44. Barbara Opall-Rome, 'Israeli Missile Defense Under Spotlight', *Defense News*, 29 October 2007, p. 10; Opall-Rome, 'Israel Speeds Iron Dome Short-Range Defense System', *Defense News*, 28 January 2008, p. 8.
45. Steven Erlanger, 'Israel's Dilemma in Response to Rockets', *New York Times*, 19 December 2007.
46. Interview with Rueven Pedatzur, Senior Military Affairs Analyst, Ha'aretz (Tel Aviv), Berlin, June 2008.
47. Mijal Grinberg, Yuval Azoulay and Avi Issacharoff, 'Jihad Claims Responsibility for Qassam Attack on Sderot', *Ha'aretz*, 15 September 2008; 'Sderot Enjoying Calm as Ceasefire Holds', *IRIN*, 22 September 2008.
48. Barbara Opall-Rome, 'Adapting Artillery to Urban War: Israel Records Drastic Drop in Rounds Fired', *Defense News*, 23 March 2009, pp. 1, 8.
49. Taghreed El-Khodary and Ethan Bronner, 'Addressing US, Hamas Says It Has Grounded Its Rockets to Israel', *New York Times*, 5 May 2009, p. A5.
50. John Mueller, 'The Obsolescence of Major War', *Bulletin of Peace Proposals*, September 1990, pp. 321–28.
51. Andrew Mack, 'Why the Dramatic Decline in Armed Conflict?' *Human Security Report 2005* (Oxford: OUP, 2005) ch. 5.
52. James N. Mattis and Frank G. Hoffman, 'Future Warfare: The Rise of Hybrid Warfare', *US Naval Institute Proceedings*, November 2005, pp. 30–2; and Hoffman, 'Hybrid Warfare and Challenges', *Joint Force Quarterly*, No. 52 (March 2009), pp. 34–9.
53. Sheila M. Bird and Clive B. Fairweather, 'Military Fatality Rates (By Cause) in Afghanistan and Iraq: A Measure of Hostilities', *International Journal of Epidemiology*, Vol. 36, No. 4 (May 2007), pp. 841–6.
54. Warren Chin, 'The United Kingdom's Strategy and Operations in the "War on Terror"', *Contemporary Security Policy*, Vol. 30, No. 1 (April 2009); 'Britain's Armed Forces: Losing Their Way?' *The Economist*, 31 January 2009, pp. 60–1; Alistair MacDonald and Charles Levinson, 'UK Pulls Out of Iraq as Cuts Curb International Missions', *Wall Street Journal*, 9 May 2009, p. A5.
55. David Kilcullen, 'Counterinsurgency Redux', *Survival*, Vol. 48, No. 4 (Winter 2006–2007), pp. 111–30.
56. Vladimir Voronov, 'Why Did Georgian Troops Withdraw From Battle So Quickly?' *Novoye Vremya* (Moscow), 25 August 2008, FBIS translation.
57. Michael J. Mazarr, 'The Folly of "Asymmetric Warfare"', *Washington Quarterly*, Vol. 31, No. 3 (Summer 2008), pp. 33–53.
58. Robert M. Gates, 'The National Defense Strategy: Striking the Right Balance', *Joint Force Quarterly*, No. 52 (March 2009), pp. 2–7.
59. An informative summary of the Obama Administration's shift toward interagency operations is Anthony Fenton, 'Obama and the Counter-Insurgency Era', *Asia Times*, 18 February 2009. Undersecretary of Defense Michèle Flournoy has been administration's most outspoken advocate of whole-of-government operations. See John J. Kruzel, 'US Needs "Pragmatic, Clear-Eyed" Defense Strategy, Flournoy Says', *American Forces Press Service*, 29 April 2009, and John T. Bennett, 'Flournoy: How Obama Nat'l Security Breaks With Bush', *Defense News*, 29 April 2009.
60. Ron Suskind, *The One Percent Doctrine* (New York: Simon and Schuster, 2006).
61. John F. Burns, 'UK On the Defensive over Basra Mistakes', *International Herald Tribune*, 7 August 2008, p. 3.

Index

For Product Safety Concerns and Information please contact our EU
representative GPSR@taylorandfrancis.com
Taylor & Francis Verlag GmbH, Kaufingerstraße 24, 80331 München, Germany

*9 7 8 0 4 1 5 8 1 5 9 2 5 *